Narrating Nature

Critical Green Engagements

Investigating the Green Economy and Its Alternatives

Jim Igoe, Molly Doane, José Martínez-Reyes, Tracey Heatherington, and Melissa Checker
SERIES EDITORS

Narrating Nature

Wildlife Conservation and Maasai Ways of Knowing

Mara J. Goldman

THE UNIVERSITY OF
ARIZONA PRESS

TUCSON

The University of Arizona Press
www.uapress.arizona.edu

ISBN-13: 978-0-8165-3967-3 (hardcover)
ISBN-13: 978-0-8165-4696-1 (paperback)
ISBN-13: 978-0-8165-4194-2 (ebook)

Cover design by Leigh McDonald
Cover photo by Mara J. Goldman
Interior design by Sara Thaxton
Typeset in 10/14 Arno Pro (text), Baskerville, and Trade Gothic (display)

Library of Congress Cataloging-in-Publication Data
Names: Goldman, Mara, author. | University of Arizona Press.
Title: Narrating nature : wildlife conservation and Maasai ways of knowing / Mara J. Goldman.
Other titles: Critical green engagements.
Description: Tucson : University of Arizona Press, 2020. | Series: Critical green engagements: Investigating the
    green economy and its alternatives | Includes bibliographical references and index.
Identifiers: LCCN 2020011734 | ISBN 9780816539673 (Hardcover)
Subjects: LCSH: Human ecology—Africa. | Traditional ecological knowledge. | Wildlife conservation—Africa.
Classification: LCC GF55 .G65 2020 | DDC 333.720967—dc23
LC record available at https://lccn.loc.gov/2020011734

Printed in the United States of America
♾ This paper meets the requirements of ANSI/NISO Z39.48-1992 (Permanence of Paper).

To Anisha, Aanya, and Shankar,

To Mom and Harvey,

And to my Maasai friends and family throughout Tanzania and Kenya

Contents

Illustrations

Figures

Maps

Tables

Preface

THIS BOOK IS the culmination of a voyage that began over two decades ago when I first traveled to Tanzania in 1993 as an undergraduate on a study abroad program about wildlife ecology and conservation. As a geographer at Clark University, I had already been exposed to the highly political social history of nature conservation, including the injustices often involved in the creation of national parks, such as the eviction of Maasai and others from Serengeti. This was not something that was covered on the study abroad program, which was focused on wildlife ecology and conservation, and did not cover the social side of such issues. I planned to conduct my required independent study in Ngorongoro Conservation Area (NCA), to learn about a place that was managed for multiple land use—wildlife conservation, tourism development, *and* pastoralism. I had read Homewood and Rodgers's important book, *Maasailand Ecology*, which provided a detailed social and ecological exploration of land use in the area. The book had been written in part to provide data for a new management plan funded by United Nations Educational, Scientific and Cultural Organization (UNESCO). The underlying assumption at the time was that the report would provide the necessary evidence to evict Maasai from the conservation area. The book did no such thing. On the contrary, the authors argued that restrictions placed on Maasai throughout NCA—particularly on grazing and controlled burning, were not only leading to increased poverty among Maasai but also to many of the ecological changes occurring in the area, such as the spread of invasive species. In other words, Maasai were not *ruining* a *natural* area, but restrictions on their use and management techniques in the name of conservation and tourism were ruining both their livelihoods and the entire ecosystem, or what was being set aside as "nature" in the first place (Homewood and Rodgers 1991).[1]

NCA was not only set aside by the Tanzanian state for conservation and tourism, but was also declared both a World Heritage Site and a Man and Biosphere Reserve by UNESCO. NCA was of global importance. It seemed that this global import was based at least in part on the unique inclusion of people *and* wildlife, culture/ society *and* conservation/ecology in one place. I was both intrigued and bewildered and became determined to understand why the multiple use area was failing. As an undergraduate with limited Swahili and almost nonexistent Maa language skills, I dedicated much of my time to reading the various successive management plans for the area housed on site, in an attempt to understand underlying motivations and attempts to run the area for multiple use. I discovered that there was never really an attempt to make things work. NCA was created as a political solution to appease Maasai evicted from Serengeti at a crucial moment when the British (formally Trustee of Tanzania under the United Nations) were already under UN review because of political unrest in Kenya. Maasai residents of Serengeti had begun rallying for support with proindependence political parties. The creation of NCA was a political necessity (Goldman 1998; Iliffe 1979, 493–503) for the colonial regime. And its creation came with promises of improved access to water for those leaving Serengeti behind.

The politics of NCA were so intense over the years that I was never granted permission to continue to work there. Yet my passion to know more and to explore how multiple land use *could work* led me to find other places in Tanzania where people and wildlife lived together despite official attempts to separate them into villages and conservation areas. I studied Swahili in graduate school and in Tanzania and came back often to build relations and find just the right place to conduct my dissertation research. I settled on two villages strategically located between two national parks— Lake Manyara, which is also a biosphere reserve, and Tarangire—in an area referred to as the Tarangire Manyara Ecosystem (TME). They were also adjacent to and dependent on a new conservation area—the Manyara Ranch—which was proposed as a multiple-use area—for community grazing, grazing for ranch cattle, wildlife conservation, and tourism. Maasai in these villages were warm and welcoming; having not been heavily researched, they were eager for me to come and live with them. And so I did, for two years straight, minus a two-week Maa language course in Kenya (outside Amboseli National Park) and a two-week visit to the United States to visit my father, whose health was failing. I took my time working there, not talking about wildlife at first, building relationships and finding my place. I also spent time traveling to other parts of Maasailand in Tanzania where friends worked, or where I had Maasai friends and connections to draw on—Simanjiro, Lake Natron, Loliondo, and Ngorongoro. My visits to Ngorongoro were hard, even when I was escorting one of the most powerful Maasai traditional leaders home or visiting a friend. Maasai lives have become so monitored inside NCA that outsiders are not allowed to stay in their homes. I did manage once to bring two Maasai friends from the villages near Manyara to Ngorongoro, and their reactions to the spectacular beauty were summed up nicely by one, who said, "It's no wonder this area was taken by the *wazungu* (white people)." To her it was spectacular. It was, in her eyes, "Maasai heaven."

As I finish the final edits on this book to send it into production, there is once again a call to remove Maasai residents from Ngorongoro. Information is limited, but a report from the Oakland Institute explains that the risk is dire.[2] A message from a friend inside, who was once employed as a game scout for NCA, and once scolded for building his house "too modern" with a tin roof, tells me they are scared. "We will refuse to go," he says, and will need to be moved by force. It wouldn't be the first time. Maasai were removed by force from the crater floor in 1974. According to the Oakland Institute Report, the new plan, supported by UNESCO, threatens approximately ninety thousand livelihoods, with the proposed creation of new restricted areas within, where Maasai are denied access for housing, livestock grazing, and crop cultivation. The proposal is the result of a joint monitoring mission from the UNESCO World Heritage Centre, the International Union for the Conservation of Nature (IUCN), and the International Council on Monuments and Sites (ICOMOS), which called on the Tanzanian government to "complete the Multiple Land Use Model review exercise and share the results with World Heritage Centre and Advisory Bodies to advise on the most appropriate land use model, including in the matter of settling local communities in protected areas." In response, the Tanzanian government produced a Four Zone Management and Resettlement Plan, where human settlement and development is restricted to 18 percent of the total area. The plan proposes to divide up NCA into different zones—for human and livestock use and then for wildlife and tourism. It also proposes annexing additional areas into the Conservation Core, what it refers to as "boundary alteration" to include Loliondo Game Controlled Area (GCA) and parts of Lake Natron GCA and Selela forests all in an effort to protect wildlife corridors coming up from Manyara Ranch and connecting TME with Lake Natron.[3]

Not only does the new plan threaten the livelihoods of thousands of Maasai residents in Northern Tanzania. It repeats the violence of colonizing nature—removing those who call a place home, to set it aside as a "world heritage" for sale on the global safari tourism circuit.

The plan itself replicates the old belief, introduced with colonialism and held up by the Tanzanian state and international conservation agencies, that people need to be removed from nature for nature to thrive. Arguments made by a local leader, circulating on YouTube, repeat the belief in the superiority of science over tradition to show that Maasai are degrading the environment and that they need to move on and accept "development."

It is these very sorts of arguments that I counter in this book, with ecological data and with Maasai voices. My goal with this book is to provide an arena in which these debates can be had in such a way that science can be called to task *by Maasai*, in their words, on their terms. Yet it is hard to stay hopeful in this task at the present moment. The UNESCO website actually states that "the most significant feature of the 1972 World Heritage Convention is that it links together in a single document the concepts of nature conservation and the preservation of cultural properties. The convention recognizes the way in which people interact with nature, and the fundamental need to preserve the balance between the two."[4] Yet at the same time UNESCO is somehow implicated in the possible removal of people from a World Heritage site, for the integrity of "nature."

Perhaps the problem lies in the very separation of nature and culture, which can even be read in this account on the UNESCO website. "Culture" can be protected next to, alongside of, but not *a part of* nature. Nature is seen as something out there, to be protected and managed, with the best available science there is. There are of course financial rewards involved in removing Maasai and maintaining a façade of pristine nature for luxury tourism. Dividing up NCA and promoting increased tourism continues the process of setting aside pieces of nature for an elite market, something well covered in the social science literature on conservation. My interest here is less about this political economy of conservation, and the financial flows, though they are of course ever present. I am interested in moving in a different direction, beyond "green economies," toward knowing and managing nature "otherwise," in the sense of outside the standard accepted Western scientific frame.

I am hopeful that the book will make a difference, that the writing style will be engaging enough for the general public and conservationists to read it and to challenge preconceived ideas of what nature is and how it needs to be managed, along with ideas of who the Maasai are and how they get on with their lives in surroundings often alongside wildlife. While much of the substantive ecological data draws from my dissertation work, the book is a product of over two decades of work, friendship, and deep ethnographic engagement with Maasai communities across Tanzania and Kenya. I only hope that it can make even a small difference in some of their lives.

Acknowledgments

THIS BOOK IS the product of over two decades of work, and there are countless people, institutions, and communities that provided guidance, support,
and assistance along the way. I apologize ahead of time for anyone whom I
may forget to name individually here. While all the efforts and kindness that helped
me get through will not be forgotten, some names might be.

Since this book is about respecting Maasai knowledge and making space for their
voices—I begin by thanking my Maasai friends, colleagues, and acquaintances in
Tanzania who welcomed me into their lives, made this work possible, and continue
to provide me with hope and inspiration for the future. The men and women of the
villages of Oltukai and Esilalei, together with the Maasai families in the surrounding
villages of Kakoi, Elasiti, and Losirwa as well as those in Simanjiro, Ngorongoro, and
Longido in Tanzania, and Kitengela in Kenya welcomed me into their homes, fed
me with bottomless cups of milky chai, spent countless hours answering my questions, and never tired of teaching me about everything from local ecology and wildlife
to Maasai ceremonies and fashions. I thank them for making my research not only
possible, but enjoyable. In particular I owe my extended gratitude to certain individuals and families who were exceptionally generous in their time and friendship:
Moinget Laibor, Letema Leiyo, Kareto Oldeyetu and his family, Oloiboni Ole-Mapi,
Mshagama Meshuko, Nangaiya Meshuko, Lengatang Lemkoko, Sikaar ("Ilmamasita")
Ngao, Loiboku and the Lekesamba family, the Well Family, Ngoe Makaine, and the
Lemanie family, Deda Sakayai, the women of the cultural boma in Esilalei, Nawoku
Mengoru, Murriet Kisamba, Senewo Kitende, Muleje Moinget, Sombete Menguro,

Njicho Papayai, and many others. I am especially indebted to Negonye Masune for keeping me fed, keeping my house clean, and keeping me sane throughout it all. She is my Maasai sister, and together with her sons Lengatang, Lenderit, and Micheal, my late Maasai *koko* (grandma) Yaiyai, and mother (Mama Le'well), they are my family away from home. I thank Kisyongo Makaa for being a hardworking and trusted assistant. The ecological and social data presented in the following pages owe much to his excellent translation skills and attention to detail. Mungai Well, who acted as an additional assistant on transects and with interviews toward the end, proved invaluable in his ability to understand and communicate across social worlds. From explaining local place-names and ecological processes to helping me map them into a GIS in Nairobi, his contributions come through this work in many ways. Tubulu Legemojino, Tauta Mappi, and Mamus Litan, who were young children when this research began, became trusted sources and interlocutors during later visits. And lastly, the late Tipilit Mkaine, who provided me a house to live in, friendship, and immeasurable inputs into this research. His integrity and dedication to his community is fondly remembered, and this book is dedicated to you, together with the communities you fought for.

Beyond the study villages, there are others in Tanzania whom I need to thank. Maika Ol'Keri in Ngorongoro, who has been a trusted friend and constant source of knowledge since my first visit to Maasailand in 1993. During later work, Abraham Lengine and Moses Ole Neselle helped me navigate meetings and interviews in Simanjiro District. Many Maasai civil society activists and NGO workers played key roles in my research over the years, providing not only answers to my countless questions, but engaging in long debates and providing ongoing support and inspiration. In particular, I thank Edward Loure, Alais Morindat, Makko Sinadea, Ndinini Lemesara Sikar, Elifuraha Laltaika, and Edward Porokwa. Your own commitment to empowering Maasai voices and management needs is humbling. I thank Saning'o Milliary for your friendship and support both in Tanzania and the United States—for your insight and advice on issues academic and personal, and for your constant translation assistance.

In Kenya, many people helped me to navigate the politics and nuance of new research terrains and talk through similarities and differences across the borders. David Nkeedianye, Ogeli Makui, and Nickson Parmisa helped me do this in Kitengela; Leonard Oneto and Jacob and Raphael Mayiani helped me navigate the politics and collect data in villages surrounding Amboseli, while Dickson Kaelo introduced me to Maasai communities in the Maasai Mara.

Other friends in Tanzania and Kenya provided support, friendship, and a sense of family over the years. Mama Lulu (Naimo Lameck) and her late husband Lemeck were my homestay family as an undergraduate, and Lameck enabled my early field work in Ngorongoro by introducing me to his acquaintances. Munka and Selina Killerai, along with their sons Killerai, Kipepiary, and Ntimama, have since that time been my home in Arusha. Long walks with Munka followed by beer at a local pub provided wonderful opportunities to talk through the nuance of Maasai translations and politics across regions. And Mama Killerai was always there for the personal support and home-cooked meals. Other friends who helped keep me going over time with friendship and conversation (and sometimes housing and food) include Paula Gremley, David Erickson, Sarah Norton, Bernadeta Kilian, Sarah Wallis, Lauren Persha, Josephine Simon, Daudi Peterson, and Annie Birch, whose home in Karatu was the ideal retreat personally and spiritually—thank you for always having space for me (and sometimes my family). My work benefited greatly through short and long exchanges with friends/scholars working at different times in both Tanzania and Kenya, including Anna Estes, Ben Gardner, Tom Morrison, Stacy Lynn, Elizabeth Garland, Msoffe Fortunata, Jeff Worden, Bilal Butt, and Mike Rainy. I owe special thanks to three individuals whom I first met in the field and have been friends and colleagues since. Amy Cooke was conducting dissertation research in Simanjiro while I was conducting mine in Manyara. The importance of her friendship, support, good food, great discussions of all things Maasai, and connections to people in Simanjiro for my later work cannot be overstated. And finally, Alicia Davis and Joana Roque de Pinho have been important collaborators and friends over the years; both read countless earlier versions of this book with excellent edits and suggestions, and have always been among my biggest supporters. Thank you.

I also need to extend my gratitude to several organizations in Arusha that helped along the way. People at Inyuaat e Maa (the Maasai Advancement Association), Peter Toima and Lobulu Sakita in particular, introduced me to the study villages, and for that I am forever grateful. The staff of TANAPA, particularly at Tarangire and Lake Manyara National Parks, were kind and always welcoming. In particular, I thank TNP chief warden at the time, Martin Oloiboko and ecologist Meing'ataki. Also at Tarangire, Mathew Langen helped me with many GIS mapping–related problems. I thank the staff and personnel at the Manyara Ranch during the time of my dissertation work, much of which appears in this book, in particular Clive Jones and the game scouts, together with the steering committee members. Clive's honesty, integrity, and kindness enabled open conversations and made much of my research that touched on the Manyara Ranch possible and rewarding.

Research in Tanzania was supported by TAWIRI and COSTECH. At the University of Dar es Salaam, I thank Adolfo Mascarenhas, who was at the Institute for

Resource Assessment in the early years and helped me navigate work in Ngorongoro. Later, Idris Kikula, principal of the University College of Lands and Architectural Studies, acted as my in-country advisor, friend, and colleague. I thank him for helping me stay on track and out of trouble. In Kenya, my research was supported by the International Livestock Research Institute (ILRI), though a National Science Foundation (NSF) Postdoctoral Fellowship. I thank Robin Reid at ILRI, Nairobi, for taking an interest in my work, funding my return trip to the field in 2005, adding me to her research team, and acting as my mentor on my postdoctoral work. Her own research was an early inspiration to me, and she was and remains an important role model in her research, her relationship with her Maasai collaborators, and her commitment to finding ways to truly manage rangelands jointly for wildlife and people. Also at ILRI, I thank Mohammed Said, Chem Mifugo, and Russ Kruska for their help on maps and ecological data analysis.

In the United States, I would like to start by thanking my mentor from undergraduate study at Clark University, Dianne Rocheleau. She introduced me to many of the critical standpoints that appear in this book, from feminist critiques of science to political ecology and the value of different ways of knowing. I thank Dianne for opening this window into a new world for me, and for trusting me to find my way in Tanzania and beyond. I also need to thank Judy Carney at UCLA, whose high standards of excellence improved my writing and taught me what research should really be about.

As much of this book comes from my dissertation, I have a tremendous amount of gratitude for my dissertation committee. I start with my advisor, Mathew Turner, whose support has always been complete—intellectually, logistically, and personally. I thank you for trusting me to experiment with my writing style while demanding all the while I maintain high standards of academic excellence. I thank you for your own intellectual rigor and friendship and for providing me with a solid role model for academic excellence, communication, and support. You have been a constant source of inspiration and guidance throughout my dissertation and the long process of turning it into a book. I cannot thank you enough. I would also like to thank my other committee members, who provided guidance in different ways throughout the research and writing process. I thank Joan Fujimura for guiding me through the science and technology studies (STS) literature and for her constant interest in and support of my work and push to make it into a book that one can "read in bed like a novel." I thank Lisa Naughton for making sure I kept conservation-related policy goals in mind and for never making me take sides. Karl Zimmerer provided an early academic inspiration with his own work in political ecology and has always been supportive and encouraging of my work. Sharon Hutchison and Tom Spear provided important feedback on the dissertation and helped me to see the way toward making it a book. I thank Tom for pushing me to look just as critically at the production of historic knowledge as contemporary environmental knowledge, and for sending a copy of my dissertation to Richard Waller. This led to focused research on Maasai stories about the past, and detailed feedback from Richard Waller on my history chapters. Thank you both. Magdalena Hauner and Aili Tripp were not on my committee but provided support and advice on translations and general Tanzania history and politics.

Also at Madison, I would like to thank those who provided friendship and peer support over the years including Rachel DeMotts, Ankur Tohan, Kristin Gunther, Liza Moscovice, Maureen McLachlan, Noah Roast, Morgan Robertson, Gordon Robertson, Eric Carter, Ryan Gault, Jessica Goldberger, Joshua Ramisch, Erica See, Chris Duvall, Brenda Parker, Leila Harris, and Abby Neely. There were many others not at Madison who over time contributed to my intellectual growth as I developed many of the ideas in this book; these include Jesse Ribot, Tim Forsyth, Suzanna Hecht, and Pete Brosius.

I am also grateful to the University of Wisconsin–Madison African Studies Program for supporting my Swahili language education through two and a half years of Title VI (FLAS) funding and to Global Studies for a Scott Kloeck-Jenson International Pre-Dissertation Grant to help with dissertation planning. Dissertation research was funded by a Fulbright-Hays Doctoral Dissertation Research Grant, a National Science Foundation Dissertation Improvement Grant in Geography, and a small grant from Graduate Women in Science (GWIS). The return trip in 2005 was funded by ILRI, Nairobi. Research since that time has been funded by an NSF (#0602034) International Research Fellowship Postdoctoral Grant, and two additional NSF grants (#0921507 from Social and Economic Sciences, and #1354542 from the Science and Technology and Society Program). Research has also been generously funded by several smaller grants from the University of Colorado Boulder, including two Innovative Seed Grants, and several small grants from the Center to Advance Research and Teaching in the Social Sciences (CARTSS).

In addition to this financial support, CU Boulder has provided me with a supportive intellectual environment to share my work and ideas over the years. Conversations with fellow geography faculty, including Emily Yeh, Azita Ranjbar, Yaffa Truelove, and Joe Bryan, about multiple ontologies, Indigenous knowledge, and decolonial processes helped me to work through many of the ideas found in this book. I also thank Fernando Riosmena, Colleen Reid, Jennifer Fluri, Elisabeth Root, Elizabeth Dunn, and Tim Oakes for their friendship and support. Outside of the department, Terry McCabe and Jane Menken provided additional support through the Institute for Behavioral Science. Colleen Scanlan Lyons, Lori Hunter, and Laura DeLuca provided friendship as well as intellectual support. In particular, I thank Laura; you have not only been a friend and copyeditor at times, but a soul sister and family for me and my family in Boulder. And you have taken our connection back to Tanzania by bringing undergraduate students to visit my field sites in Oltukai village, making our connection that much stronger. I have also had the privilege of working with several talented graduate students as primary advisor or committee member, whose ideas shaped my own over the years, in particular Eric Reiff, Eric Lovell, Meaghan Daly, John P. Reid-Hresko, Nicole Smith, Mason Auger, Michelle Olsgard Stewart, Sierra Ross, and Shruthi Jagadeesh.

Earlier versions of this work have been shared in different places and with different people where feedback contributed to an improved final version. In particular, I thank Garth Myers and Rick Schroeder; Andrea Nightingale and her graduate students at the Swedish University of Agricultural Science (SLU); Kathy Galvin, Stacy Lynn, and Robin Reid, at CSU-Fort Collins; Joel Wainwright and Mathew Coleman at The Ohio State University, and Ryan Unks. Portions of chapter 2 were published as Goldman, M. J. 2018. "Circulating Wildlife: Capturing the Complexity of Wildlife Movements in the Tarangire Ecosystem in Northern Tanzania from a Mixed Method, Multiply Situated Perspective." In *The Palgrave Handbook of Critical Physical Geography*, edited by Rebecca Lave, Christine Biermann, and Stuart Lane, 319–38. London: Palgrave Macmillan. Portions of chapter 6 were published as Goldman, M. J., and S. Milliary. 2014. "From Critique to Engagement: Re-Evaluating the Participatory Model with Maasai in Northern Tanzania." *Journal of Political Ecology* 21: 408–23.

I wish to thank Dan Brockington and Jim Igoe, for inviting me to submit this manuscript to the University of Arizona Press Critical Green Engagements Series. Drawing from both your work over the years made your support and interest in my work that much more meaningful and important. Your feedback and suggestions throughout the process helped to make this a better book. And of course, none of this would have been possible without the support, encouragement, and patience of Allyson Carter.

I also need to thank my family, starting with my mother, Roberta Penziner. Despite the fact that she hates having me out of the country, she has always supported my love for, and work in, Tanzania. Together with my stepfather, Harvey Penziner, their love and support (emotional, logistical, and at times in the early years financial) has been constant and unquestioning. This was affirmed by their visit to Tanzania to see what it was all about in 2002 and their ongoing support of my research endeavors over the years, which often took me to East Africa for long stretches of time. I love you both and hope that the culmination of all that hard work in this book will bring you some sense of pride. I also thank my sisters, Jodi Goldman and Alysa Pasqua, whose constant love and support no matter where I am has helped me get through the best and worst of this. They are my best friends as well as my sisters, and I thank them both for just always being there. I also thank my Aunt Sylvia and late Uncle Bob for their interest in my work and for their house in Vermont, which was the perfect getaway to draft the first outline of the dissertation.

Unfortunately, though to be expected given the time frame of this project, there are several loved ones who are no long with me today. My father, Neil Goldman, grew sick during the course of my dissertation research and passed away at the start of my writing. He was always so proud and so full of love and is greatly missed. My grandparents, Gene and Frances Cooperman, both passed away during the time I was in graduate school. In many ways they were my early intellectual inspiration, especially my grandmother, who received a college degree in her late seventies and was an ardent feminist. When everyone was skeptical of my first desire to go to Tanzania, she introduced me to a friend and teacher of hers, a Tanzanian woman.

Finally, I express my sincere gratitude to my husband Shankar Ayyalasomayajula and two daughters: Aanya and Anisha. This book project began well before you all came into my lives, but it could never have been completed without your love, support, and patience. You have all put up with my long work hours and time away from home, come with me to Tanzania to see what it was all about, and heard me talk about it for far too long. Anisha and Aanya, thank you for your smiles and hugs, for your curiosity and ability to relate to people and places far away from home, and for your desire to actually read this book someday, and to work with me on a children's book. Shankar, thank you for your support and enthusiasm for my work, for reading and listening, and mostly for your unconditional love and respect. I owe the final product of this book to you all.

Abbreviations

AWF	African Wildlife Foundation
CBC	Community-Based Conservation
GCA	Game Controlled Area
JKT	Jeshi kujenga Taifa (National Army)
KEEP	Kwa Kuchinja Environmental Easements Project
LMNP	Lake Manyara National Park
MR	Manyara Ranch
TANAPA	Tanzania National Parks Authority
TLCT	Tanzanian Land Conservation Trust
TMCP	Tarangire-Manyara Conservation Project
TME	Tarangire-Manyara Ecosystem
TNP	Tarangire National Park
UNDP	United Nations Development Program
WMA	Wildlife Management Area
WWF	World Wide Fund for Nature

Narrating Nature

Introduction

THOUGH IT WAS NOT yet noon, the hot sun beat down on us relentlessly as we walked home from a morning's work counting animals by Lake Manyara. I was with two Maasai young men, my regular research collaborator, Mollel, along with Laizer, who had joined us for the day.[1] We were walking through the short grass plains, in an area called *Ang'ata Olowaru* in the Maasai language (Maa), which means the plains of the lions.[2] While the area may not be frequented by lions as it was in the past, it was certainly full of zebra and gazelle that morning. The short grass plain was so named because it attracts zebra, wildebeest, and gazelle, which in turn attract lions. It is also a favorite grazing area for cattle. Yet there were few cattle here today. It was a hot dry day, and cattle had been brought into the neighboring Manyara Ranch to graze, where there was plenty of water and grass. They had been brought in to graze illegally, for the ranch had recently become a conservation area, and livestock grazing by local villagers was allowed only on a limited basis. Yet for neighboring Maasai villagers, the ranch remained an important grazing area, so despite its conservation status, they continued to graze as they could, whenever they could, against the rules that some of them were involved in creating.

Mollel commented that if the *village* managed Manyara Ranch, and wildlife were bringing in benefits they could *see*, then they would regulate grazing in the ranch better, and would even think about giving up their farms to better protect wildlife, because the ranch would be *theirs*, they would *own* it. Laiser had worked in the tourist industry for a hunting company locally and then as a guard at a hotel in Zanzibar and had a more cynical outlook. As he explained,

What I see, and I don't know if you do, or if others do, is this. . . . Maasai and wildlife
bring in the largest percentage of tourist money into our country. Tourists come here
and they want to see Maasai. People make carvings of animals and of Maasai. They
make carvings that look just like you and they sell them and we get nothing? Nothing
at all.

He paused, and then continued, "If you see animals, Maasai are not far. If you see cattle, animals (wildlife) are not far." Looking in my direction, he said, "Why?" Before I
could ask, knowing I would, he continued: "Because they are both things of the *pori*
[Sw: bush/wilderness]," he said simply. But was it really that simple?

My goal with this book is to show that it is not that simple; that there is no singular story that can easily be told through the well-worn binaries of nature and society,
Maasai and conservation, and even politics and ecology. On the contrary, throughout
the book I introduce and work with different storytelling practices *to create ontological
openings for knowing and being with nature otherwise*. In this way, I seek to uncover
the complexity surrounding what many in "the West" have come to call nature and
culture and introduce other ways of understanding these categories, and living in and
across them, in a place populated by people who call themselves Maasai, which is
also surrounded by world-famous wildlife conservation areas. I start by introducing
the familiar stories to situate the less familiar reader, before disrupting these stories
to expose multiple simultaneously existing (sometimes overlapping, and sometimes
disparate) stories *and enactments* of nature-society relations.[3]

Stories of Wildlife Conservation in "Maasailand"

It is not that I want wildlife *to not be here*. We see wildlife as a regular thing. There are
seasons when there are a lot [of wildlife], and they run around freely and come near
the *enkang'* [homestead]. I don't hate wildlife and not want them to be here. Nor do
I like them for [the sake of] tourism because we don't really see tourists. Animals on
the side of tourists are not the problem. It is the people who protect the wildlife that
are the problem.[4]

Many stories have been told in words and pictures of the landscapes and people of
East Africa. Of a place where large charismatic wildlife roam the vast acacia-studded
savanna grasslands, and proud Maasai Indigenous "tribesmen" continue to protect
age-old traditions with pride and grace, and sometimes live "in harmony" with

nature. These stories are ubiquitous—covering the windows of travel agent offices, the pages of coffee-table books, novels, the travel section of the *New York Times*, and performed live across the big screens of IMAX theatres and home televisions through BBC, Nature, Discovery, and Disney channels.[5] These stories have become accepted by many as a true reflection of real Africa: an Africa worth visiting and saving as a living romantic relic of wild nature and premodern society. Yet other stories also circulate—of Africa at risk of environmental and social collapse. These stories depict the same charismatic megafauna suffering from overpoaching and loss of habitat. In these stories, African Indigenous "tribesmen" are no longer noble, but destructive, unaware of the value of nature, misusing their land, carelessly hunting or poisoning threatened species, and at a loss for how to get on in the modern world. Such stories are also found in the newspaper and on TV, in novels and academic books, and the web pages of big international conservation organizations (BINGOS), such as the African Wildlife Foundation (AWF), the World Wide Fund for Nature (WWF), The Nature Conservancy (TNC), and the Wildlife Conservation Society (WCS).

These sets of stories are, of course, not innocent. They come from a particular ontological framing based on Cartesian dualisms that separate nature from society, object from subject, landscape from viewer, and science from other ways of knowing. The stories, and their associated policies and boundary-drawing practices, were born out of imperial conquest of African lands and peoples. Yet the outcomes have persisted over time, with uneven and often devastating effects on people, animals, and landscapes. Much has been written about this process, and I will not detail those stories here.[6] My goal is rather to provide enough of a context for the storytelling I do in this book; to disrupt the common stories about nature in this particular part of the world and create ontological openings for new sets of stories and storytelling techniques— for *knowing and being with nature otherwise.* For there are many stories that have yet to be told—stories that do not fit easily onto the templates outlined above, for they are neither romantic embellishments of a "traditional" Indigenous people living in harmony with nature, nor racist depictions of a savage people destroying nature. It is to these multiple, overlapping, and constantly changing stories of differently situated Maasai that I attend to in this book.

SITUATING THE MAASAI

It is not an accident that Maasai feature strongly in the stories told about African nature. Maasai are an Indigenous people who occupy the same semiarid rangelands of Tanzania and Kenya as many of the globally famous charismatic wildlife.[7] They historically practiced a predominantly pastoralist, seminomadic lifestyle. This meant that vast areas of land left open for grazing by livestock were also used by wildlife. For the most part, Maasai did not hunt, nor did they historically cultivate on a large scale, instead relying on regular trade with agriculturalist neighbors.[8] As a result, "Maasailand has retained one of the world's largest concentrations of wild animal populations" (Parkipuny 1979, 137).[9] Rather than benefiting from this situation, Maasai have been disproportionately impacted by land loss through the creation of national parks in Tanzania and Kenya, starting during the colonial regimes in both countries (Germany and Britain in Tanzania, Britain in Kenya) and continuing today.[10] Many of the areas that Maasai inhabit today continue to contain relatively large wildlife populations and are thus afforded some form of conservation status, with subsequent limitations on resource use. Yet Maasai are rarely recognized by conservation professionals, tourists, or scientists as knowledgeable actors regarding the land they live on and the wildlife they often share it with. They are not asked to contribute their way of knowing and being with wildlife, their knowledge and intelligence, to conservation planning, as doing so would challenge standard scientific knowledge production protocols relied on by conservation science and practice. This fallacy has been pointed out by Maasai scholars and activists for some time (Parkipuny 1979; Parkipuny and Berger 1993; Laltaika 2013; ole Ndaskoi 2002; Parkipuny 1989) and was recently articulated in the fight by Maasai in northern Tanzania to resist new boundary-drawing practices on their lands adjacent to Serengeti National Park (Ngoitiko et al. 2010).[11]

While boundary drawing has always been integral to conservation management (Harris and Hazen 2006; Zimmerer 2000), it has also always been a tricky business, particularly with regards to wildlife (Western 1989; Western and Gichohi 1993; Whatmore and Thorne 1998), which are not usually inclined to follow national park boundaries. In northern Tanzania and southern Kenya, many wildlife spend much of their time outside protected areas where they overlap and intermingle with Maasai livestock in village spaces. Maasai, for their part, often continue to rely on resources inside protected areas to which they are legally denied access yet which they regularly obtain by crossing the physical boundaries under the cover of nightfall or with the protection of bribes.[12] On the other hand, Maasai are often marketed as a part of the Tanzanian and Kenyan "natural" treasure, with most safari itineraries now including a stop at "cultural bomas"[13] where "traditional" Maasai livelihoods are on display and performed as "close to nature."

Conservation agencies are prone to ignore such boundary transgressions or address them through community-based conservation (CBC) endeavors that create official and accepted links between "nature" and "society," such as economic benefits for local communities to win their support for wildlife conservation and, by exten-

sion, wildlife use of village lands. This often translates into microenterprise development projects, provision of water projects and health clinics, and the promotion of
Maasai "cultural" activities, *outside* of the spaces of nature, along with the training of
local game scouts in scientific methods and military skills to protect nature outside of
parks. In this way, rather than breaking them down, CBC projects reinforce boundaries between nature and society, conservation and development, "traditional" and
"modern" (Goldman 2003).

While CBC practices have been critiqued by myself and others, in this book I
am interested in doing more. I am interested in following the border crossings that
regularly occur to see how some wildlife can (and do) survive outside of protected
("natural") spaces, within community lands; what this does to common conceptions
of the nature-society binary; and what differently positioned Maasai, conservation
scientists, and practitioners have to say about it. I am interested in producing new
possibilities for talking about multiple knowledge production processes that move
beyond the incorporation of traditional ecological knowledge (TEK) or "Indigenous
knowledge" into Western scientific management protocols. For doing so only reinforces existing knowledge hierarches associated with another boundary, that between
categories of Indigenous/traditional and modern/scientific, and continues processes
of colonizing knowledge (Simpson 2001; Watson and Huntington 2008). I am interested in decolonizing knowledge and methods to explore—in an academic text—
ways to take seriously multiple ways of knowing, narrating, and being in the world, or
"worlds and knowledges otherwise" (Escobar 2007; see also Smith 2013).[14]

|| || ||

In trying to understand the complex and multiple ways in which Maasai feel about,
know, and interact with wildlife, I made a point when I first went out to the field to
not talk about wildlife. I did not want Maasai to think that I was a "wildlife researcher"
like many others in the area, which would have biased their discussions with me. I
wanted them to feel free and comfortable talking to me about anything, including
wildlife. And so they did. They would talk to me about local and national politics,
about who was sleeping with whom, about the latest fashions (in beadwork and cloth-
ing), about the strange ways of white people they had seen on TV or with tourists
they encountered, about cattle colors and breeds, the birthing patterns of goats and
sheep, and about wildlife. They would speak with awe about the mass birthing of the
wildebeest (if I could only see it, they would insist). On trips to the national parks
they would remark on the skill and agility of impala, observe with great affection the
way mother baboons carry their young, and exclaim with anger and excitement, if
only they had their spears, when we saw a lion. At home, they would also show me

the poison arrows they used to shoot animals that entered their farms, and they would tell me when the *ilmurran* (young men of the warrior age-set) were going on a lion hunt. Maasai feelings about wildlife, I quickly learned, were multiple, complex, and changing; they were also closely associated with their feelings about conservation. They would simultaneously insist they were the original conservators of wildlife and talk about wildlife conservation as occurring "over there," inside the national parks and the Manyara Ranch (MR). They spoke with pride about their decision to have the MR be a "community conservation area," where wildlife and livestock would share the pastures as they always have, and they would benefit from conservation tourism. Yet they respected the MR boundary by farming up to it, making sure it did not shift, that "conservation" did not move into "their land."

One of the men whose farm was up against the MR boundary was a game scout for the ranch, and a good friend, Tipilit.[15] When I visited Tipilit on the ranch, he showed me around, talking about all the wildlife, especially the wild dogs that had just set up home there. "There are no wild dogs left in Serengeti," he explained, but they were here and that was something to be proud of. He showed me his GPS unit and all the recordings he had made of various animals. And then we spoke a bit about wildlife and cattle co-use of the ranch, as we passed a herd of cattle that belonged to the Manyara Ranch.[16] There was plenty of grass in the ranch he suggested, "but AWF just wants the place to be for conservation and thinks that if there are cattle around that could ruin it. They only want wildlife so are thinking of even getting rid of the ranch cattle" (something that was broadly opposed so never happened). In the dry season, villagers would request permission and enter with some of their own cattle. "They are going to build hotels," he said excitedly. Back in the village, I had moved into an old house of Tipilit's, in the *enkang'* (Maa for homestead/settlement, *inkang'itie* pl.) where his mother lived.[17] I was surprised to find poison arrows hidden away in the thatched roof. Poison arrows that were used to kill wildlife.

Then one day I had a conversation with Tipilit's best friend, age- and *enkang'*-mate, Mpake. I simply asked Mpake if his farm was on the border of the Manyara Ranch. "Yes," he said, "it's right on the border." But he did not stop there. "No one can stop me from farming," he insisted. "It's *my* land." He continued to explain that it was not like in Ngorongoro Conservation Area; it was not an area where people could stop him from farming. He spoke in a self-assured way, like he knew what his rights were and would not compromise; he was luckier than those Maasai in Ngorongoro because he had these rights. He insisted that the Ngorongoro Maasai were poor because of all the restrictions placed on them by the conservation area authority, including the restriction on farming. "The problem" in Ngorongoro, he said, "is that the entire area is *hifadhi* [conservation]." "But isn't this area also *hifadhi*?" I asked. "No!" he said, defensively. "This is *our* village and we can farm the whole area if we want to. No one can stop us. Manyara is over there," he said. He then informed me that his farm used to extend into the ranch, but he was told that he had to move it to respect the conservation area boundary. He was told to move the farm by an MR game scout—his friend, age-mate, and business partner, Tipilit.

But Tipilit also had a farm on the border, right next to Mpake's farm. Being so close to the ranch, both farms suffered from high crop raiding by wildlife. When I asked if wild animals came to his farm, Mpake responded by snapping his fingers up in front of his face in a fast, Maasai gesture of exaggeration. "Eh-heh-heh-heh," he said, "too many animals come to the farm! Buffalo, elephant, gazelle, all of them!" And then he explained quite matter-of-factly how he would shoot these animals (with the poison arrows, oh, but if he had a gun!). There was a *Swahili*[18] woman hired for the purpose of guarding the farm. And what about Tipilit? I inquired. I was assured that he too would kill animals that entered his farm. So I just openly asked, "Tipilit cares a lot about wildlife inside the conservation area [MR], but outside he doesn't care?" "That's right," Mpake replied. Then he explained, with a slight smile on his face, how Tipilit *worked* for the MR. He worked for the "government" (and *their* animals). It was a job. Outside the ranch *boundary* was another story; it was *his* farm, *his* personal business, which was about his family's survival. It was that simple.

But it was not (and is not) that simple. Both Mpake and Tipilit were also intrigued by and extremely knowledgeable about wildlife. Mpake constantly requested I take him to the national parks, and always dreamed of seeing Serengeti. When I was in the field, he had the opportunity to go with a tour company working in his village and was thrilled to see so many animals, some different than those he was familiar with near his home. And he was always informative about wildlife we saw inside the village (but far from his farm). Both men had been involved with different wildlife-related research projects, and both have actively deterred *ilmurran* from killing lions inside the MR on several occasions.

Things have changed since my research in this area began in 2002 and I found the poison arrows tucked away inside Tiplit's house. A wildlife-based tourism enterprise was established inside Oltukai Village by Corbett Bishop Safaris. They hired local community members, paid an annual rent and a "head fee" for every overnight tourist, and brought tourists to visit Maasai houses and purchase beadwork. This company left when the owner passed away in 2009, another company came and left, and another started building in 2018. A high-end tourist tented camp was established inside the ranch, the Manyara Ranch Conservancy, and a tourist camp was established in Esilalei Village. And finally, the prime minister officially (at least on paper) returned the Manyara Ranch to villagers in December 2016, though it remains in the hands of district politicians. For Maasai living in this area, wildlife have come to have financial value and political meaning. They bring tourists and money, as well as special interests by politicians and outside groups. As such, Maasai have learned to "milk wildlife" like second cattle.[19] Yet they have also learned that *wazungu* (white people) often want to protect wildlife in ways they don't agree with, and that even "community-based" conservation interventions can disenfranchise them and threaten their livelihoods.[20]

Both Tipilit and Mpake, along with many other villagers (men and women, youth and elders), have also come to realize, through participation in my research and inter- actions with other researchers, that their *knowledge regarding wildlife is valuable*. They have begun to use this knowledge and their confidence in it to challenge conservation projects that attempt to draw more boundaries in their land for the exclusive protec- tion of wildlife, such as wildlife corridors and wildlife management areas (WMAs), the Tanzanian version of state-mandated "community conservation areas."[21] Maasai have contested these projects on political grounds ("The land is ours and no one can tell us what to do with it!") and on ecological grounds (corridors don't make sense; wildlife move everywhere). This is important. It suggests that there is not a singular story here based on nature-society binaries, such as Maasai versus Conservation. It is more complex, with multiple simultaneously existing (sometimes overlapping, and sometimes disparate) stories and *enactments* of nature-society relations.

Complex Political Ecologies

The different stories I have begun to tell in this introductory chapter suggest a certain set of seemingly contradictory possibilities—of Maasai living *with* wildlife, of Maa- sai *resenting* and sometimes hunting wildlife, of conservation *benefiting* local people and of conservation *infringing* on Maasai society. I do not intend to resolve these contradictions. I rather draw on them to highlight the complex multiplicities involved in knowing, being with, and planning for nature in this part of the world, about which many simplified stories have been told. I use the stories to highlight the ongo- ing *multiple enactments* of nature-society relations that are constantly occurring in this place, which also entail boundary-making and boundary-crossing practices—by Maasai, animals (wild and domestic), conservation science, and researchers (myself included). But neither is my goal to tell a story of boundary making or policing in this area, for we already have many of these stories to refer to.[22] Work by political ecolo- gists has uncovered the politics of land appropriation, livelihood destruction, and knowledge marginalization involved in the boundary-making processes associated with conservation in East Africa and beyond (Brockington and Igoe 2006; Gardner 2012; Goldman 2003; Goldman 2007, 2009; Igoe 2004; Neumann 1995a; Neumann 1997; Schroeder and Neumann 1995).

While I draw from and contribute to this scholarship, my goals with this book are slightly different. I am concerned with the *socioecological processes and ontological politics* that occur at the boundary zones between what Western scholarship has come to call nature and society in its various guises, including "Maasai," "science," and "conservation." *It is to these politics of nature-society enactments and narrations that I attend in this book.*

I use the terms *enactment* and *narration* with purpose, to suggest that more than knowledge politics is at stake in talking about, understanding, and planning conservation practices in Maasai-dominated rangelands of East Africa or elsewhere. While it is certainly important to argue for the validity of multiple ways of knowing nature, our work (as scholars, activists, practitioners, translators) should not stop there. Knowledge generation practices are inseparable from world-making practices (Barad 2007). It follows that just as there are multiple ways of knowing the world, there are multiple ways of being in the world and thus multiple possible worlds (Mol 2002). These are not separate, bounded worlds, but worlds that overlap, intermingle, and sometimes conflict; worlds that are enacted through the practices of humans and non-humans, leading Blaser (2010, 3) to use the terms *ontology* and *worlds* as synonyms. As researchers, we participate in creating certain worlds over others (Law 2004). We do this partly through the research methods we employ, through our own positionality, and through the books that we produce. In this book, I take responsibility for that process and work to create ontological openings (de la Cadena 2015), where different enactments and narrations of nature-society relations come into view and become possible—different worlds where nature and society are not bound into discrete material and analytical realms. In doing this work, I draw from the insights of Maasai interlocutors, friends, and activists, as well as scholars who have grappled with questions of how to get on with difference (Verran 2001; Watson-Verran and Turnbull 1995; Green 2013), "foster worlds and knowledges otherwise" (Blaser 2010, 37), build Indigenous alternatives (Simpson 2017), and call for situated solidarities across worlds in ethically responsible ways (Nagar 2014, 2019).

ENACTING NATURE—IN THEORY AND METHOD

In her theory of agential realism, feminist scholar Karen Barad (2007) highlights that how we know the world (epistemology) is intimately connected with what the world is for us (ontology), as well as the types of worlds (material and discursive) that we participate in creating, with the associated (ethical) consequences. For instance— there are worlds created where nature is walled up inside national parks and sold through tourism for profit to an elite few, and other worlds were reciprocal human- nonhuman relations are fostered and respected. These are ethical issues, with certain worlds related to evictions, displacements, and social and ecological disruptions, and others holding on to hope for social and ecological justice. In challenging received ideas of "expert" knowledge I seek to make an ethical intervention into conservation practice, by taking seriously other ways of knowing and being in the world.

In doing so I draw on Barad's theorization of the inseparable nature of epistemol- ogy, ontology, and ethics. I quote her at length here to capture her contribution in all its complexity (2007, 90–91, emphasis in original):

> According to agential realism, knowing, thinking, measuring, theorizing, and observ- ing are material practices of intra-acting within and as part of the world. What do we learn by engaging in such practices? We do not uncover preexisting facts about independently existing things as they exist frozen in time like little statues positioned in the world. Rather, we learn about phenomena—about specific material con- figurations of the world's becoming. The point is not simply to put the observer or knower back in the world (as if the world were a container and we needed merely to acknowledge our situatedness in it) but to understand and take account of the fact that we too are part of the world's differential becoming. And furthermore, the point is not merely that knowledge practices have material consequences but that *practices of knowing are specific material engagements that participate in (re)configuring the world*. Which practices we enact matter—in both senses of the word. Making knowledge is not simply about making facts but about making worlds, or rather it is about making specific worldly configurations—not in the sense of making them up ex nihilo, or out of language, beliefs, or ideas, but in the sense of materially engaging as part of the world in giving it specific material form.

Barad's call aligns with the work of other science and technology studies (STS) scholars, who have called for ways to see the world as "an unformed but generative flux of forces and relations that work to produce particular realities" (Law 2004, 7). Both Barad and Law provide useful points for how to get at this "becoming" through theoretical framings and a move beyond standard methods. To begin with is a recog- nition that "practices of knowing and being" are not isolatable, but rather "mutually implicated" in configuring the world in different ways, not all of which come to matter equally (Barad 2007, 185).

To return to my discussion of boundaries above, we can see that boundary-making practices are material and discursive, epistemological and ontological, and produce certain worldly configurations. One must think about nature and society in particular ways and use certain tools to reveal sets of boundaries that create the categories of nature and society on the ground, in maps, and in policy documents. Yet these boundaries are not permanent fixtures that we can know or study independent of our relationship to them (in creating, respecting, abiding by, challenging). The boundaries are created and recreated (materially and discursively) through the work of conservation practitioners, wildlife, livestock, Maasai herders and farmers, researchers, cartographers, fire, rainfall, and so forth. Barad's agential realism forces us to take the boundaries seriously, while focusing on the *ethical, ontological, and epistemological practices* of their differently becoming. In other words, it is not just a question of how different Maasai, scientists, and conservation practitioners know nature, but also about their simultaneous enactments of certain types of natures, and which come to matter, in both senses of the word—ones where wildlife and livestock are separated in space or ones where they coexist.

Barad provides two additional framings that I find useful: *intra-action* and *diffraction*. Her concept of intra-action gets at the relational aspect of worlds becoming, moving away from a focus on individual, *preexisting* entities, to focus on the relations that bring all entities into being. As she explains, "The object and the measuring agencies emerge from, rather than precede, the intra-action that produces them" (2007, 128). This framing enables a move away from preconceived categories such as Maasai, Indigenous, scientific, domestic, wild, nature, and society, to look at how categories come into being through ongoing intra-actions. This is not to deny the politics behind certain actions, but to complicate our understandings of the categories themselves and to enable more robust ways of *getting on with difference*, as we follow knowledge and practice.

The value of intra-action as a point of entry in unpacking taken-for-granted categories comes through discussions in the book of what it means to be "Maasai," as a set of ongoing intra-actions across different understandings, memories, and enactments of this identity among various Maasai and others. Similarly, the chapters on wildlife and livestock in the landscape should be read as a set of questions regarding the sort of *phenomena* created at the intra-action of different ways of knowing and being in the world where wildlife, livestock, farmers, soils, rainfall, Maasai, conservationists and others intra-act; as well as the politics in choosing which phenomena come to matter for conservation and community planning. I do this by following Annemarie Mol's methodological call of praxiography (2002)—by attending to the practices of particular individuals, groups, and processes. I also follow the call of Law and Mol (2002, 6) to work with "other ways of relating to complexity, other ways for complexity to be accepted, produced, or performed."

This all requires a constant checking of my own assumptions at the door, which is difficult and sometimes impossible to do. There will be slippage along the way, and I use this moment to outline my intent, in the hopes that the reader will see it come through in the following pages. One way in which I do this is to draw on a final valuable contribution made by Barad: the use of diffraction (Barad 2007, 2014), together with a focus on storytelling (Haraway 1991, 1994), and a move "beyond method" to keep messiness and complexity in full view (Law 2004).

Beyond Method: Diffractions and Storytelling

Donna Haraway proposed the term *diffraction* as a useful counterpoint for the notion of reflection/representation, as "an optical metaphor for the effort to make a difference in the world." Diffraction patterns can be read as a record of "the history of interaction, interference, reinforcement, difference" (1997, cited in Barad 2007, 71; see also Haraway 1994). Barad expands on this and proposes diffraction as a method "for reading insights through one another" (Barad 2007, 71). I use this method throughout the book to read different ways of knowing/being/narrating into conversation. I do this by presenting stories and contrasting narratives and knowledge production practices, and by presenting interview data, reports and published material side by side in the format of a dialogue, in the structure of a Maasai meeting. The latter may not be considered storytelling in the strict sense of the word, but is an oral forum and decision-making process, and thus storytelling in the performative sense, and in many ways a diffraction methodology itself.[23]

Social science writing has recently tapped into storytelling, not as "representing a stable, outside reality or developing an argument in a conventional sense, but rather a form of play with possibilities" (Cameron 2012, 585). I am interested in storytelling as oral literature, as history, as a decision-making and knowledge-production device, as open and nonlinear, as an African medium (Mbembe 2015), and thus as a fundamental challenge to preconcieved ideas of "the expert" (see Nagar 2019). I present stories told to me by Maasai, tell stories of my own experiences, and create new stories by diffracting the words of differently situated Maasai, scientists, and my own research into an oral performative device (in written form) of the Maasai meeting, or *enkiguena*. An *enkiguena* is a discussion, meeting, consultation, or debate for Maasai. The *enkiguena* illustrates the strength of the spoken word, the importance of (nonlinear) debate and discussion, and the value of both divergence/diversity and unity within Maasai society. It is a central component of Maasai governance, leadership, knowledge generation, and management systems. As a narrative format, the *enkiguena* maintains a sense of fluidity, motion, and knowledge as active (Furniss and Gunner 1995). I argue that the ideals encompassed in the *enkiguena* provide a valuable template for diffracting the enactment of truths through dialogue among, between, and across multiple (and partially connected) voices.[24]

I thus use stories in the broadest sense of the word: to invoke history, produce new realities, share ideas, debate, and perform what the world is and should be. It is through storytelling and debate that nature is (at least in part) enacted and conservation landscapes produced. This is most visible in the *enkiguena* chapters (1, 3, and 5), which are written to mimic an active Maasai *enkiguena*, with knowledge performances diffracted as a dialogue, and my voice presented as one among many, so as to decenter the perceived "expert." I suggest that the ebb-and-flow style of the *enkiguena* provides the space to follow multiple enactments of nature-society relations simultaneously, without having to delineate between an explicit "Maasai" way of knowing versus a specific "scientific truth." In building the *enkiguena* dialogue I draw on interview and observation data as well as published and unpublished scientific texts. As is customary with academic writing, citations are provided either in text or in footnotes, and quotation marks are used to indicate direct quotes (either from interviews or written material). Yet the style itself attempts to disrupt standard academic knowledge production protocol. I elaborate more on the specifics of a Maasai *enkiguena* and how I used it as method in chapter 6.

MORE ON METHODS AND SOME WORDS OF CAUTION

> Positioning implies responsibility for our enabling practices. It follows that politics and ethics ground struggles for the contests over what may count as rational knowledge.
>
> —HARAWAY 1991, 193

In using Maasai forms of communication and narrative, there are a few words of caution in order. First, my intent is neither to romanticize Maasai as a people or the *enkiguena* as an idyllic form of knowledge production. I am rather doing my best to take seriously Maasai forms of knowledge production and expression in a way that is at least familiar to them, and that challenges Western linear storytelling practices. This attempt follows Ngugi's call to "decolonize" literature (Wa Thiong'o 1992) and similar calls to decolonize methods (Smith 2013) and take seriously Indigenous intelligence and forms of communication (Simpson 2017).

However, my efforts are limited by my own positionality as a non-Indigenous scholar.[25] As such, like Blaser (2010, 36), I "warn the reader against taking this ethnography as an exercise of ventriloquism." In this section, I outline my own positionality within the communities where I worked and how I came to gather and create the words that appear on these pages. I see my writing as performance, to simultaneously bring into being different worlds (nature-society relations) while also opening space for different ways of talking about such worlds—past, present, and future. In doing so, I take inspiration from Nagar's call to build ethically responsible forms of storytelling "with an acute awareness of the tones and textures, memories and feelings, logics and poetics—of people, places, and times as well as the seemingly mundane truths of life that remain distant or insignificant in the imagination of mainstream academia" (Nagar 2019, 32).[26]

Partial Connections: A View from Many Places

My broad goal with this book is to create ontological openings for knowing and being with nature otherwise. Yet I am not interested in doing so in the abstract. I do this in part to make sense of what I have learned, seen, and participated in with Maasai in Tanzania and Kenya over the past two decades. I also want to make this knowledge do some work, to have it speak to ongoing challenges Maasai in both countries grapple with to control their land in the face of ongoing land dispossessions in the name of conservation. To do so, I tell stories from one place in great detail—the *Emanyara* part of the Tarangire-Manyara Ecosystem (TME), among the *Ikisongo* Maasai in Tanzania—while also making connections to other places where different groups of Maasai encounter similar struggles and enact similar processes of nature-society relations. All the areas discussed can be considered semiarid savanna landscapes that support wildlife and pastoralism, and all were historically part of what was considered "Maasailand," which was and continues to be divided into different territorial sections (Maa: *iloshon, olosho* sg.), and subsections (*inkutot, enkutoto* sg.). Discussions about Maasai in this book draw mostly from research within the *Emanyara enkutoto* with additional insight gleamed from visits to Simanjiro and Ngorongoro *inkutot* within the *Kisongo olosho*. Research also draws from time spent with *Ilkisongo, Ilkaputei,* and *Purko iloshon* in Kenya. See map 1.

Material presented in this book draws from ongoing ethnographic fieldwork over two decades with Maasai communities in Tanzania (2002–2004; January–May 2005; October 2006–July 2007; January–July 2009) and Kenya (October 2006–July 2007;

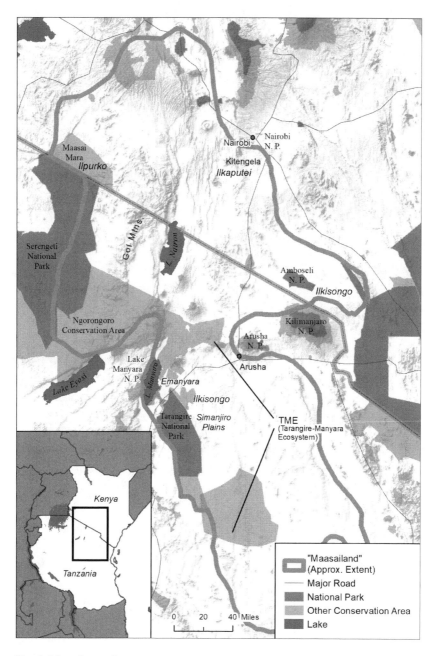

Map 1 Map of research areas

January–July 2009), with shorter trips made in 1993, 1997, 2000, 2010, 2011, 2013, 2016, and 2019, with the majority of work and residence at least in the early years being in the TME. Over time, my own partial connections made me part local, foreigner, student, expert, woman, child, elder, honorary male, honorary Maasai, and so on. As I began this journey as a single white woman, working and living in a Maasai village, people needed to know how to relate to me.[27] This meant placing me within their own social categories (age-sets, clans, gender), which taught me a great deal about how these categories regulate social relations. I also quickly established individuals who acted as my fathers, mothers, grandmothers, brothers, and sisters.

These multiple positions exposed me to a variety of everyday relations that I was not always prepared for, such as the complex nature of gender dynamics, the importance of clan politics, the ongoing and shifting role of "traditional" Maasai governance structures alongside official government demarcations (Goldman, forthcoming), and the overlapping and often conflicting views of wildlife and conservation.

During my time in Maasailand, I relied predominantly on in-depth ethnographic methods. These included hundreds of hours of participant observation (at meetings, ceremonies, during ecological data collection, while herding, at home, in national parks), formal and informal group and individual interviews, participatory mapping, and short surveys. Short interviews with a representative sample ($n = 70$) of household heads in TME in 2003 assessed wildlife and livestock grazing patterns by season, as well as views about wildlife corridors and "troublesome" animals. I also worked with Maasai interlocutors to gather wildlife and vegetation data using ecological field methods along (walking) transects in eight different ecological zones (2003–5), presented in the *enkiguena* chapters. See map 2.

Details regarding the transect methods are described at length in Goldman (2018). To summarize, we counted live animal sightings and estimated the distance from the transect line so that we could produce estimates of animal densities. We also collected data on "signs" of animal presence (dung, footprints) along the transect line from within a few days of our transect walk. These methods were designed to combine Maasai intimate knowledge of wildlife, livestock, and the local landscape with scientifically recognized methods.

Additionally, short postmeeting surveys were conducted (2007, 2009) with the help of Maasai interlocutors in Kitengela and Amboseli in Kenya, Simanjiro, and *Emanyara* to address meeting topics, power dynamics, and decision-making processes, totaling over 400. These data contribute to my understanding of meeting facilitation within Maasai communities, which I draw on to construct the *enkiguena* chapters. In chapter 6, I explain the set of guidelines followed in an *enkiguena*, and

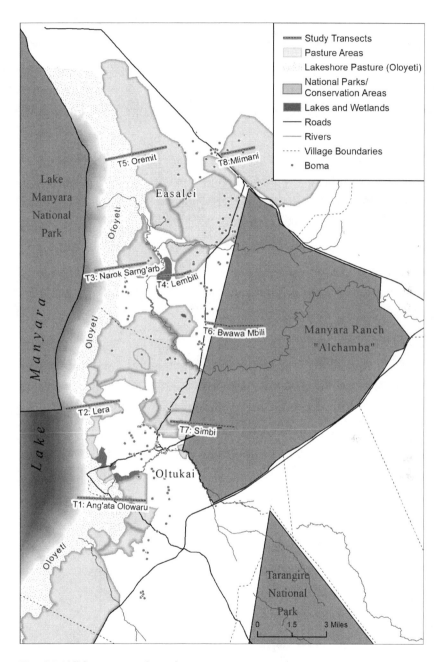

Map 2 Wildlife transects in the study area

how a consensus is constructed. For now, I provide a basic outline of the format and participants to set the stage for the coming chapters.

Setting the Stage: The *Enkiguena* Method, Setting, and Participants

Knowing is not about seeing from above or outside or even from a prosthetically enhanced human body. Knowing is a matter of intra-acting. Knowing entails specific practices through which the world is differentially articulated and accounted for. . . . Knowing is not a bounded or closed practice but an ongoing performance of the world.

—BARAD (2007, 149)

As method—for writing and presenting—the *enkiguena* follows the law of symmetry as proposed by STS scholars, which suggests that we not let our ideas about what is true or false affect how we approach research, with "truths" and falsehoods, nature and society, science and ethnoscience all treated *symmetrically* (Law 2004, 40). I try to do this by weaving together different voices without partitioning off ethnoscience, belief, religion, science, or anecdote in addressing different thematic questions as if they were agenda items in an *enkiguena*: wildlife movements in time and space (chapter 1), rangeland ecology and wildlife-livestock relations (chapter 3), and wildlife corridors (chapter 5). While I bring each chapter to a close, the consensus is not presented as a coherent singularity. I work rather to expose (and create) the *overlap* and *diffraction patterns* between different ways of knowing and being with nature (within and across assumed "groups"). This means that I present individual words, thoughts, and statements from different Maasai and conservation practitioners and scientists, citing them accordingly and providing information on their positionality in the *enkiguena* chapters, rather than presenting "the Maasai" way and "the conservation science" way. In the final chapter, I discuss what the *enkiguena* offers as a larger framework/presentation format, and what a consensus is. For now, the reader should see the consensus as an ending that is sufficient enough to end the discussion with an agreement, but without hiding the multiple contributions that created it.

It is important to note that while I do draw from some actual meeting dialogue, much of the *enkiguena* I produce in the following chapters (from ecological, ethnographic, and secondary sources) *never actually took place*. The dialogues presented would not occur as I have enacted them, not within the current social political context, which prioritizes certainty and coherence, politicizes knowledge regarding wildlife, and privileges scientifically verified ways of knowing. Maasai participation in conservation, even if encouraged by outsiders, is often inhibited due to epistemological hierarchies, the meeting format itself, and relations of "respect" (Maa: *enkanyit*) among Maasai and between Maasai and outsiders. My intent is not to ignore or minimize these complex, historically situated, and constantly changing relations of power. I attend to them in chapters 4 and 6 and again in the conclusion. By presenting the *enkiguena* chapters first, I am in some ways asking for a suspension of belief to enable the possibility that things could be otherwise. It is a strategic attempt to engage the reader in decolonial possibilities for knowing and being with nature, without getting mired in analyses of power. Power is always present, and is always deflected, transformed, and remade. Of course, we are not dealing with a tabula rasa, but neither should we feel confined to a set of preconceived categories and possibilities. I do make note of power dynamics throughout the *enkiguena* chapters, in line with structural categories of wealth, gender, clan, and age, while also noting other processes at play that mediate speaking at an *enkiguena* (i.e., personality, speaking ability). And I provide some guidance below on how these categories play out so that the reader can see the power woven into the *enkiguena* dialogue.

The *enkiguena* I enact in the coming chapters reflects much of the ebb and flow and rhetoric as practiced at a Maasai *enkiguena*. Drawing on Haraway's account of the "kinship" of fact and fiction—both rooted in the experience of human action and both apparent in scientific narratives—what I present is *both* fact and fiction. Haraway explains the difference as such: "Fact seems done, unchangeable, fit only to be recorded; fiction seems always inventive, open to other possibilities, other fashionings of life." But, she also warns, "in this opening lies the threat of merely feigning, of not telling the true form of things" (1989, 4). I avoid this by citing my sources and explaining the experiences behind my narrative. My story is fiction in that the meetings enacted in the following chapters never actually occurred as presented. Yet my story is also fact, (re)presenting statements, knowledge claims, and numbers, that *were* made, stated, and calculated, through the experiences of different actors, at particular times and places. I now briefly introduce this context.

THE MEETING PARTICIPANTS

The major participants in the *enkiguena* are Maasai and conservationists (scientists and practitioners). While these are not homogenous groups, there are general statements that can be made regarding different methodological approaches used by conservation scientists, regarding wildlife census techniques, rangeland management, and conservation management, compared to Maasai ways of knowing the landscape and wildlife around them.[28] The specific positionality of individual participants in the *enkiguena* that I construct is presented in the dialogue when possible or in footnotes, keeping in mind that many of the individuals (if not all) share partial connections with others, within and across groups. There are Maasai trained in conservation science and practice. There are scientists engaged in conservation practice, and some working with Maasai, and conservation practitioners engaged with science. And there are state civil servants, working for "conservation" (i.e., in the game department, forestry department), through their involvement in conservation projects. Here I briefly outline the participant groupings.

Conservation scientists. My use of "conservation scientists" includes a wide range of people, institutions, schools of thought, and disciplines concerned with wildlife conservation in Tanzania. Through the course of the *enkiguena*, these differences are articulated, particularly between scientific researchers and conservation practitioners. However, with regards to wildlife conservation in Tanzania (and Kenya) there is an amazing coherence between the work of scientists and the words, concerns, and work of practitioners. In many cases, they are one and the same person, with conservation interventions often proposed by researchers (Borner 1985; Mwalyosi 1991; Newmark 1993; Prins 1987).

Generalizations can often be made regarding the ways in which "conservation science" knowledge, expertise, and respect are defined as associated with education, understanding of scientific tools and theories, or scientific literacy. However, expertise within the conservation science community in Africa is also highly racialized. People of Euro-American decent are more readily accepted as experts than many of their African contemporaries (Garland 2006). Euro-Americans who begin as tour guide operators or safari drivers become conservation project directors or managers. They can quickly learn the skills of the trade, talk the scientific language, impress their scientific (and Maasai) colleagues, and gain respect as knowledgeable (and capable) in their field, even with little or no formal scientific education. Tanzanian conservation workers can also gain respect through formal education, research, and participation in science. They are more likely, however, to be questioned on their judgment and ability to be "objective," and also more readily accused of corruption. Some Tanzanian conservation actors take on a strong Western stance and directly challenge Maasai knowledge, while others are more open to Maasai ways of knowing; much of this depends on education and social position.

Maasai participants. Maasai too should not be viewed as a homogenous group but rather as the enactment of an identity that is "more than one and less than many"

(Mol 2002). Through a series of sociospatial boundaries, Maasai are both united as a group and divided into various categories based on geography (section/*olosho*), age (*olaji*), clan (*enkaji*), gender, and class, which I briefly outline here to provide some context for the micropolitics at play in the *enkiguena* chapters. The ways in which these categories mediate power dynamics and how this is changing is elaborated on further in the second half of chapter 6.

Location/Iloshon. The various groups of people discussed today as "Maasai" belong to different sections (*iloshon*; sg: *olosho*), that were previously described by historians as distinct social groups or "tribes" that fought wars against each other prior to the arrival of Europeans (Jacobs 1975, Waller 1979).[29] There are seven territorial sections (*iloshon*) usually recognized in Tanzania, including *Serenget, Salei, Purko, Laitayok, Loita* of Ngorongoro District and Southern Kenya, and *Kisongo*, which is the largest section and includes much of northern Tanzania into Kenya where they are known as the *Loitokitok* (Ndagala 1992). *Kisongo* is further divided into subsections, *inkutot* (*enkutoto* sg.), with geographic and social overlap as well as distinctions, each with its own customary leader (*ilaigwenak*).[30] According to Maasai I worked with, the *Kisongo* section in Tanzania is comprised of the following *inkutot*: *Kisongo, Emanyara, Ngorongoro, Longido, Simanjiro, Kiteto/Moipo*, and *Enguruka. Emanyara enkutoto* is the focus of the *enkiguena* chapters. Research was conducted predominately in Oltukai and Esilalei Villages (Monduli District, Arusha Region), with some spillover into Losirwa, Elasiti, and Kakoi Villages, all of which maintain strong cultural ties and shared resource use as one *enkutoto* (*Emanyara*), which are mediated through clan and age-set affiliations. Maasai refer to places within this space with place-names, detailed in chapter 2. See map 3.

Clan/Enkaji: Maasai also divide themselves into two moieties (*enkaji*, "house" in Maa) and multiple clans and subclans (*enkishomi*).[31] Clans are patrilineal descent groups, which are nonlocal and connect Maasai across *inkutot* and *iloshon*, while dividing them locally (Homewood and Rodgers 1991). While there are multiple clans and subclans, the major division is into two overarching moieties, often referred to by the dominant clan within each, *Ilmolelian* for the *Nado-Mongi* (those of the red oxen); and *Ilaiser* for the *Narok-kiteng'* (those of the black cow). While conducting field work, the Ilmamasita were the most dominant clan within the *Emanyara enkutoto*, much less dominant across *Kisongo*, barely recognized in Kenya, and only a subclan in the other sections.

Clan relations are solidified through marriage, facilitating access to grazing land and water resources across *enkutoto/olosho* boundaries. In this way, clans unite Maasai across space—helping a stranger find a place to stay in a faraway *olosho/enkutoto* and

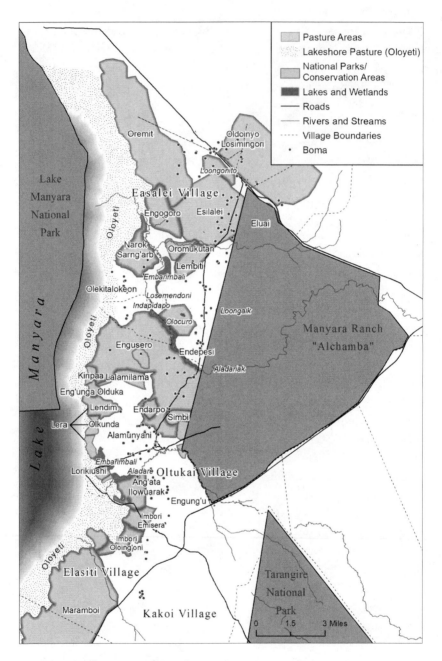

Map 3 Maasai place-names in the study area

enabling a woman to feel comfortable and free with a "brother" or nervous and shy around a senior male in-law. Clan membership is embodied in cattle markings, clan-based practices and rituals, and traditional clan leaders (*ilaigwenak le nkaji*). Historically, clan membership mediated access to point-source resources, such as water from hand-dug wells, with clan members given priority of use. Today, access to education, leadership, jobs, outside income flows (from development/investments), farms, and land is often contested along clan lines. In this way, clan affiliations also divide Maasai and mediate power between and across age-sets and gender.

Age-sets/Olaji: The age-set system is perhaps the most well-known and visible aspect of Maasai society to outsiders. Everyone knows of the famous Maasai "warriors" or *ilmurran*—often poised with one leg bent against the other, proudly holding a spear as they look off into the endless plains. With their colorful beads, plaited hair, and proud demeanor, *ilmurran* have long commanded the attention of tourists, scholars, and administrators—either in admiration, scorn, or both. Myths and exaggerations of their behavior abound, from the hunting of lions with a spear as an assumed "rite of passage" to the casual planting of their spear outside an age-mate's house to claim sexual relations with his wife.[32] While exaggerations, these stories reflect the strength of age-set relations, the protective role played by *ilmurran*, and their role as coveted lovers of young girls and married women alike. But this is only part of a larger age-grade system that officially organizes Maasai men's lives into a series of socialized stages, along with their mothers, the girls they dance with, and the women they marry. As with clans, the age-set system both brings people together and divides them into conflicting groups; it calls on collective responsibility and respect, while also generating fear.

Central to the age-set system is a series of age-grades that divide men into distinct groupings once they move on from being uncircumcised boys, *ilaiyok* (sg. *olayioni*): circumcised young men, *ilmurran* (warriors; sg. *olmurrani*); and elders (*ilmoruak/ ilpayiani*), with further breakdowns into junior and senior *ilmurran*, junior, senior, and retired elders. Circumcision for a new age-set is opened approximately every fifteen years, and the period of warriorhood, the climax of the age-grade system, lasts approximately twenty years. In this way, Maasai can use age-sets to tell time and history, referring to the name of the age-set that were *ilmurran* at the time, often further referencing ceremonies to mark finer temporal scales (see table 1). A complete age-set is referred to as an *olaji*, the masculine noun for house, as it is another "house" that men claim allegiance to alongside that of their *enkaji* (feminine version: house, moiety/clan).

Age-set names have historically been the same across Maasailand, with shared ceremonies marking the passage of time. While much of this has changed over the years, I

Table 1 Age-set names and dates

Common names (with different names given at different ceremonies)	Important dates	Representation in this story
IlNyangulo	2011– Eunoto: 2019	**Recent initiates to *Ilmurran*** Most were children when I started field work.
IlKorianga *Irimireh*–Enkipata OR *imirishi* *Ilkiponi*–Olng'esher 2017	1998–2017 Eunoto: 2005	**Warriors (*Ilmurran*)** Were junior warriors at the beginning of the study, with some circumcisions still occurring. They then became warriors (with different senior and junior subsets), when Landis graduated to elderhood in October 2003.
IlLandis *Irkimunyak*–Enkipata *Ilkidotu*–Eunoto *Irkidotu*–Olng'esher	(1981?) 1983–2003 Eunoto: 1991 Olng'esher: 2003 (20 years)	**Junior elder (*Ilmoruak*)** Were senior warriors at the start of research (2002). Graduated to junior elders 2003.
IlMakaa	1971–1988 Eunoto: 1978 Olng'esher: 1987 (17 years)	**Senior elder (*Ilmoruak*)** Were junior elders at the start of the study; graduated to senior elder status 2003.
IlSeuri	Circumcison: 1955 Eunoto: 1965 Olng'esher: 1974 (19 years)	**Retired elder (*Ilmoruak*)** Most populous group of senior respected elders at the start of research.
IlMeshuki (Ilnyankusi)	Circumcision: 1935 Olng'esher: 1958 (23 years)	**Retired elder (*Ilmoruak*)**
Ilterito	Circumcision: 1926 Olng'esher: 1947 (21 years)	**Retired elder (*Ilmoruak*)** Very few remained alive from this age-set, with one passing away during the study and two being blind and homebound.

was able to find commonality in the formal names of age-sets across sections, although for the last three age-sets "nicknames" were more commonly used. As such, I only use the formal names for the older age-sets, which during my fieldwork consisted of the *Seuri, Meshuki* (Or *Ilnyankusi*), and *Ilterito* (in terms of living members). The other age-sets in descending order were the *Makaa* (nickname in Tanzania, official name *Ilkishumu*), *Landis* (*Ilkumunyak*), *Korianga* (*Ilkiponi*), and the *Nyangulo* (2017). See table 1.

The age-set system coordinates social relations across houses (men of different age-grades) as well as between men and women and between and within clans. It sets rules for eating (*ilmurran* are not to eat meat seen by women or eat in front of any women except their mothers), sleeping (*ilmurran* are to sleep together), sexual relations (informally tolerated outside of marriage only *within* the age-set of the husband), and even greetings and ways of speaking (or not) in social settings and at an *enkiguena*.[33] Elders play an important role in the age-grade system, often mediating the rules and determining when an age-set can graduate to the next level. They have historically dominated discussions in *enkiguena* and can silence *ilmurran* with threats of a curse. Relations are generally tense between members of adjacent age-sets, which vie for power and respect, often leading to direct conflicts. On the other hand, men of alternate age-sets share a supportive father-son-like relationship (referred to as *ilpiron* or firestick elders), which nonetheless is still mediated by the elder's power over the *ilmurran*, as discussed more in chapter 6.

Women play an essential role in the age-set system—as wives and mothers—in all the major ceremonies that mark turning points in men's lives.[34] Women also have their own places within the system. They are socially affiliated with the age-set of their husbands, or the age-set with which they danced as uncircumcised girls. Women are also recognized as belonging to a certain life stage: uncircumcised girl (*entito*; pl. *intoyie*), married young wife (*esiangiki; isiangikin*), mother (*yieyio*), and grandmother (*koko*), each associated with different responsibilities, social standing, and public image. Women often discuss their progression into becoming a mother (*yieiyio*) and then a grandmother (*koko*) as bringing increased levels of joy, freedom, and respect—over younger women and with their husbands. Throughout much of *Kisongo* Maasailand, women also belong to named *esirit* (circumcision) groups like men, depending on when they were circumcised. Not recognized as formal age-sets, these groups act as important indicators of social solidarity and a woman's place within the society, particularly as a young wife, often embodied in beadwork designs, dress, dance, and speaking styles.

Throughout the *enkiguena*, while I use pseudonyms, I reference the age-set, or the general age-grade for women, and sometimes clan affiliation or leadership status. All these overlapping social alliances are linked to a decentralized system of customary leadership, *ilaigwenak la mila* (pl., *olaigwenani* sg., in Maa, *mila* is Swahili for "traditional"), that historically acted less as autonomous leaders and more as "spokesmen" for age-sets and clans in each locality. There are also ritual "leaders," *iloibonok* (*oloiboni* sg.), best understood as ritual expert, medicine man, prophet, diviner (Mol 1996, 299).[35] Today, *iloibonok* of different ranks and *ilaigwenak* of different groups are still feared and respected across Maasailand, though the system has weakened in parts of Kenya. The respect that customary leaders instill is embodied in the *olkuma*, a black ebony club often beaded in elaborate designs, which carries the power to curse, which *ilaigwenak* hold as they speak at an *enkiguena*. In Tanzania, there is also a parallel system of decentralized government leaders both elected and appointed. These government leaders do not carry an *olkuma* and do not necessarily garner the same respect (Goldman, forthcoming).

MYSELF

My own voice comes through the *enkiguena* as a mediator (in boxed asides), explaining and tying different points together, and as a participant (as MG) presenting transect data and explaining conservation interventions. This reflects my multiple (and partially connected) identities: social science researcher, feminist, ecology researcher, westerner, woman, and honorary man. I do not let my voice dominate the meeting but try to present my views, knowledge, and opinion as one among many. Now, on to the first agenda.

| Chapter 1 |

Enkiguena Agenda I

Where Are the Animals?

I MAGINE, IF YOU WILL, the setting: an octagon-shaped Catholic church in Esil-alei, just off the dirt road. The building is cement, painted a burned brown on the outside and white on the inside, which has long since dirtied to a nondescript tannish color, resembling the surrounding soil. The roof is corrugated iron, with no ceiling board. Along the walls are large, open windows, screened with a thick, wide, metal mesh that keeps flies and rain out. There is a population of bats and birds that occupy the rafters, littering the floor with droppings and making constant sounds that echo throughout the one-room building. Along the front wall are various items—a drum, papers, and drawings—all attempts to Africanize and personalize the teachings of the church. Rows of narrow and rickety wooden benches face the front of the room, where there are two red, overstuffed, badly torn cushioned stools and a podium, where the leader of the services usually stands.

Maasai meetings do not utilize the podium, and most often take place outside, in a shaded patch of grass in a stand of *oldepesi* trees (*Acacia tortilis*). The two overstuffed stools are brought out for the most important and oldest elders to sit on. Sometimes a bench or two are brought out, if there are other guests, but most of the Maasai participants sit on the ground, on the low-lying tree limbs, or on piles of rocks they form into makeshift stools. It is only when an outside group comes in or the weather is bad that the meeting will be held inside the church. Meetings inside the church facilitate the display of maps, papers, and figures, which can be taped to the walls or put on a podium without being blown away by the wind. Yet this makes it difficult for the speaker to stand in the middle of the gathering. Imagine our meeting taking place in the space just outside of the church. You should get the feeling of an oddly hybrid place—at once foreign, organized, and modern, yet simultaneously so very African, Maasai, and local. The meeting agenda is to better understand where wildlife are in village lands throughout the year.

The meeting is opened with a blessing from a respected elder. He stands up, holding on to his robes, which drape over his large stomach—a sign of his wealth—to keep them from blowing in the wind. Leaning on his tall, thin walking stick (*engudi*), he speaks in a low, melodic tone. He blesses all of us at the meeting, our cattle, and our children. He begs for *Engai* (God and rain), to make the land and the cattle healthy, and for cattle and children to be many. Throughout the blessing, at each appropriate (but barely noticeable) pause, all the participants respond with "*Nai*" (the response to prayer, "O God!" [Mol 1996, 268]). He sits back down on one of the overstuffed, torn chairs. The meeting is now ready to begin.

Chairman of the meeting: *He is also the village chairman and former customary leader* (olaigwenani) *for his age-set, the Makaa. He is well respected, but his close association with conservation organizations has led many to challenge his intentions and integrity. He opens the meeting.* Welcome everyone, especially our guests who have come from afar. *He motions over to the guests all sitting together on the wooden benches brought out just for them, in the best shady spots. Looking directly at them he smiles broadly.* Thank you for coming to visit us today. I hope you can stay the whole time. Our meetings take a while, but we will try to be quick! *He then circles around to face the many Maasai present and continues.* We have only one agenda today, that concerning wildlife presence in our village lands. Our guests here have their scientific data to share with us, and I think MG does too? *He looks over at MG, who nods; he continues.* But we Maasai, we also have a lot to say about this, so everyone, welcome! Please tell us what you know/see about wildlife in our lands. *He sits down and invites everyone to contribute. He gives the OK for the local conservation manager to start.*

Local conservation manager:[1] *A white British man, he has lived in Tanzania working on conservation-related issues for many years, starting as a safari driver and moving into community conservation management. He is well liked by the community, who see him as honest. It helps that he is married to a Maasai woman. He introduces himself to the meeting, although they all know him anyway, so he does so in a joking manner, and everyone laughs. He switches to a more instructional, almost paternal tone.*

As you all know, this area that you call home is an important place for wild-life. Back in 1964, a scientific study showed that wildlife move out of Tarangire National Park (TNP) into the Simanjiro Plains and into this area in between TNP and Lake Manyara National Park (LMNP), referred to as the Kwa Kuchinja corridor. *He waves his arms around to indicate that he means right here, where we are all gathered.* In fact the man who conducted the study (Lamprey 1964) referred to certain animals, such as zebra, wildebeest, buffalo, eland, and elephant, as "dry season immigrants" of Tarangire National Park because they only came into the park in the dry season for water. The Tarangire River provides an important source of water for these animals. But they seem to prefer the areas outside the park, and research has pointed to why this might be the case. *He nods over in the direction of the two young researchers sitting next to him.* The quality of the forage is higher outside of the park, particularly in the Simanjiro plains [Tarangire Conservation Project (TCP) 1998; Voeten 1999]. *He looks over again at the young researchers for their agreement; they nod in approval, and he continues.* Lamprey also found that the "northern end of Lake Manyara" is "an important dry season area particularly for wildebeest" (Lamprey 1964). However, as many of you can attest to, a lot has changed since 1964. *The elders make signs of agree-ment and exclamation around the circle . . . oosho . . . ee pae (yes, of course). He nods and continues.* With an increase in population and farms we cannot be sure anymore if wildlife are really safe outside of the parks. And the wildlife here are of importance **globally**. *He pauses and looks around as Maasai look at each other and seem surprised. "Globally?" they whisper to each other. He continues.* There are people in America and Europe who are interested in wildlife here in Tanzania; and this is not just so they can come over as tourists. *Laughter from Maasai.* This is about **biodiversity conservation**, a global concern. The creation of Manyara Ranch as a conservation area was done with international support, to protect an important habitat for wildlife between the two parks. But the ranch is only a small piece of this larger area, and before we can talk about doing more, we need to have a better idea of where wildlife are, not just in the ranch but in vil-lage lands. Markus Borner (1985, 91–92) suggested that this "area east of Lake Manyara is still important during the early rainy season, when several thousand wildebeest and zebra move [here]."[2] The guest researchers here also have data to present, so maybe today we can get a better idea of which animals are where at what times of the year. That is the starting point for any conservation plans.

Maasai talk among themselves, some quite loudly, particularly a group of women. Surprised to hear them speaking up, the manager looks in their direction. Speaking to the chairman, he says, It seems the women have something to say. Perhaps they should be given the chance to speak next? *The chairman nods in the direction of the women.*

Yeiyo Esirit:[3] *The first wife of one of the wealthiest and most respected men in the village, she takes the opportunity to speak but looks in the direction of the researchers and not in the direction where her husband is sitting.* There are a lot of wildlife in the village. "We see them when we go to collect firewood. Especially during *alare* [wet season], in the *osero* [bushed area] of *Lera,* we see all kinds of animals but especially wildebeest and zebra [see map 4].[4] During this time and during *orkisirata* [the early rains, see table 2 below], the animals pass right by our *enkang'* in Oltukai, especially zebra, going back and forth between *Alchamba* [MR] and *Lera.* And ostrich! *Oosho,* so many of them stay near our *enkang'.* But in the dry season [*alamei*], most of the animals run away because of water, only a few zebra and wildebeest stay, but the gazelles—*Oosho,* many of them stay."

Seuri OL:[5] *A safe man to speak after a woman, he is a retired elder, kind and respectful. He was born here and is well liked.* It is true. There are a lot of wildlife in the village nearly all year round. "In *orkisirata*—wildebeest and zebra will use *Oremit* and *Oloyeti* where there is usually water here and there. In *oladalo* [break in the rains] wildlife and cattle both just go wherever the water is. . . . It depends on where it has rained. They follow the rain and good grass," sometimes that is in the village and sometimes it is not. During *engakwai* [heavy rains] all the wildebeest move; you don't see even one! But in *koromare,* the wildebeest return. The zebra are just here; they don't leave. And in *alamei,* wildebeest and zebra fill up Manyara Ranch. They drink water there and then visit the village. *The younger Maasai men look at each other grinning with respect for this elder who just so quickly and effortlessly explained the "way things are."*

> *A note on seasons*: At the broadest scale, Maasai refer to the dry season (*alamei*) and the wet season (*alare*).[6] Yet, on a daily basis, they utilize a more detailed seasonal calendar, along with a set of corresponding Maasai months, that today most Maasai discuss in relation to the Gregorian calendar, breaking the months down for a more detailed discussion of when one season begins and another ends. Seasonal boundaries are not fixed in time, but can shift as seasons come early or late, and move across space. Keeping this in mind, one can outline a general breakdown of how the seasons are expected to behave, as shown in table 2.

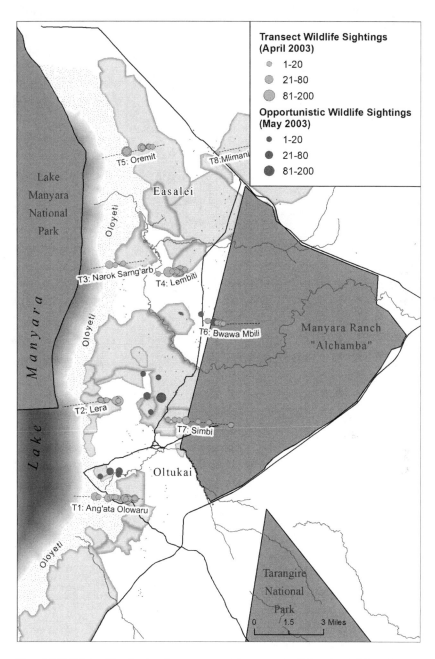

Map 4 Wildlife in village lands using transect and "opportunistic" data, April–May 2003

Table 2 Maasai seasonal breakdown

Season name	Timing	Description
Orkisirata –Oltumerin	Oct./Nov.–Dec.	Short rains scattered, then every-where, combined as *orkisrata* in TZ[a]
Oladalo	mid-Jan.–mid-/late Feb.	Short hot dry month with a break in the rains
Engakwai	mid-May–June/July	Long heavy rains
Koromare	mid-May–June/July	End of rainy season, beginning of dry season, with grass and rain puddles still available.[b]
Alamei	July–Sept.	Dry season

[a] In *Kisongo* Kenya, *oltumerin* was used to refer to both, with *orkisirata* used for the scattered rains (Ryan Unks, personal communication).

[b] As the dry season is becoming more severe in many places, Maasai in Longido have suggested the loss of this season (Lovell 2018).

Scientists A and B stand up:[7] *Two young Italian women, they worked together on the Tarangire-Manyara Conservation Project (TMCP), a partnership between Instituto Oikos, the University of Insurbria, Tanzania National Parks Authority (TANAPA), and the World Wide Fund for Nature (WWF). Their work is widely accepted by conservationists as the best word on what is happening in the ecosystem. Since they have charts and maps to display, they would like to go inside the church. However, the smell of the bats and the trouble of moving everyone inside discourages them. They opt instead to lean the large display board they have up against a tree. They will stand here to speak, rather than the middle of the circle. They unroll large papers with maps and charts and clip them to the board. As Maasai begin to talk among themselves, the older of the two women clears her throat and they both look around. The chairman hushes everyone, then motions for the women to speak.* Just like the local conservation manager explained, we are interested in finding areas that are important for wildlife at different times of the year across the TME. We combined methods and data to find trends in wildlife numbers across time and space. *They point to a table clipped to the board* [see table 3]. We found this area, "between the eastern shore of Lake Manyara and Tarangire National Park," as an important wildlife distribution area for elephant, zebra, buffalo, and wildebeest in both the wet and dry season (Tarangire-Manyara Conservation Project [TMCP] 2002b, 5). And, if we combine data from different years for the entire TME, we

Table 3 Data collection methods used by the Tarangire-Manyara Conservation Project (TMCP) with corresponding Maasai seasons in bold

	RF (reconnaissance flight)	SRF (standard reconnaissance flight)	TC (total count for elephant and buffalo)	RT (radio-tracking)
Wet season	May 1998 **Engakwai (WS)** Mar. 1994 **Engakwai (WS)**	Feb. 1996 **Oladalo** June 1996 **Koromare**	May 1996 **Engakwai (WS)** Feb. 1998 **Oladalo**	12 wildebeest and 13 zebra (1995–1997) 7 elephant (1997–1999)
Dry season	Sept. 1990 **Alamei (DS)** Oct. 1994 **Orkisirata**	Nov. 1995 **Orkisirata** Sept. 1996 **Alamei (DS)**	Sept. 1995 **Alamei (DS)** Oct. 1994 **Orkisirata**	

can see that for this area, which we call "Esilalei (between LMNP and TNP),"
wildebeest and zebra have a "medium abundance" in the wet season. Zebra and
buffalo show a "low abundance" in the dry season, and there are no wildebeest
(Tarangire-Manyara Conservation Project [TMCP] 2002b, 6). *They display a
map of the TME and point to the large collection of different-colored symbols indicating wet and dry season presence of different animals in the "Esilalei" area. Scientist A
gathers the papers and returns to her seat. Scientist B remains standing.*

Scientist B: Yes, this is true, *she explains.* However, our research on a smaller
scale shows a slightly different picture. We conducted driving transects on
designated roads. *Pointing on the map she speaks slowly.* One of the roads goes
through the village, down to the lake. Another comes up through the center of
Esilalei, this road right here that we came in on today. The other transects are in
adjoining villages and in the Manyara Ranch. *She looks up making sure everyone
understands the area she is referring to. There is much commotion as Maasai point
out that the first road she mentioned is not in Esilalei but in Oltukai. She seems
confused by this and is not quite sure how to proceed. The village chairman from
Oltukai stands up to speak.*

Oltukai village chairman:[8] *Tall and proud, he turns around the circle, smiling at
everyone and then talks directly to Scientist B in an authoritative but calm, almost
patronizing voice.* It is all a bit confusing sometimes to outsiders. We used to
be one village, but now we are two. I am the chairman for Oltukai Village.
He pauses here for effect. She nods, and he continues. The first road that you

mentioned, that goes down to the lake? That is in *Oltukai Village*. And the elders just want to make sure you know that. You should change your tables and maps to show this. It matters. Researchers, like yourselves, often come into our village and do research without visiting our office, asking for permission, and telling us you are here. Then we don't even get the credit (or benefits, *he says with a smirk*) of the research and the findings—that we have wildlife in **our** village! *He stresses this last part and then laughs; others do as well. The conservation manager shakes his head with annoyance.* Well, that's it. We just want to make sure you know when you (and your transects) are in Oltukai and not Esilalei.

Scientist B: *She stands up again and, looking at the maps, continues where she left off, a bit frazzled now.* OK now . . . regarding zebra, these data concur with what my colleague said, "The abundance of *zebra* in the area is higher during the wet season (March–June) compared to the dry season (October–December)."[9] But, for wildebeest, our findings differ. The road transects found that *"wildebeest* abundance shows the opposite trend, being higher during the dry season (October) and almost zero in all other periods. Thompson's gazelle seem to use the area throughout the year" and "Grant's gazelle seem to be more abundant during the wet season, as well as impala, which use the area during the whole year" (Tarangire-Manyara Conservation Project [TMCP] 2002b, 28, emphasis in original). The transects richest in wildlife were those inside the Manyara Ranch. *She points to her map. There is more uproar among the Maasai men and women as they look at where she is pointing to on the map, and they explain to her that all but one of the transects she is pointing to are NOT inside the Manyara Ranch but are inside village land—both Oltukai and Esilalei.* Oh, OK, well then, we can say that wildebeest, zebra, and gazelle numbers were particularly high on transect 10, which is this road that heads down to the lake shore through Oltukai Village? *She looks around and gets nods of approval. Maasai start talking among themselves, naming places through which the road passes*: Ang'ata Olowaru, Lera. . . . *They make sounds of agreement. She continues.* We found a lot of wildlife across the whole area (nineteen species in total), but we also always saw livestock. And if you average across all transects, livestock were always a good deal more abundant than wildlife.[10] But zebra and ostrich were also common, "being present on all the Road Transect Counts. Other common animals were Thompson's gazelle, giraffe, and impala. Zebra were the most abundant wildlife species with a maximum relative abundance of 6.6 animals/km. Wildebeest, while less common, also had a high relative abundance (4 animals/km in October 1999)." *She notices some confused faces and pauses to clarify.* The Index of

Presence says how many months we saw the animals along transects, so while we often saw a lot of wildebeest when we saw them, they were not always present in the area, while zebra were always present, if in varying amounts. *Men and women nod and make sounds of agreement. She returns to her seat.*

Maasai elder:[11] *An elder stands up to speak. He stands in the middle of the circle and, leaning on one leg, holds up his* olkuma *and speaks with an air of authority.*[12] It is true; zebra are here all the time! And yes zebra, wildebeest, and gazelle like the area by the lake. This is **their** area. We call this area *Oloyeti,* but another name for it is *Naong.* That is the sound that wildebeest make when they are there with their small calves during calving time, although [*and as if an aside, he says with some curiosity*] they have not been here in the past few years. But [*he refocuses his attention and circles slowly to look at the gathering of people sitting around him, before stating*] I would like to say that perhaps the difference the researchers observed between animal presence in what they call the wet and dry season can be explained by the fact that October is not *always* the dry season, or *alamei,* as we call it. Sometimes the season of short rains, what we call *orkisirata,* starts in October, if we are lucky. "Long ago, *orkisirata* always came in October. December too is not really the dry season, unless we are in trouble! It is *orkisirata.* And *orkisirata* **always** brings the animals."

Elder group #1E:[13] *A second highly respected elder from Esilalei stands to speak.* What the elder said is true. "During *orkisirata,* wildlife are many [in the village]." And while, it is true that cattle are here all the time, during *orkisirata,* the wildlife can even be more than livestock in certain places like *Esilalei, Narok Sarng'arb,* and *Kiripaa.* [See map 5.]

   Murmurs spread around the gathering, particularly those from Esilalei, who raise their eyebrows in approval, nod, and discuss among themselves: "Narok Sarng'arb? Which wildlife, not wildebeest? Oh yeah, in the Oloyeti area." They are hushed by the meeting chairman, who scolds them to be quiet. The elder continues. Much of the wildlife remain in these areas after the short rains have stopped, during a season we call *oladalo.* However, during this time, some move to *Alchamba* [MR], where there is usually water in the dams.

MG: *She exchanges a few words with her two research collaborators (K and L), who are sitting next to her.* We should say something shouldn't we, in relation to what the elder just said? *she asks. They both agree but are hesitant to speak after such a respected elder and run the risk of contradicting him and his knowledge. They decide that MG should stand to speak. As a foreigner, she is subject to different standards, and so she stands to speak, with K and L handing her a pile of papers. As many*

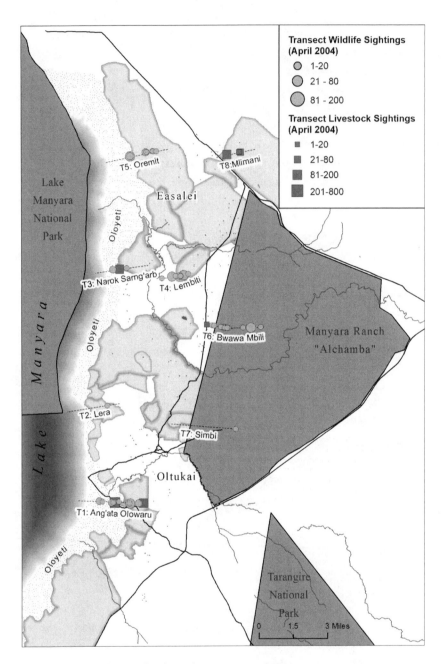

Map 5 Wildlife and livestock sightings by transect, April 2004

of you know, we also conducted transects and have wildlife data to present. Ours were walking transects, and not on the roads. They were designed to pass through places that Maasai say are important for wildlife and livestock grazing, as shown on the following map [see map 2]. *She holds up a map and passes it over to the scientists so they can see it and pass it around to others.* We walked transects every other month for the first year and then every month after that. We report our data by month because, well, [*she pauses and looks around*] the seasons don't always occur at the same time every year. And we used Maasai seasons, which I find much more helpful as they reflect smaller scale changes in rainfall. Here is a table where I have tried to map out the Maasai season for the different transect months. [See table 4.] *She hands a piece of paper to the two scientists.*

She looks around and then back down at the papers she is holding and continues. Like the elder said, we did find that the wildlife were most abundant during the season that Maasai call *orkisirata*. However, for our transects, this was in December 2003 and January 2005, not October. *She glances over at the elder who just spoke to see his reaction. He smiles and raises his eyebrows in agreement. She continues.* December is nearly always *orkisirata*, although the two earlier researchers called this the "dry" season. January on the other hand can be tricky. We called our data for January 2005 *orkisirata* because we walked the transects in the first week. Later in the month is *oladalo*, but this is not set. It all depends on the rains. Zebra numbers were quite high in both *orkisirata* seasons (Dec. 03, Jan. 05; see figure 1), as were wildebeest, although not as much.

I have a graph of rainfall recorded from Manyara Ranch, and we can see that in 2004 there was not much rainfall until December. In 2003, there was some rain in October, but wildlife and zebra abundance was still quite low. If

Table 4 Breakdown of transect data collection organized by Maasai seasons

Season	2002–2003 transects	2004–2005 transects
Orkisirata	Dec. 02 (21/02–Jan. 4); Oct. (Oct. 27–Nov. 6); Dec. 03 (17–27)	Nov. 04 (8–21); Jan. 05 (5–10)
Oladalo	Feb. 03 (Feb. 16–Mar. 1)	Jan. 04 (23–30)
Engakwai	Apr. 03 (16–25)	Mar. 04 (1–14); Apr. 04 (5–16); May 04 (2–6)
Koromare	June 03 (June 18–July 4)	June 04 (1–6)
Alamei	Aug. 03 (Aug. 21–Sept. 1)	July 04 (1–6); Aug. 04 (4–10); Sept. 04 (18–24); Oct. 04 (22–28)

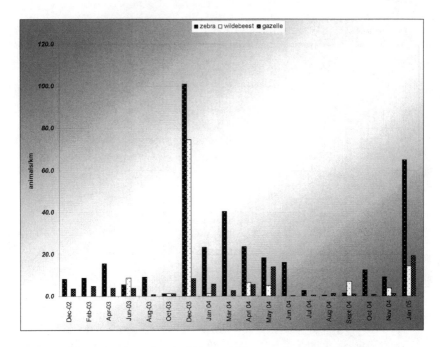

Figure 1 Relative abundance (KIA) of zebra, wildebeest, and gazelle across all transects

you look at the graphs of wildlife alongside rainfall as plotted in figure 2 [*she holds up a piece of paper so it can be seen by all, and then passes it to an elder to pass around*], you can see that wildlife patterns closely follow rainfall, particularly for wildebeest and zebra.[14]

These graphs combine data across all transects. But [*she pauses and looks around*] the transects are in different places, with different types of vegetation, soils, and rainfall patterns. So, in order to really understand wildlife dispersal patterns, it is helpful to look at breakdowns by transect. The transect that had the highest concentrations of wildlife in October was T5-*Oremit* [see figure 3], likely due to pools of water from rain a few days earlier. We know this because we recorded these details when collecting data. Rains during *orkisirata* are extremely variable, and while all the other transects were still dry at that time, *Oremit* had fresh water, in the *Oloyeti* part of the transect—the area by the lake that the elder just referred to as *Naong*. T1-*Ang'ata Olowaru* also had some standing water during our October transect (2003) but there were almost no wildlife there (only two gazelle and two ostrich [see figure 4]). This may be related to the fresh poaching tracks we saw in the *Oloyeti* portion of that transect.[15]

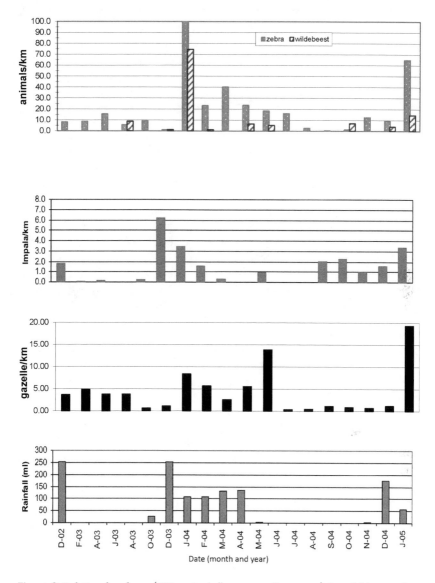

Figure 2 Relative abundance (KIA, animals/km across all transects) for wildebeest, zebra, gazelle, and impala, and rainfall records from the Manyara Ranch across transect months

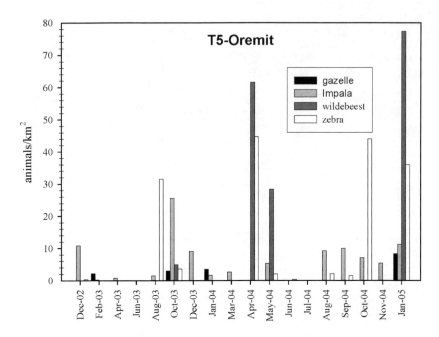

Figure 3 Wildlife density (by species) for T5-*Oremit* (scrub savanna)

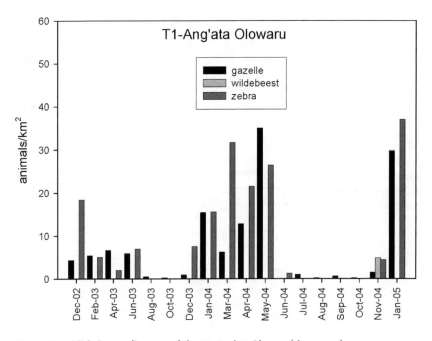

Figure 4 Wildlife density (by species) for T1-*Ang'ata Olowaru* (short grass)

So, it is likely that the presence of wildebeest and zebra in the *Oremit* (T5) transect in October 2003 is directly related to rainfall. There were also a lot of wildebeest in *Oremit* (T5) in April ($61.5/km^2$) and May ($28.3/k^2$), the season Maasai call *engakwai*—the heavy rains. However, this is the only transect where wildebeest appeared at all at this time. Now, to return to October. While the presence of some wildebeest and zebra in the *Oremit* transect at this time may be related to rainfall, there were other animals, like impala, which is most likely not related to water. We found impala around most of the year, but there were more in October 2003 in *Oremit*. This might not reflect a real change in numbers, but rather be a function of visibility. *Oremit* is a scrub savanna, and by the end of the dry season, which it was in October that year, much of the grass is gone and the scrub is thinned out, making it easier to see impala and other animals in the bushed areas. This might also explain the high numbers of zebra and impala in 2004 in *Oremit* again, despite lack of rainfall in October that year. *Looking over at scientists A and B, she states,* None of your transects covered *Oremit*, so it would be hard to directly compare.

Scientists A and B: *Shift in their seats and exchange words between themselves. One of them stands to speak, a confused look on her face, and, speaking in English, she directs her words not to the whole group but to MG and the meeting chairman, who are sitting next to each other.* I am sorry, I am confused. First the elder said that October was not really the dry season and thus might explain our high abundance of wildebeest sightings during this time. But now what you are saying seems to be both in agreement and disagreement with this statement. You seem to be explaining the high abundance of wildlife as a function of both rainfall and it being the dry season![16]

MG: *Begins to stand in preparation to speak, rustling through papers to look again at her tables, charts, and notes, but one of the men who have been doing the transects with her, Landis M, stands up first. He is a Maasai junior elder [Landis] who is very knowledgeable about the "Maasai" way of things, has been doing the transect work for three years, and has a special talent as a "negotiator" or "mediator" to arbitrate or settle disputes, translating between different people and across cultures. He speaks clearly and concisely but in Maasai fashion, slow and musical.*

Landis M: It is true. It is complicated. Let me try to explain. The season we call *orkisirata* normally begins in November, and for this reason we have labeled the transect months of October as *alamei*, like MG has explained. However, sometimes, we get lucky and rain comes in October, like it did in 2003, which is labeled as *orkisirata* in the tables [table 4]. Then we say, "*Orkisirata* has come early this year." However, even if it comes early, there is usually not enough rain for grass and trees to grow. So, when MG spoke about having more visibility, this is because by the end of October we are usually almost out of grass. And we noted this in almost all the transects, except in the *Oloyeti* part of the *Oremit* transect in 2003, which is where the wildebeest were seen. *Oloyeti* is different from other areas because sometimes as the lake recedes, grass grows, which we noted happened in October 2003. And often in October, **if** we get rain, small pools of water form, and that also attracts animals. That is how it can be possible that wildlife are coming for water in an area but that there are also "*alamei*" (dry season) like conditions in the vegetation. Does this make sense? *After a pause, where he looks around at the faces, particularly of the researchers, and MG, he continues in a slightly different tone (more certain and concise, less negotiating).* However, in *orkisirata*, **whenever** it starts—October, November, December— that is when the wildlife are many, usually more so than any other time. They can be so many in certain places that they can outnumber livestock, like the elders have said. And I believe that we found this sometimes on the transects? *He looks back at MG, who starts ruffling through her papers. The chairman holds off speakers and looks over at MG, anxious for her reply. She speaks while sitting but hands the papers to Landis M, who is still standing.*

MG: In fact, for the time that we have been talking about as having the highest wildlife numbers, *orkisirata*, specifically December 2003 and January 2005, we saw more zebra than cattle [see table 5]. And if you add in wildebeest it would be even higher. *There are murmurs throughout the crowd, the conservation crowd looking at each other with slight surprise, and Maasai exclaiming, "ee pae" (of course!) and "enkerai" ("child" from the men, as in "I tell you it is so!").*[17] But [*MG interjects, standing now, to look at the papers that Landis M is holding*] I should say that it is only in these two months that wildlife outnumber cattle and only in certain places. But that is something to discuss another time [see chapter 3]. *They both return to sit down.*

A Note on Methods

The different sets of measurement tools used to understand wildlife phenomena cannot be separated from the phenomena themselves. In other words, the apparatus—which includes the measurement device used together with the discourse and practice associated with it and the people involved in doing the "seeing"—don't just see different phenomena, but produce different phenomena (Barad 2007). Driving transects produce different counts of wildlife than walking transects—partly based on different biases and limitations. But also because the wildlife react to the measurement process themselves and move or stay still, are seen or not, get counted or not (even if seen), and come to matter or not (i.e., if wildlife or livestock, inside the village or the MR). The TMCP scientists combined several different methods to reduce the errors in their counts and expand their "vision" of wildlife in the area. But in so doing, they combined data from different months into one season that is assumed to stay put (as a dry season or a wet season) but does not always behave as described. Our transect data were limited in other ways. They were devised to provide sample counts for different representative vegetative zones important for wildlife. But in attempting to protect valuable Maasai grazing areas from future conservation incursions, we purposely excluded some important locations from our analysis (Goldman 2018). Additionally, the walking transects were analyzed to present wildlife densities within the transect area using a modified variable fixed width method (Norton-Griffiths 1978), which is biased toward large mammals and animals in groups (zebra, wildebeest, and cattle), prone to high errors, and transect specific. For discussions of wildlife across the entire area, we utilized a kilometric index of abundance (KIA), as used by TMCP, so that our data were comparable. This entailed calculating how many animals were counted (which is not the same as "seen") over the total number of kilometers covered, across transects, in a given month (an average of 25.5 km), shown in table 5. These are all different ways of manipulating measurement apparatus to reflect wildlife presence as best as possible. The apparatus are integral to the production of the phenomena that get seen and reported.

Scientist Prins: *Unrelated to the prior scientists, he is an elder to them, both literally and figuratively. He is older, male, and has worked on Tanzania wildlife ecology for many years. His own work and that of his students have contributed significantly to the scientific understanding of wildlife grazing and plant ecology in this ecosystem* (Loth and Prins 1986; Prins and Loth 1988; Prins and Douglas-Hamilton 1990; de Boer and Prins 1990).[18] *He stands quickly and with confidence speaks to the crowd.* I am happy to hear that there is at least one time of the year when wildlife may outnumber cattle, but I suspect that won't last long if people keep accumulating stock at the rate they do and with cattle outcompeting wildlife (see my articles on this: Prins 1987, 1992, 2000), but that is a topic for another day [see chapter 3]. I'd like to speak to this discussion of rainfall and plant

Table 5. List of relative abundance of species recorded during all transects for each month, measured as a kilometric index of abundance (KIA)[a]

	Animals' relative abundance (kilometric index of abundance, KIA)								
	Dec. 02	Feb. 03	Apr. 03	June 03	Aug. 03	Oct. 03	Dec. 03	Jan. 04	Mar. 04
Zebra	8.11	8.69	15.53	5.61	9.10	1.28	100.92	23.31	40.35
Wildebeest				8.77		1.09	74.66	1.21	
Gazelle	3.65	4.91	3.76	3.79	0.62	1.13	8.39	5.71	2.61
Giraffe	0.16	0.37	1.60	0.28	0.59	0.44	0.48	1.65	0.31
Impala	1.77	0.04	0.17	0.00	0.24	6.20	3.47	1.54	0.31
Dikdik			0.08		0.03	0.07	0.15	0.11	
Ostrich	0.91	0.32	0.25	0.35	0.62	0.44	0.22	0.88	1.01
Lesser kudu		0.32	0.08	0.14					
Reedbuck				0.04	0.00	0.00	0.00	0.04	0.00
Warthog	0.05	0.24			0.00	0.00	0.22		
Elephant		0.04							
Lion								0.07	
Jackal					0.03		0.18		
Leopard					0.03				
Cattle	132.9	13.20	35.41	30.85	56.04	88.95	81.23	108.72	82.49
Goats	21.23	1.62		12.62	0.00	4.78	8.13	41.72	15.56
Donkey				0.81	0.83	1.60		0.73	

[a]List of relative abundance of species recorded during all transects for each month, measured as a kilometric index of abundance (KIA), which equals the number of animals seen across all transects in a given month divided by the total length covered by all transects.

availability in October. In our studies, we found that the early rains are so sporadic in time and space that vegetation growth during this period is extremely variable and grass seeds do not "immediately germinate following a first rain after the long dry season." Most grasses stay dormant until a certain threshold of rainfall is reached (50 mm; cf. Pratt and Gwynne 1977). The chances that this threshold is met will be more likely during the long rains than the early short rains (Prins and Loth 1988, 462).

Local conservation manager: *Stands up and blows his hair out of his eyes, which brings laughter to most of the Maasai. He then clears his throat and speaks in a serious tone. Looking over at the last speaker, he says,* Thank you Professor Prins for your valuable contribution. *He then turns to face the gathering and straightening*

Animals' relative abundance (kilometric index of abundance, KIA)									Index of presence
Apr. 04	May 04	June 04	July 04	Aug. 04	Sept. 04	Oct. 04	Nov. 04	Jan. 05	
23.47	18.30	16.05	2.64	0.46	1.36	12.54	9.21	64.82	1.0
6.45	5.16				7.04		3.94	15.54	0.5
5.57	13.86	0.34	0.44	1.15	0.84	0.71	1.17	19.33	1.0
1.25	0.84	0.34	1.21	0.52	0.23	0.29	0.38	0.83	1.0
0.00	0.96	0.00	0.00	2.04	2.25	1.05	1.59	3.36	0.8
0.04				0.11	0.09	0.57	0.14		0.6
1.05	1.56	0.69	0.55	0.69	0.56	0.43	0.38		0.9
0.12			0.33		0.23				0.3
0.08						0.05	0.09	0.21	0.3
							0.51	1.01	0.3
									0.1
									0.1
0.04		0.11							0.2
									0.1
37.95	56.39	64.93	19.61	19.53	71.66	79.10	67.81	47.97	1.0
0.00	1.83	16.70	11.05	46.01			0.47		0.7
									0.2

himself to stand tall, he says, Again, I would like to draw on the work of Lamprey. Based on his observations from inside TNP he stated that "in most years light and very localized rain falls in late October and early November in widely sep-arated showers in Masailand [*sic*]. At that time, the effects of the four or five rainless months are most pronounced, the ground extremely dry, and the grass either dry and yellow or burnt off." The large herds of animals inside the park congregate around the few remaining water spots, pools in the river, and near hillside springs. "When the first rain falls there is an immediate response from the wildebeest and zebra. Both species travel towards the site of the rainfall sometimes moving 25 miles in a night. . . . In zebra, a congregating activity has been observed in October which has in each year coincided with the falling of rain at some point in the Masai Steppe [*sic*]" (Lamprey 1964, 168). *He pauses, and with his hands on his hips looks around, then toward the scientists before stat-*

ing, Others have also found this no? Ah, yes, James Kahurananga [and Silkilu-washa 1997]! *Pausing again, he leans in to focus on the Maasai elders and leaders before stating,* the director of the Maasai Heartland Project at AWF. *He waits for these men to nod in recognition before continuing.* So, it seems that while I greatly respect what Professor Prins is saying, even if the early rains are not enough to bring grass, the animals are surely reacting to the rains! But of course, there is no good data on rainfall! *He says this final line with a degree of exasperation in his voice.* So, I commissioned a study from the U.S. Forest Service to analyze over twenty years of rainfall data from Tarangire to come up with patterns to help us better understand all this variability. The analysis reflects what has been spoken so far. October, as a month, was extremely variable—sometimes wet, sometimes dry. The researcher suggested calling October a "semidry" month, with November and December being more consistently "wet." But he also suggested that months were not the best breakdown for discussing rainfall patterns, which seem to cross over and split up months [Bevenger 2004]. Anyway, I just thought this might be a useful contribution to the conversation.

Makaa LM:[19] *A serious man and respected elder, he speaks briefly and to the point.* I would like to just point out that the rains during *orkisirata* are not only variable in terms of **when** they come, but also **where**. Not all places are blessed with these early rains. And *Oremit*, the area that MG was talking about, usually receives the first rains during this time. For this reason, we usually go there with our cattle and the same with wildlife—it is usually full of zebra and wildebeest during *orkisirata* because there is often water there when the rest of the country is still dry. If it doesn't rain in *Oremit* then I will go elsewhere with my cattle. It is the same with wildlife. **We are all following the rain**. But also, when the rains stop again, during *oladalo*, the wildebeest are here in the village and they usually go toward the lake [*Oloyeti*] and toward *Oremit*. They like it down there. It is their place.

Makaa LS:[20] *Thin and poor, he comes from a strong family where many ritual and political leaders have been chosen, although he is not one. He is modest and unassuming but knowledgeable. He speaks softly but with confidence.* "In *orkisirata*, [there are] wildebeest and zebra in *Oremit* and at *Olotorro* [the dam by the side of the tarmac road by the school in Esilalei]. They move back and forth between *Oremit* and *Olotorro*. They leave the lake and come to the school, to *Olotoro*, looking for water and green grass. Long ago when it rained (more regularly), *oladalo* would be when the wildebeest would give birth. They don't give birth during the rains; they wait until it stops and then the calves can enter the water to bathe. But today, it doesn't rain very much. Now *oladalo* is longer, one to two months when it used to just be half a month. The calves (of wildebeest and cattle) get very thin because they don't get enough milk. In the dry season (*alamei*), wildlife start to suffer. They can't leave the lake, they go to the *korongo* [seasonal river] in Mto wa Mbu town, where there is water and wildebeest stay at *Oloyeti*."

Elder Seuri LL:[21] *As an olegwenani [customary leader] for the Laiser clan and a respected elder, he is sitting on one of the overstuffed cushioned seats. He waives his* olkuma *in the air but does not rise to speak. Despite common accusations of him being political, he is respected for his knowledge of the area (having been born here) and his skills as an orator. He is also quite good at keeping discussions on track. All attention focuses on him as he speaks in a strong but calm voice.* During the dry season, the wildlife move to get water, except for the gazelles, which don't need water, and the warthogs, which stay here and get water by digging in the *korongo*. The wildebeest and others move toward the lake, and the livestock use the hand-dug wells in the *korongo*. We can talk about the places that wildebeest like, such as by the lake [*Oloyeti*]. Long ago, wildebeest didn't go to all places, only to the short grass near the lake. There were no dams up here long ago. *With his hands he motions to the area around us and farther up on the slight slope into the forest.* So Maasai would say, "Let's go to the place of the wildebeest." That is why it is called *Naong*. But today, if it rains everywhere, the wildebeest go to *Lera, Oloyeti, Narok Sarng'arb, Ang'ata Olowaru, Oremit*, even toward the mountain like this young elder just explained [in the open plains area near *Olotoro*] because they like places that are open, especially when they give birth, so they can see predators. But it is not just giving birth that the wildebeest do here. During *koromare* [end of the rains], the wildebeest like to come to places like Esilalei to mate because there is usually green grass and water here.

Elder group O1:[22] *A group of elders discuss among themselves. One of the younger but outspoken Landis stands and speaks with confidence.* During *orkisirata*, the animals are many, even more than livestock until March. We cannot speak as well for *Oremit* as the others have, because we do not go there as much. But we know that there are many wildlife in *Emborianda* [*Oloyeti*],[23] *Lera* through to *Endarpo*, and *Ang'ata Olowaru*. *He pauses for a moment, but just as someone else is about to get called on to speak, he begins in a quick tone.* This year [2003] it did not rain. But if it does rain, the wildebeest will come. This rain the other night [early December 2003] brought a lot of water and Friday of last week a lot of wildebeest came. They filled the area near the *enkang'* of Lohola [near

Lorikiushi; see map 3]. But they moved because poachers came on Sunday. The wildebeest usually stay through the season we call *koromare* until May, then they start to leave, but they come back to *Oloyeti*, all of it, all the way to *Maramboi*, to rut, just like the elder said.

Note: All the areas named by the elder, *Oloyeti, Lera, Ang'ata Olowaru, Endarpo,* and *Maramboi,* are places where water collects quickly and sits after a short rain. They all have seasonal streams flowing through them. *Endarpo* was recently selected for dam construction to catch the steady trickle that comes across the slightly sloping landscape during the rains (see chapter 3). *Maramboi* gets runoff from the seasonal Oltukai river and has historically been one of the most important grazing areas for cattle during *orkisirata* and *koromare* but was recently turned into a conservation area (a WMA). *Oloyeti* and *Ang'ata Olowaru* have many places within them, referred to as *impoorri*—hard, rock-like places (or solid, crusted soil) where water stands and grass does not grow, but animals come to drink. See map 3.

Jr. Elder, Landis P:[24] *Also a member of the Landis age-set, he is on the older side and someone who wields a great deal of respect across age-set and clan lines for being knowledgeable, agreeable, and a good speaker, all the qualities Maasai respect. He lives on an uplifted area close to the lake called* Oleketalokeon *in Maa, which translates into "to look back at oneself," referring to the stunning 360-degree view one gets at this location. He holds his* olkuma *in the air only slightly, to show the respect he knows he commands as an emerging* oloiboni, *but to not outdo the senior elders. He speaks softly.* It is only during this time, during *orkisirata,* that the wildlife will be so many that they will outnumber livestock. *Amongst murmurs of agreement between Maasai sitting around, there is a strong scratchy voice, full of authority but clearly mellowed with age, that speaks out above the crowd in disagreement. But. . . . There is a hush. He is one of the most respected elders in both villages and across clan lines. The others wait for him to stand up and speak to the meeting properly. Landis P moves swiftly to sit down.*

Seuri K:[25] Yes, yes, it is true that there are many wildlife during *orkisirata,* but, "there are still a lot of cattle; it is just that you cannot put all the cattle in one place at one time and the wildlife all stay in one place, and so if you look it seems that there are more wildlife than cattle."

Scientist B:[26] *Holding on to her papers, and flipping through the tables, she looks around the group and speaks with confidence.* Our data from the road transects in this area show that "all livestock (cattle, donkey, goat and sheep) intensively use the whole area. Livestock are always present and much more abundant than wildlife (20 times more, considering the average of all the [transect counts])." *She pauses for a moment, looking at one of the graphs a little more closely, and flipping to a graph on another page. She continues.* However, if you look at it by individual transect, and by individual months, there are times (like October) and places, like on the transect (10) that runs through Oltukai village [*she says with a smile and to nods of recognition from the crowd*] to the lake, where wildebeest numbers do actually outnumber cattle numbers, but not every year [Tarangire-Manyara Conservation Project (TMCP) 2002b]. *Others raise their eyebrows in agreement and talk among themselves. MG stands to speak.*

MG: As I said earlier, our transect data does suggest that most of the time, in most places, cattle are more than wildlife, which makes sense. This **is** a Maasai village [*Maasai exclaim*—"ee-pai! *(of course)* . . . eeaa"]. However, if you look at the graphs per transect with cattle added, we can see that in *Lera,* zebra and gazelles far outnumbered cattle in the months of February, April, June, and October in 2003, as well as March and June of 2004 [see figure 5a]. According to Maasai, this would be *oladalo, engakwai, koromare,* and *alamei. She looks around at some of the Maasai elders as she says this, and they grin, proud that this foreign* "mtaalamu" [*Swahili for expert, pl.* wataalum] *is trying to use their classifications and language in front of her fellow* wataalamu. However, our transects are biased toward wildlife because they were walked early in the morning, when cattle are not out grazing yet. So we also counted marks of animal presence (footprints and dung from within a couple of days) on the transects, and this data also suggests that there were many times when wildlife outnumbered cattle, such as on February 3 and in March through till June 4 [see figure 5b]. *Lera* isn't really used by cattle in the wet season. It's muddy, and Maasai say that the grass there [Maa: *Olkereyan,* Latin: *Sporobolus pyramidalis*] isn't good for cattle at that time, it's saved for dry-season grazing. Wildlife marks were also higher in December and January, which could be considered *orkisirata.* While the grass may be finished then, wildlife come for water.

But . . . *she hesitates, looking over at the other researchers, not sure how they will respond* . . . I would like to speak to data that we collected outside of transects, in a more opportunistic fashion. Since the transects were only conducted at certain times on certain days, in certain places, we think it is important to also talk about animals we saw and recorded when out doing other work, or just visiting people in the village. And I tried to record information told to me by

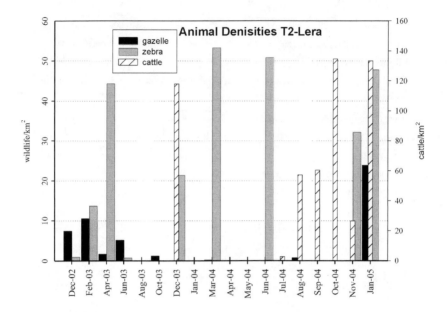

Figure 5a Wildlife and cattle densities for T2-*Lera* (wooded savanna)

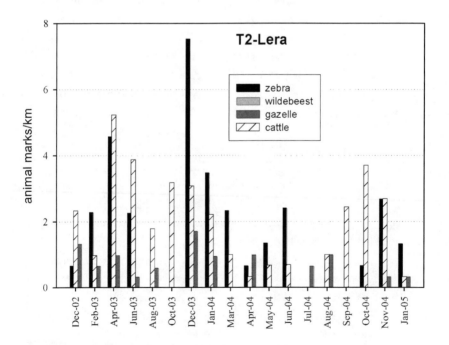

Figure 5b Marks of wildlife and cattle (by km) for T2-*Lera* (wooded grass savanna)

villagers about where and when they see animals pass by their homes, or while they are herding. Naibor is extraordinarily good at this; he always seems to know the whereabouts of wildebeest in particular. *She looks at him in the crowd, and he grins. Others make joking comments at him for receiving special attention.* Maybe this is because wildebeest like to pass by his *enkang'*. He gives me regular reports of how many animals passed on which days, as they move between *Lera* and the MR. There were also times when I myself, together with Landis W and Landis K, saw a lot of wildebeest out farther in the *Engusero* part of the village, an area where there are no transects, particularly in March and April, which can be categorized as the wet season, or *engakwai*. The animals were either seen by the *inkang'itie* or walking to them at night from the MR. We spotted them all over *Engusero* for several days once, and even marked their presence by GPS, so that I could map them [see map 4]. They were just in *Engusero* grazing, near the homes of Landis W and Landis K actually!

Elder Makaa KAL:[27] *A thin junior elder of the Laiser clan, stands and enters the circle sheepishly to speak. He is an elder, but poor and does not usually speak at meetings. Yet he has much to offer. He looks down at the ground as he speaks in a soft voice, leaning over on his engudi* [walking stick], *which he clutches fiercely.* During *orkisirata* I go with our cattle to *Lera* and *Lorikiushi* and we usually see wildlife, like zebra, wildebeest, gazelle, ostrich, giraffe, dikdik, reedbuck. During *oladalo* zebra and wildebeest start moving, they can go to Manyara Ranch, they follow the water, same with giraffe. Gazelles stay though. In *engakwai* we go with the cattle to *Lera Lentim*, because there is water there and all the wildlife are there, especially zebra, giraffe, wildebeest, reedbuck, ostrich, dikdik, warthog, gazelle, porcupine, hyena, and lion. There are also eland and leopard. Many of these animals stay into *koromare* if there is still water. "In the dry season only those animals that don't really need water stay around, like gazelle, reedbuck, dikdik, mongoose, porcupine, ostrich. The others go looking for water."[28]

The women, sitting in the corner of the meeting, have been paying attention and talking among themselves throughout the meeting, sometimes in agreement with what is being said, sometimes not. The meeting chairman leans in their direction and asks them to speak up. But everything has already been said, *they argue.* We agree with it all, *they say as a group.* He pushes them to speak, nonetheless. There are visitors here, and it would not look good if the women didn't speak. One of the older women, the mother of the Oltukai Village chairman, volunteers. She is assertive and confident. Her husband is one of the oldest men in the village, but his other wives *care for him; she lives with her son and so is free from his gaze, which has nonetheless become weak with old age. She does not stand, but speaks loudly, while sitting.*

Mama P:[29] There are animals everywhere throughout the village, especially during *orkisirata* and *engakwai*, like the elders have been saying. Even [now,] in December [December 7, 2003], there are a lot of zebra out in *Engusero*, by our *enkang'*, like MG explained. During the day they go to *Lera*, or to *Alchamba* [MR] to eat, but they come by the *inkang'itie* at night because then they are not bothered by *ilowuarak* [predators, *olowuaru* sg., often used to refer to lions]. *She says this last bit in a particularly strong tone, and the women around her all laugh. The men start to compete again to speak, when another woman starts to speak; the chairman hushes them and turns his attention to the women again.*

Koko Y:[30] *Considerably older, this woman is highly respected by men and women, young and old. She is the local midwife and brought many of these people, and their children, into this world. Yet she does not usually speak at meetings and stays out of village politics. She is partly blind and sits calmly looking off into the distance as she speaks.* What my sister says is true. During the big rains of *engakwai*, the animals are many, and they get chased by lions until they can even run inside an *enkang'* to escape! *Laughter among the young women and elders.* At the end of the rains [*koromare*] the animals start to move because everything has become open, there is no *pori* [closed bush, tall grass], and so they are not afraid of the lions anymore. Many will leave until the rains come again, during *orkisirata*. During the break between the rains [*oladalo*], wildlife are not so many, they will be in places where they get good grass and water like *Kakoi* [near to Tarangire NP], *Maromboi, Lera,* and *Aliperipera. She looks over at MG and adds,* Oh, *Aliperipera* is a part of *Ang'ata Olowaru*, an important part, where water lies. The name means a flat place where water rolls over slowly. MG did not put it in her map but it is there.[31]

Elder Makaa Lak:[32] What the women say is true, *he begins, and the women all beam. He is a well-liked man by both men and women, congenial, lighthearted, and knowledgeable.* "During *engakwai*, when water is plentiful, there are a lot of wildlife [*iti tukol*]! There are a lot of lions because there is a lot of tall grass. If there is too much grass, the wildlife will leave the *pori* places like the MR and go to the lake (and near our *homes!*). Only a few will be left in the ranch, like the large, male gazelles and the zebra because they are not afraid of tall grass. During *koromare*, there is still a lot of water and grass [but] the wildlife become fewer and often go to the Manyara Ranch at this time."

Landis K: *He does not usually speak at meetings, being uncomfortable around the elders, and even men of his own age-set. Yet his participation in MG's research and* *his recent training as a game scout has brought him confidence and a greater sense of pride in his knowledge. He is pushed on by MG and Landis M, who have already spoken and would prefer a different voice to express yet more information from the transect data. He clears his throat and, looking down, speaks in a loud tone to hide his nerves.* Just as the elders have pointed out, we also found in our transects that *orkisirata* is a time when the wildlife are many here. This was especially the case for December 2003, as MG has already spoken about, even though there were very few wildlife in general that year; most of them were seen during *orkisirata*, with some seen during *engakwai* (March, April). During *orkisirata* (December 2003) most wildlife were inside the Manyara Ranch and *Lera*, two places that get the early *orkisirata* rains.

But, that year (2004) during *engakwai* (March, April, and May), wildlife were counted in high numbers across all the transects.[33] In *koromare*, the beginning of the dry season, zebra were only really present in the *Lera* transect, where there was still a lot of grass, and some places of water. Wildebeest were few [*he looks around at the elders and then back at the papers*], but there were some wildebeest around during *koromore* in 2003, mostly in *Mlimani* (T8) (42.7/km^2) [see figure 6]. They were down near *Oloturo*, where there was water in the dam. They were still there in July, although we don't have transect data for that month because in 2003 we only did the transects every other month. But we don't need transects to tell us where the animals are. We were in that area on July 7, 2003, and we counted 192 wildebeest in *Oloturo*. Later that month (July 29), we counted 120 wildebeest coming to *Oloturo* from an area called *Engososi*, where they probably had gone for grazing. This matches with what Makaa LS said about *Oloturo* as the place that wildebeest like to come to in *koromare*. Others (Elders O1) mentioned the wildebeest coming to places like *Lera*, *Oloyeti*, and *Maraomboi* in *koromare*. We can't speak for *Maramboi* because we didn't have a transect there nor did we go there very much; it is far, and it is a conservation area [WMA] now. But we did not see any wildebeest at all in June (2003 or 2004) in the other places named by the elders (*Lera* and *Oloyeti*). *He pauses, and looks around.* There were other places, though, that we saw wildebeest during this time [*koromare*], when we were not conducting the transects, like in the Bwawambili [T6] area, inside the MR. We went out there on June 2, 2003, and we saw over 150 wildebeest, near *Laangaik* dam.[34]

Landis R:[35] *Young, poor, and considered by many as not really Maasai since his father was of the related but seen as quite different Waarusha tribe, he is a good speaker and cannot sit through a meeting without saying something, and people listen.*[36] *He*

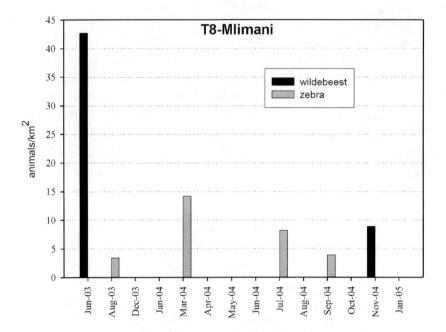

Figure 6 Wildlife density for T8-*Mlimani* (mountain/wooded savanna)

speaks quickly and with confidence. I would just like to say what I think, just a few words, regarding the dry season. Really in the dry season, the animals are few. Thompson's gazelles don't leave, but the Grant's move. The reedbucks stay, they come at night to look for water in the wells. Giraffes are here but not many. We don't see them every day, if we are lucky, maybe every few days. They pass everywhere looking for food. They usually stay through *koromare*, with some leaving in July and then most leaving in August for the ranch where there are lots of trees.

Elder Molita:[37] *An elder from Esilalei, speaking for a group of men who were discussing this topic, enters the center of the gathering.* "It is true that during *engakwai* the wildlife are here," but not everywhere, like some of the people have been suggesting. "If it has rained hard, then there may not be so many. Wildebeest are afraid of the mud. Zebra will go to uplifted places like *Lembiti*. If water stays in the dams then they will stay the whole year, as long as there is water."

Elder group O1:[38] Yes, it is true, if it rains a lot during *engakwai*, the wildlife leave because there is too much water and mud. They go to mountainous areas, especially wildebeest. If the rains are not very big, they can stay in *Lera*. And then in *oladalo* [when the rains stop] there are still a lot of wildlife here. Especially wildebeest, they come to birth during that time, especially in *Oloyeti*, *Ang'ata Olowaru*.

MG: *MG stands again. She tries to sit; she is tired and a woman, and since the women sat while they spoke, she figures maybe she too can sit. But this is not allowed; she is treated as a man at these meetings, and is told to stand. Someone even hands her their* engudi *to lean on as she speaks.* It is true that if you look at the *Lembiti* transect [T4, an uplifted place] alone, most wildlife, zebra in particular, were found there during the wet season (*engakwai*—March and April [see figure 7]). Also in March, *Lera* (T2) had the highest density of zebra (53.3/km² [see figure 8]). While I hear what the elder has said about the wildebeest coming to give birth in February to March, down by the lake, I have yet to see it. I hear this all the time, and yet I have been here for two years and have yet to see this happen! I don't know where the wildebeest are. Does anyone else?

Korianga M:[39] *A young, arrogant warrior stands to speak; he is from the wealthy family that lives by the road against the mountains in Esilalei. He leans on his* engudi *and speaks confidently, despite his young age.* At the beginning and end of the rains, wildebeest come near our *shambas* [Swahili: small farms] below the mountain, by the side of the road; they don't enter places with trees. When the rains just started this year [2003] they came, but then left, they went to *Engasosi*, and to Manyara Ranch.

MG: *Since she had barely sat down, she is quick to turn around and continue talking. She looks at the chairman for approval to speak, then speaks in an excited tone.* It seems to me that there are different places that the wildebeest frequent at different times (along with other animals). Different people [*she pauses and looks around, then continues*] have different knowledge about that. This warrior who just spoke, he is talking about an area that our transects did not cover. We have a transect in *Oldoinyo* [T8-*Mlimani*], that is meant to represent the mountain area in general, but we do not have a transect by his *enkang'*. Nor has anyone else here from his *enkang'* yet spoken, so we don't have much information regarding wildlife in that area. We all know that where this *ilmuraran* lives is an important area for wildlife because AWF is working hard to obtain it![40] *She pauses and looks around, then more calmly continues.* There are many things the elders have said that our transect data agrees with, such as the importance of *Oremit* (T5) during *orkisirata* [short rains], but only some of the time (e.g., January 5) and *Ang'ata Olowaru* (T1) during *engakwai* (heavy rains, March–May). But we also found *Oremit* to be important in the rainy season (April,

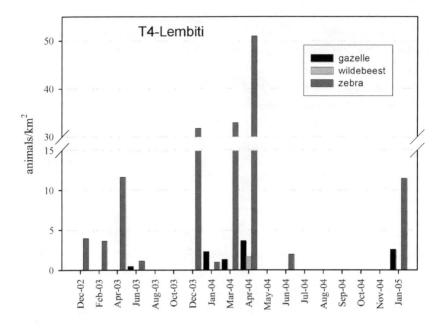

Figure 7 Wildlife density (by species) for T4-*Lembiti* (mixed wooded/grass savanna)

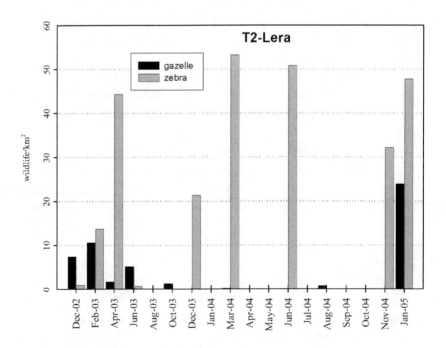

Figure 8 Wildlife density (by species) for T2-*Lera* (wooded grass savanna)

May 4), and *Bwawambili* (inside Manyara Ranch) to be important during *orkisirata* (December 3), something none of the elders spoke about. Our data, and
that presented by the other researchers, matches what everyone is saying, that
orkisirata (December, January) brings a lot of animals to village lands. However,
lots of people spoke about *Lera* as an important area for wildlife, especially
during *orkisirata* and our transect data doesn't show this. In fact, we show peaks
during the rainy season here when some people even said that animals leave!
*Murmurs of confusion around the crowd, among Maasai in particular. Looking
around she corrects herself.* Or maybe that was just the wildebeest. *Sounds of
agreement now, "aiya, eh-heh, that's it."* But others did say that there were a lot
of animals during the rainy season (*engakwai*), so I guess it depends on where
one lives, where one goes with the cattle, and what one sees.

Maybe our transect is in the wrong place in *Lera*. Or maybe things have
changed, and people are speaking from what they remember rather than what
they see today? *She says this a bit nervously and in a questioning, uncertain way,
and then adds with a smile,* I think this might be true of some of the elders here
who don't really go all the way out to *Lera* with the cattle anymore! *Laughter
among the younger men.* The rainfall changes every year, and it seems that, if
nothing else, we are all in agreement that many of the animals move to follow
rainfall. This seems to be particularly true for wildebeest. *Sounds of agreement,
"ee-pai! [of course!] . . . eeaa," come from the Maasai men and women and nods
from the researchers.* This seems also, perhaps to a lesser extent, true for zebra
and gazelle. It does seem, however, that wildebeest may be reacting to rainfall
at a larger scale than we have been measuring. That is, if it rains in other places
that wildebeest prefer, they may not come to these two villages, but instead go
to those places (like *Engososi* in Selela, as the *olmurrani* said). For this reason,
it would be nice if we could have larger-scale data of the entire TME, including areas in Selela and Engaruka to compare with our data on an annual and
seasonal basis. If we look at the map that Scientist A presented, we can see that
there are areas in Selela that are heavily used by wildebeest in the wet season,
but also in the dry season. *Maasai men and women speak out loud. "Ee-pai [of
course]! The wildebeest love Selela, haven't we said that?"*[41]

To really understand wildlife movements and population trends we need
data at multiple scales. Maybe we can continue to document wildlife sightings
by herders and continue the transect work? There are now many men here
trained as game scouts. They are traveling through the village all the time and
probably have a good idea about wildlife presence. *Many of the young men look*

up and smile, proud of their new status and value to the village. There are also many women who have a lot of knowledge about wildlife movements now and in the past. Maybe we could find better ways for them to participate in this work? *The older women smile and laugh aloud; the younger women giggle and hide their faces in their hands or the corners of their capes draping over their shoulders.*

Anyway, that is what I have observed about our discussion so far. If anyone disagrees or has anything else to add please say so. *People talk among themselves, and several people call out: "I don't disagree. I have no problem with this." There is a hum across the crowd as people whisper to themselves. It seems the meeting is going to end; there is no one who disagrees with what has been said by the last two speakers. But there is a lot of more active and anxious whispering occurring among the women, and just then one of the eldest women in the group starts talking loudly from where she is sitting with other women.*

Koko B:[42] *One of the oldest women in the village, she speaks in a scratchy voice.* I just want to say a few words. *Everyone looks over at her, surprised.* I agree with what has just been spoken. I think we are all in agreement now. I just wanted to speak to the statement that MG said about never seeing wildebeest here. I hadn't heard what she said, and it was just explained to me by one of these young girls! *Laughter among the women.*[43] She needs to understand that things have changed. *As she says this, she holds her hands up in the air around her and looking up, says, Eng'ai* [God/rain/sky]! The country is dry. If there is no water, how can the wildebeest stay? In 2003 there was no water! Many people from both Oltukai and Esilalei moved to Mto wa Mbu town for water. Don't the wildebeest need water too?

Seuri K:[44] This is true what my sister here has said, and I am glad she has said it. People have talked about poachers, and this is a problem. But I think that the wildebeest not being here is about rainfall. "I believe that if it rains during *orkisirata*, the wildebeest will come to *Oloyeti* and not leave again until they give birth. But if the water finishes then this makes them leave, especially while birthing. They need to be near water when they have their children. So if there is water here, they will give birth here. These days they are not here that often because they cut that river, *Lochokolenyi*, inside Lake Manyara National Park to divert it into the park, and so it doesn't enter *Oloyeti* anymore the way it used to. Now it just goes through the park to Mto wa Mbu. It used to come through here and provide fresh water in *emborianda* [*Oloyeti*]. But also the rains have changed. For this reason, there has even been a change in the wildebeest birthing patterns. The time for the wildebeest to birth is from February to March.

Long ago there was rain during the time for rain, but now the country is getting dry. The rain used to start in October, like people have said, and then by January the wildebeest would start to birth. But today! Today, you can see them giving birth in March and even April!"[45]

Meshuki L: *He is an* oloiboni, *on the MR board, and the richest man in the area. He is also thought to have a generous heart, liked and respected by all, not as being exceptionally knowledgeable or wise, but for being kind. He stands, with difficulty, and speaks with a sense of authority but a hint of laughter and ease in his voice.* As I think we can see now, there are regular patterns when it comes to wildlife, but there is also a lot of change because of rainfall and grass growth. And from development like the elder just explained. The same is true with our cattle. So just like we say that our season *orkisirata* starts in November, it can start as early as October or as late as December. Or it can refuse to come at all, which brings us much trouble. And it is then that we need to go looking for water and grass. It is the same for the wild animals, because animals are animals. Have things changed and are things changing? Of course. The country is getting drier, people are increasing, and the land is filling up with farms. Long ago, we were few. And we didn't farm. But I don't think that this has impacted the wildebeest numbers, they are still many. But they have not been here much in recent years, as others have already spoken about. They are many in the Manyara Ranch. My boys go in there to graze our cattle and they see them. And the ranch is a conservation area, and so the animals are protected there. They are safe with Maasai too, but there are other people that come here to hunt, and we are powerless to stop them. We don't hunt wildlife, so we don't know so very much about them. But we live with them, and so we understand them. We have told you what we know. *He shifts his stance and his gaze to look at the place in the circle where the researchers and conservation manager are sitting together.* I hope that you can fix your maps to show that wildlife are in our villages for much of the year— especially places like *Lera, Engusero, Oloyeti, Oremit,* and out by our *enkang'* in the mountains! Maybe it would help if you would put these places and their Maasai names on your maps.[46]

MN:[47] *As a junior elder, he is a bit nervous standing to speak after the last elder, but he is prodded on by others and is not usually too constrained by power dynamics. He is a well-respected, well-liked, and extremely knowledgeable junior elder.* I think that we can all see that there are a lot of wildlife in our land [*enkop ang*]! *He speaks loudly with pride but also in a jokingly obnoxious way that makes everyone laugh, as he looks at the researchers and people from the conservation agency.* Knowing exactly where they are likely to be at different times can be hard, but it is not impossible. All animals have different needs and different ways to meet them. For instance, impala, like MG said earlier, like it in *Oremit*. They have always liked it in *Oremit*. That is their place, together with the area by the *korongo* inside the MR. There are other animals that like it inside the MR and can't be found in the village because it is not *pori* enough for them, like waterbuck. And even hippos! There were times when we needed to move our cattle down south of the lake and we saw a lot of hippos there, but there are none here in the village. Hippos have a certain grass they like to eat that no other animal eats. None! It is just the food of the hippo! So you can see, there are certain animals that have certain needs. Lesser kudu likes *pori* [bushed/wooded places], like *Oremit* and the *korongo*, just like impala. They eat grass and *imbenek* [dicots, such as shrubs and tree leaves] and they don't drink much water, so they can stay in the dry country even once the rain has stopped and water dried up. So, lesser kudu, impala, reedbuck, waterbuck, and even eland like the bush. Buffalo like the bush too, but usually more forested areas like in *Olmukutan* and *Mlimani*. There used to be a lot of buffalo in *Olmukutan*, but then we Makaa killed so many [*he imitates spearing an animal*] to make shields.

Zebra and gazelle are easy; they are not afraid of people or of the bush and can eat anywhere. But wildebeest are different. They like the wide-open places near the lake as everyone has been saying, and I believe that the times that MG talks about seeing them on her transects in *Oremit* she is referring to this area down by the lake. They like open areas, and they are afraid of thirst. They need water. But knowing where the animals are can be difficult because they move around a lot. So there are lots of times that MG, Landis M, and Landis K didn't see any wildebeest on their transects, but they were here in the village. I live right near a place where the wildebeest pass all the time. And I will come and tell MG that twenty-five wildebeest passed yesterday morning from *Lera* going to the MR [*he acts this out as if he was in conversation with MG*]. And she will be surprised! "But we did a transect in *Lera* and we didn't see any!" [*he says in a feminized Swahili*], she'll tell me, all flustered. "Well maybe they weren't in *Lera* but were just moving through and maybe you were there at the wrong time!" *As he finishes this little skit, he laughs out loud and others laugh with him.* The wildebeest move a lot, and that is why it helps to have lots of eyes if you really want to know where they are—my eyes are good, and some of the *ilmurran* herding see a lot, but not all [*as he says this, he scowls at some of the* ilmurran *he knows spend most of their time in town or have even started drinking*], but not the *ilaiyok* [young herd boys], they don't know anything. *More laughter from the crowd.* Anyway, this is what I say/think. And like MG said, we Maasai, we know a lot about where the animals are and what they like. We may not have studied, but we know. You know, "you see a bird that has no hands, only a beak, and it builds a house that you don't know how to build."[48] But. . . . *He pauses, looking down, and then directly at the researchers and conservation manager with a very serious look.* What will be done with this information that we have shared with you? Will those interested in "global conservation" take our land to protect wildlife? Like what happened with the Manyara Ranch? Or will we be rewarded for keeping them alive when all our farming neighbors have killed them or chased them away? *He points his arm in all the directions around him to areas dominated by agricultural groups.* Will we be allowed to just continue as we always have? Together with the wildlife [*he says this loud and bold, and then lowers his head to whisper*]—well most of the time [*with a smirk*]. I have nothing more to say.

Conclusion

Tracking wildlife is hard. There is no "god-trick" of seeing everywhere from nowhere. Variability matters. Wildlife movements are both regular and not. Knowing patterns of regularity in the movements is important for management purposes for all involved. Pinning them down and simplifying them into strict boundaries, such as wet and dry season dispersals in time and space, is to lose the variability vital to the movements themselves. Patterns exist but are based on different factors that are not often appreciated by conservation scientists/practitioners and cannot easily be boxed into discreet categories or boundaries. For instance, the "wet season" may bring animals, but too much rain may push them away; October may be the wet season one year, the dry season the next, or may exhibit both wet and dry season characteristics, affecting not only wildlife presence but what we *see*. Animals have preferences, needs, and personality traits. Animals act and react to rainfall, people, and other animals. They shape the landscape as they react to it, and their movement patterns change accordingly. And these patterns, actions, reactions, and intra-actions are not separate from people (Maasai, poachers, scientists, conservation practitioners, game scouts), who also react to and change the landscape as they move across it, study it, mold it, intra-act with it.

There was general agreement in this *enkiguena* that there are a lot of different ways of knowing "the way things are," that things are changing, that all knowledge is always only partial, and that knowledge is also power. Knowledge can either empower Maasai to be more involved in conservation planning or can further disenfranchise them of their land if those in power use it in certain ways. In other words, there are lots of different politics involved here. Where the wildlife are matter. Knowing where they are also matters. And how that information gets used matters too.

Of course, there are also the familiar politics of access and control. What does it mean to show that wildlife rely on village land? Can Maasai gain respect for their knowledge of wildlife and their way of life that has kept wildlife (mostly) intact? Or does sharing this knowledge risk appropriation of their knowledge and their land? Does it challenge ontological framings that separate nature from society and posit science as superior over other ways of knowing? Or does it provide fuel for policy initiatives based on this framing, regardless? My hope is that the *enkiguena* format provides the possibility for ontological openings—to know and be with wildlife differently, and the potential to bring such differences into conversation. To move beyond colonial appropriation of "indigenous technical knowledge" into an appreciation of Maasai ways of knowing and being with wildlife, of Maasai intelligence, theory, and practice (Simpson 2001, 2017). Without doing so, conservation science risks more than ethical compromise. It misses the complexity of the very wildlife movements it seeks to understand and protect. The result is a landscape that is simplified and bounded into places for people and places for wildlife—a compartmentalized way of world making that does not always work as it is meant to. For we learned that wildlife can be found in village lands throughout much of the year, where they sometimes share pastures with livestock. Yet there is little agreement over what this means ecologically or ontologically, or even just how wildlife and livestock co-use the landscape, something addressed in more detail in the next *enkiguena* agenda, chapter 3. For now, I step out of the *enkiguena* for a moment to present or "map" the study site, from differently situated standpoints.

| Chapter 2 |

Mapping the Study Site of
Emanyara Maasailand

Boundaries are drawn by mapping practices; "objects" do not preexist as such. Objects are boundary projects. But boundaries shift from within; boundaries are very tricky. What boundaries provisionally contain remains generative, productive of meanings and bodies. Siting (sighting) boundaries is a risky practice.

—HARAWAY 1991, 201

IT WAS a nice overcast morning as we set out on foot to "ground-truth" the maps I was trying to make of the two villages I was calling my "study area." I had my handheld GPS with me and three interlocutors: my regular field assistant, Landis K; another man of the Landis age-set (Landis M), who had been helping out with the wildlife transects and had additional knowledge of the local landscape; and Naibor, an extremely knowledgeable Makaa junior elder who had agreed to lead the expedition. While they were all men, our goal was to get GPS points for place-names that had been delineated through "mapping" exercises with separate groups of men and women. While that exercise had proven quite problematic at first, it eventually led to some great hand-drawn maps of different discrete places named and used by Maasai women and men in the area.

I put "mapping" in quotation marks because Maasai do not draw maps, nor do they have an equivalent word in Maa for map, or mapping. It was not until I asked them to make maps for me that I realized the problematic nature of my request. I had become frustrated with my inability to talk to Maasai about where they took their livestock, or where they saw wildlife, without knowing how they saw and spoke about the landscape. When I realized how heavily Maasai relied on their own place-names, I became determined to create "Maasai maps" of the study area. To do so, I called different groups of individuals (men, women, *ilmurran*) for participatory mapping exercises (on paper or in the dirt, whichever they were more comfortable with). I asked them to think about what they were going to do on any series of days and draw a "map" (Swahili: *ramani*) of the areas that came to mind. I realized how flawed my approach was when I noticed that the Swahili word for map, *ramani*, was not being translated into Maa. I then began to notice that the word was actually used by Maasai, even when speaking amongst themselves in Maa, to refer to official state delineated boundaries, the marker of the "map" between two separate state recognized entities (e.g., villages, districts). When I first asked some elders to draw a *ramani*, I was told, "But we, we Maasai, we do not have maps." Another elder remarked, "I don't have anything to really say, but it's very good if you could explain to us more about the map. There is no map at all in all of Maasailand, but there's a map between Babati and Monduli [districts]."

Once I realized my mistake I clumsily tried to remedy it by asking them to instead draw a picture, before realizing that this too reflected my own ontologoical bias associated with mental mapping proccesses (Crampton 2009; Turnbull 2000). I finally settled on rather lengthly explanations that seemed to reflect what I had observed and was different for the different groups. For the elders, it went something like this: "When you wake up in the morning, you have an idea of where you want the cattle to go that day, and you need to explain it to the *ilmurran*, right? How do you do that? What are the various places you can think about, and could you draw them for me (on paper or on the ground)?" Realizing this too was limiting, I asked them to include all the places they think of as important. I did the same with the *ilmurran* (but rather where they would go, what they think about/picture/know), and the same for the women. This seemed to work reasonably well and resulted in unique maps from each group, reflecting their own areas of expertise and interest. Whereas the elders began their drawing far from the village, at the place where the main water source comes from upstream, the *ilmurran* began with the dirt road that passes through the center of the village. And the women mapped locations of water in far greater detail then either of the groups of men. They also mapped stories about wildlife encounters that are often associated with men, such as places where the lions hide or the elephants go.

I was quite pleased with the final results and now wanted to make proper GIS maps to display them. I originally thought this would be difficult and would somehow betray Maasai spatial ontology of place-names by forcing them into standard cartographic classifications. But to my surprise, all the mapping exercises resulted in the drawing of discrete shapes that could quite easily be turned into polygons in a GIS map. So that is how I ended up on this refreshingly overcast day walking with three Maasai men to gollect GPS points of place-names on the ground. And here, once again, what seemed like it should be a simple and straightforward exercise proved far from. We started off, Naibor in the lead, instructing me when to take a GPS mark—which we did at the beginning, middle, and end of a particular place, more if the place was particularly large. At one point, he told me we had reached the end of a place (*Lera Olkunda*, see map 3) and for me to mark it with the GPS. I did so, and we continued walking.

Naibor: *As we are walking, he looks over at me and with a forward gesture of his arm he says,* And up there ahead is *Lera Lentim.*

Mara: *Stopping where I am standing and taking out the GPS.* So we are in that place now?

Naibor: No. It's just up there. *Keeps walking.*

Mara: *Catching up to him, but then stopping again.* So then we are still in *Lera Olkunda*?

Naibor: *Confused, he looks at me and back in the direction we came from.* No, we have already left *Lera Ollkunda*, didn't you mark it?

Mara: I did mark it. But then if we have left *Lera Olkunda* but we are not yet in *Lera Lentim*, where are we?

Naibor: We are in between!

Mara: So there are in-between places that are not a part of one place or the other?

Naibor: *Stops walking to look at me with an exasperated look on his face, leaning in an authoritative pose on his walking stick* (engudi). **Yes, we are in between.** In America, one person's house and land goes all the way up to the boundary of another person's land? There is no *space in between*?

At this I just stopped and laughed. Laughed at my own inability to see otherwise, and at Naibor's inability to imagine it.

Recognizing and drawing boundaries is always a contested process. This short vignette describes a moment of ontological conflict when I tried to align Maasai boundary-making practices with those by which I know and live, those of Western cartography—first in having Maasai "map" their landscapes and then to put Maasai place-names into a GIS map. I resolved the conflict, at least in part, by more carefully choosing my words, and then by stretching the methods of GIS to accommodate Maasai spatial framings—by leaving spaces in between on the map that I created or so I tried. We blurred the boundaries of adjacent places in the GIS, but unfortunately the final printed map conveys them as dark boundaries instead of spaces in between (see map 3). The ontological conflict provided an opening to explore different techniques to bring Maasai ways of knowing and being into a format visible to the Western trained eye, and thereby useable for conservation planners, by being on the maps.[1] My goal in doing this was initially far more than academic. As conservation agencies and Maasai NGOs rush to complete land-use planning exercises around Maasailand, through "participatory mapping" they begin with Western informed boundaries for seasons and places. Maasai are just asked to fill in the appropriate spaces (i.e., wet season grazing area) on the map. This process and others like it silence Maasai ways of being and knowing the landscapes spatially and temporally. My hope was that in reconciling Western mapping techniques with Maasai boundary-drawing practices, I could provide a template for mapping and planning otherwise, in a way that recognizes Maasai intelligence practices.[2]

If my use of Maasai place-names in the last chapter was jarring and uncomfortable, that was intentional. Part of decolonizing conservation entails changing the language of the conversation. And for Maasai, they know, use, and talk about space with their own place-names, yet they are usually asked to use the names imposed by others (i.e., the state, conservation agencies). This chapter acts as a nonconventional introduction to (or "mapping" of) the study site—as a confluence of overlapping (and changing) boundary demarcations and units of spatial, cultural, administrative, and ecological organization. This entails moving beyond the map, toward a narrative presentation of space, through Maasai place-names. I then introduce the other boundary enactments—ecological, cultural, and administrative—that Maasai in the study site also utilize almost daily. The final section explores how these different boundary-drawing practices are linked to different ways of knowing wildlife in and across this space—primarily in Oltukai and Esilalei Villages (Monduli District, Arusha Region), in the *Emanyara enkutoto* in the *Kisongo olosho*, within the Tarangire-Manyara Ecosystem—all diffracted in the pages below.

Maasai Spatial Enactments

> We experience the contours of the landscape by moving through it, so that it enters . . . into our "muscular consciousness." . . . In their journeys along paths and tracks, however, people also move from place to place. To reach a place, you need cross no boundary, but you must follow some kind of path. Thus there can be no places without paths, along which people arrive and depart; and no paths without places, that constitute their destinations and points of departure.
>
> —INGOLD 2000, 204

The savanna landscape where Maasai live is covered in the footpaths of people, livestock, and wildlife, crisscrossing space and connecting various named places. The paths themselves are not named, except to connote the places they connect (Lovell 2018). In discussing wildlife and livestock movements, or giving directions, Maasai will often suggest the movement pattern with the use of their arms, the roll of their eyes, or the shift of their head. These bodily gestures are accompanied with the names of the various places along the pathway of movement. Places are known through movement and stories of ecological, physical, and social features that are visible to the trained eye and shift over time. Sometimes these features result in discrete boundaries, such as the closed shapes that participants drew during mapping exercises and as seen on the landscape where the tall grass ends or trees grow. I rarely if ever heard cardinal directions used for explaining space, with the same word used in Tanzania for both north and south (*kopikop*). Though there was an understanding of its original mean- ing (still used in Kenya), as one elder woman explained (May 29, 2003): "*Kopikop* is the place where neither the sun nor the moon comes from or goes to. But it is really the place to the right of god, and god is in the east [where the sun comes from]. It is the place of *Yemate*, the rift towards Kerio, where Maasai come from."[3]

I present my own description of Maasai place-names for the village lands as a ver- bal tour, but I use cardinal directions to help the reader find her way. This should be viewed as only a surface presentation of a much richer oral spatial knowledge to help the reader navigate the *enkiguena* chapters, while decolonizing discussions of space and providing a glimpse into Maasai relations with their surroundings. The scale is small, and the places mentioned can all be located on map 3. Names that will come up often throughout the book are noted with an asterisk. Many of the names can be found throughout Maasailand, as they refer to common ecological or physical features.

WALKING THROUGH PLACE-NAMES

We start our tour outside of Oltukai Village in the southwest corner of the map in a place called *Maramboi*, a wooded savanna, dominated by the *Olduka* date palm trees (*Hyphaene ventricosa*), and historically an important dry season grazing area for Maasai in Oltukai. It is now in a separate village and within a WMA, with sub- sequent restrictions on land use. Moving north, one passes through different areas called *impoorri*—places where grass does not grow, where the soil is hard and small pools of water collect during the rains. Surrounded with the short grass of *Oloyeti* (see below), they are favored locations for cattle during the early rains. Continuing north through alternating patches of *impoorri* and short grass, we enter *Ang'ata Ilowuarak**— the plains of the lions, also referred to as *Ang'ata Olowaru* (figure 9). In the not

Figure 9 *Ang'ata Olowuarak* (also: *Ang'ata Olowaru*) with cattle calves and zebra

too distant past, when wildebeest and zebra heavily populated this area during the
wet season, it was also frequented by lions, with *Elang'ata Olowuarak*—the river
crossing of the lion—referring to a specific location where the animals crossed the
river. Closer to the river it is called *Aliperi pera*—the place that is flat in elevation
so water stays for a while as it slowly makes its way toward the lake. We approach the
river, *Olkeju Loltukai*,[4] a bit farther south, and enter *Alo-adare*—where the water is
red from high mineral/alkaline content and spreads out into small creeks on its way
to the lake. The name refers to an important grazing area around this source of water,
which overflows into the surrounding pasture at the beginning and end of the rainy
season. The Oltukai River forms the southern boundary of the village and supports
dense riparian vegetation dominated by *Acacia polyacantha* (*elasiti* in Maa) but is dry
most of the year and thus is referred to as a *korongo* [ditch] in Swahili.

　　Crossing the *korongo*, we enter Oltukai Subvillage, which gives the name to the
village, after the date palm tree, which dominates the uplifted sandy area where most
homesteads are located. Today this area is an open grass-scrubland, with scattered
regrowth of *olduka* trees (see figure 10). The trees are prized for poles and smaller
wooden stems for house construction, while the palm fronds make good rope for
building, for carrying water, and for young children to play with, and the fruit provides
a treat for children at the peak of the dry season.

Figure 10a Oltukai with the main meeting place of the baobab tree (*olmesera*) and Oltukai River in the background. Note short palm regrowth in the foreground.

Figure 10b Meeting held under the *olmesera* tree, Oltukai Village.

Once inside Oltukai, the first smaller area we enter is called *Embaribali**—small depressions that hold water during the rains. Just south of *Embaribali* is *Lorikiushi**— the place of termite mounds, a grass plain without trees. While there is only one termite mound there today, there used to be many. Some suggest that the El Niño floods (1998) changed the landscape. Embedded within this area is *Nalkeldenyo*—the name of a well that used to be here, named for the man who enhanced the work begun by a warthog. Neither the man nor the well remain.

Walking down a bit, we approach the western boundary of the village, which lies against *Emakat*—soda, soda-ash, or Lake Manyara. Running the length of the lake is an area called *Oloyeti**, a short grass plain seasonally inundated with water from the lake. As the lake recedes in the dry season, the dominant grass, *oloyeti* (*Sporobolus spicatus*),[5] "spreads rapidly by runners and produces a perennial sward" of a highly palatable grass for cattle and wild herbivores (White 1983, 267). The only other grass that grows here is *emurua* (*Cynodon dactylon*), in the small crevices where water collects. The area is also called *Emborianda*, referring to the saline hard crusted soil that produces patches where grass does not grow. A third name is *Naong*—the sound of wildebeest communicating with their calves. *Oloyeti* is a popular destination for wildlife and cattle because of the salt, the near constant supply of grass, and the small pools of water that collect after the rains (see figure 11).

Continuing north, we enter the important grazing area of *Lera**, named for the presence of *ilera* (sg. *oleria*), yellow fever tree (*Acacia xanthophloea*), but also full of *olkereyan* (*Sporobolus pyramidalis*) and *ologoraing'ok* (*Pennisetum mezinium*) grasses, both

Figure 11 Oloyeti short grassland during the dry season with injured gazelle and two men of Landis age-set investigating the situation

valuable for grazing during the dry season. *Lera* is further divided into smaller named places: *Lera Shingo, Lera Olkunda**, and *Lera Amuret,* all of which refer to the names of *inkang'itie* (homesteads) that used to be located there. Today, there are no *inkang'itie* in *Lera,* now designated a grazing area, and many of the tall *ilera* trees are gone. Maasai cut large branches to make the thorn fences (*esita*) that encircle the *enkang'* to keep predators out. The decline in these trees means that many *inkang'itie* in the Oltukai part of the village fence only the cattle kraal (*olsinko*) and not the entire *enkang'* as is customary. While outsiders blame the deforestation on Maasai, Maasai blame the combined forces of El Niño floods, a disease that afflicted many trees, and deforestation by villagers. As for why settlements were relocated out of *Lera,* people suggest it was due to increasingly limited access to fresh water, the desire to farm, and the need to preserve dry season pastures. *Lera* used to be a regular place for *eronjo* (temporary settlements) during the dry season, but this is no longer the case, because of the declining water table.

During the rainy season, water passes through *Lera* in three small streams, *Enkeju Olkereyan* (the stream of *Olkereyan* grass); *Naikurkur,* the sound that water makes as it roars through the tall grass toward the lake; and *Enkeju Olowuarak**, the stream of the lions. The northern portion of *Lera* used to be more densely vegetated and is thus called *Lera Lentim**—"in the bush/forest." Today it has a sparser coverage than the name suggests, with a dense thicket of *ilera* regrowth. On the eastern and northern

Figure 12 Cattle grazing in *Lera Lentim*

edge of *Lera Lentim*, the thicket gives way to open grassland (*Sporobolus pyramidalis* dominated), named *Alalili le Lentim*. *Alalili* refers to reserve pasture areas for calves and sick cattle in the dry season and this was the *alalili* for the families that once occupied *Lera*. Today, the name recalls this history, but refers to a narrow swath of tall grass, good pasture that is no longer restricted in access and fills the "place in between" *Lera* and *Enkung'u Olduka** to the north. *Enkung'u* is Maa for knee, used to refer to a small, slightly raised area, in this case, one dominated by the date palm. *Enkung'u Olduka* is an important dry season grazing area, as well as the location where two hundred acres were designated in 2003 for the creation of a high-end tourist campsite (see chapter 3). North of *Enkung'u Olduka* we enter *Kiripaa**—to enclose, keep secret, a place filled with tall and thick *Olkereyian* grass that provides the perfect hiding place for lions, keeping their presence "a secret."

On the other hand, if we walk east from *Enkung'u Olduka*, as many herders do on their way home with cattle, we continue into more open wooded grassland. At first, we enter an area called *Kimorijaki*, dominated by the date palm but also with a wider mix of grasses, forbs, and shrubs. The name suggests that the fruit here is so sweet that all the fibers (normally spat out after sucked on) are swallowed whole. Continuing east, we walk into *Lalamilama**, where trees are *separated* out at a slight distance, bordered on the south with the short grass plains of *alamunyani*.

This distinction of an area as *alamunyani* matters and refers both to a soil type—mixed sand and clay with a high saline content that is seasonally flooded—and the type of vegetation, which it supports: annual grasses, what Maasai referred to as *nyepesi* in Swahili, meaning "light, quick grasses," and dicots/forbs/scrub that Maasai call *imbenek* in Maa.[6]

Walking north we enter *Engusero*, a term employed throughout Maasailand to refer to areas of black cotton soil which support nutritious grasses such as *ologoraing'ok* (*Pennisetum mezinium*) and *emurua* (*Cynodon dactylon*). Here, it refers to a designated subvillage, an area that was discussed as the most important grazing area for livestock for people in both villages, as well as by migrating wildlife. Inside *Engusero* are several small hand-dug dams (*elueni*), *inkang'itie* (Maasai settlements), and *shambas* (small farms). *Endarpo* is a separate, slightly raised place inside *Engusero* that refers to the sausage trees there (*Kigelia africana*; *oldarboi* in Maa). A dam was built in *Endarpo* in 2005 with the assistance of Corbett Bishop Safaris to collect water running down toward the lake from *Simbi*, which is the flat stretch of land or "valley," (Maa: *ayarata*), where water collects during the rains. Simbi is now also the name of a new subvillage, as well as a dam located inside Manyara Ranch, where one of the transects is located.

Figure 13 Giraffe family in short grasslands just outside of *Lera* in *Enkung'u Olduka*

The Manyara Ranch is also called *Alchamba*, a Maasai rendering of the Swahili word *shamba*, recalling a time when the ranch was divided into small farms by an earlier owner. *Engusero* takes us to the northern boundary of Oltukai Village, marked by *Olkeju Loorg'abolo*, the river dominated by *Orgaboli, Ficus sur* trees. This river is also seasonal and thus called a *korongo* in Swahili, though water stays here much longer then in the Oltukai *korongo*. Just over the boundary with the Manyara Ranch lies *Aladariak*, the places of red water (plural of *Aladare*), a windy part of the river where small wells (*ilcorroi; olcorro* sg.) are dug in the dry season to access water. In some places the water is "salty" or mineral rich (and thus red), yet in other areas the water flows clean. Maasai have maintained rights to these wells through the various forms of ownership of the Manyara Ranch.

We now enter Esilalei Village, which gets its name from a tree that once covered the landscape, *Commiphora schimperi*, and is today found only in small patches, individually referred to as *esilalei**.[7] We first enter the subvillage of *Endepesi*, a small area of *Oldepesi* trees—*Acacia tortilis*. Today this place is filled with Maasai homesteads and farms. Local stories suggest deforestation for charcoal production by neighboring tribes as the leading cause of land use change, combined with a disease that spread through the shared root system of the trees. There is a natural dam just inside the Manyara Ranch used regularly by *Endepesi* residents, along with wildebeest and zebra, called *Loongaik** (arms), because its shape resembles two arms spread wide. The surrounding pastures of the dam provide valuable (if illegal) grazing inside the Manyara Ranch. This area used to be called *Olpurkel*, a Maasai reference to dry hot places, and *Olcorro*, the name for the soda lake, the adjoining, now silted dam, and surrounding pastures, a name that is still heard today. West of *Olcorro* down a slight slope are two important sources of water—*Losemendoni* and *Embarimbali**.

Embarimbali again is a depressed area that holds rainwater and spill off from the river, but this one is much larger than that in Oltukai, supplying herders in both villages with water well into the middle of the dry season.[8] Once water was dried up in *Embarimbali*, villagers dug wells in the river, *Olkeju Loorg'abolo*, in a place called *Indapidapo*. The name refers to the cement-like soil in the dry riverbed, which can maintain deep wells, even when water in the *Aladariak* wells run dry.[9] Continuing toward the lake, we cross the river and enter *Narok Sarng'arb**—black mud. This place, named for the black cotton soil, which turns into a thick clay mud when it rains, is different from the soil in *Engusero*; not as heavy, it does not crack when dry and supports a dense coverage of long grass, dominated by *olkereyian* (*Sporobolus pyramidalis*) and *ologoraing'ok* (*Pennisetum mezinium*), which lasts well into the dry season. *Narok Sarng'arb*

Figure 14 *Engusero* view from an *enkang'*, with small stock coming home. Wooded area in the background is the Manyara Ranch.

Figure 15 *Olkeju* (river) *Loorg'abolo* with woman collecting water from a hand-dug (shallow) well in front of *orgaboli* (ficus) tree.

Figure 16 *Oleketalokeon*, with a view down toward the lake and the pastures of *Engogoro, Oremit,* and *Losirwa*. See trees in the foreground planted by the local resident.

is bound on the east and south by hometeads and farms, called *Engaramangu* (Maa for farm) on the east.

On the southern edge is *Oleketalokeon*—"to look back at oneself," referring to the stunning 360-degree view one gets at this location (see figure 16). When the river is full, residents here are unable to leave, forced to graze in *Narok Sarng'arb* year-round. When the river is dry, there is a regular back-and-forth movement of people and livestock into the pastures surrounding *Embarimbali,* particularly *Lembeti*,* which is a slightly raised area of mixed rocky and sandy soil that supports a diverse range of grasses, forbs, shrubs, and trees, and is recognized as a "corridor" or pathway for wildlife.[10] Adjacent to *Lembeti* is *Olmukutan*,* a small, closed forest of *Albizia anthelmintica* to which the name refers; that used to be heavily populated by buffalo and today supports some wildlife, as well as cattle grazing on the edges. Stories abound about the ways in which the Makaa age-set slaughtered buffalo here when they were *ilmurran* to get skins to make shields and to "display their fierceness," before they were stopped by the elders.

Descending from *Olmukutan* we cross *Enkeju Olaiyen,* the "stream of the young boy," where water flows heavily in the wet season, supporting dense vegetation, and one day carried away a small boy. On the northern side of the stream we find ourselves

Figure 17 View of Esilalei Village from the main road, with mixture of pastures, farms, and homesteads

in *Esilalei* proper, while the subvillage is *Kanisani*, a Swahili word referring to the Catholic church that lies at its center. It is this area that gives the larger village its name: a mixed wooded grassland with pockets of *esilalei* (*Commiphora schimperi*) thicket, particularly as one heads to slightly higher ground, and east, toward the boundary with Manyara Ranch. To the west, we also move up slightly in elevation into an area called *Engogoro*, which means dispute/fight. According to an elder who lives here, this area used to be full of wildlife, "and if you passed they would get angry and the people would also get angry," and so the place is named accordingly.[11] *Engogoro* runs into a large scrub savanna, *Oremit*, Maa for *Salvadora persica*, the twigs of which are used as a toothbrush.[12] This is an important grazing area for wildlife and livestock during the early rains and spans the border of the next village, *Losirwa*, which is Maa for an open, whitish, expansive area.

On the northeastern boundary of Esilalei Village is a tarmac road, on the other side of which are the *Losimingori* Mountains, referred to by Maasai in the area simply as *Oldoinyo**, meaning mountain, but the official name (*Losimingori*) refers to a genet. There are several water supplies near the road in this area—a natural depression called *Loongaik* (spread-out hands), and two larger natural dams, important sources of water for cattle, people, and wildlife, *Olotoro* and *Loongonito*.[13] *Eluaii* sits just inside the Manyara Ranch but is frequented by members of Esilalei for pasture, fuelwood, and *olcani* [Maa: medicine, often from plants]. *Eluaii* is Maa for *Acacia drepanolobium*, prized by Maasai women as a potent medicine used to clean out the uterus after childbirth.

There are many other places with names, many of which are embedded within the places mentioned, referring to smaller scale distinctions. Place-names reflect differences in vegetation composition and structure, water sources, animal presence, social history, soil type, elevation, and more. Place-names are used in conversations between Maasai men and women, adults and children. When I asked elders to tell me about their grazing patterns, they were often at a loss for what to say until I informed them that I knew the place-names. This inspired an almost universal sigh of relief and then they would begin talking: "Today they went to *Lorkiushi* for water and then to *Enkung'u Olduka* for grass."[14] It is for this reason that I use the Maasai place-names in the *enkiguena* chapters, to provide a space where Maasai contributions can be made more freely.

Place-names help Maasai navigate their use of resources. They are used to direct *ilmurran* where to go to capture seasonal change and resources for livestock and to talk about rainfall patterns and animal movements. They overlap and exist across other sets of boundaries—administrative and conservation based, in addition to already existing Maasai territorial/cultural delineations of the *olosho* and *enkutoto*.

SOCIOSPATIAL CATEGORIES OF MANAGEMENT: *OLOSHO/ENKUTOTO*

The place-names above are all within the *Emanyara enkutoto*. *Enkutoto* distinctions remain relevant to Maasai for cultural events and resource management, though they are rarely recognized by conservation agencies or even Maasai NGOs working on land-use planning. Historically, *iloshon* (and in *Kisongo inkutot*) were managed as separate common-property systems, with social rules directing resource management, yet with porous boundaries (Galaty 1981; Homewood and Rodgers 1991). They were essentially management units that encompassed all the resources needed for a transhumant grazing system, including *osupuko*—forested uplands with permanent water sources and year-round but lower-quality pasture—and *olpurkel*—hotter lowlands with salt licks and mineral-rich grasses but often without permanent water (Homewood and Rodgers 1991; Potkanski 1994). Grazing rules were—and to some extent continue to be—managed at the *enkutoto* level by community elders, with daily grazing practices coordinated by the *enkang'* and the family (Maa: *olmarei*).[15] This is illustrated in the above mapping of places that cross village boundaries. Within *enku-toto* and *olosho* boundaries, resource access can also be mediated by clan and age-set affiliations, government boundaries such as villages and districts, and conservation boundaries (i.e., national parks, the Manyara Ranch, and WMAs).

This means that while Maasai can still graze and relocate their *enkang'* anywhere within *enkutoto* boundaries, they often need to negotiate with village government leaders when crossing village land to build a temporary or permanent *enkang'*, gain a farm plot (*shamba*), or access grazing or water. And mobility, even just for daily grazing, can be restricted when one village designates land for conservation.[16] During initial field work, many families in Oltukai Village relocated to Losirwa Village during a drought year because of better access to water and the main road. Several families never returned to Oltukai but remained connected through clan and *enkutoto* ties. Others moved to Simanjiro District to set up a temporary ronjo *enkang'* for grazing, but because this is outside of the *Emanyara enkutoto*, negotiations were needed that often included both local traditional leaders and village government. The various boundaries and associated powers overlap and have changed over time, sometimes causing conflict between elders and youth, as well as constantly shifting negotiations. While elders are often associated with customary/traditional law that historically managed common property at the *enkutoto* level, younger men are often in govern-ment positions and thus responsible for management at the village level, as explained in the following quote from a Maasai elder regarding resource management:

> There have been many changes because today we follow a village with a government. Today tradition [Swahili: *mila*] and the elders can't say anything about land and gov-ernment. Like yesterday, we met to plan how to bring the water from Mto wa Mbu [a pipeline] that is being built and they're trying to get it extended to the village. The land committee and the water committee met. Long ago, it would have been the elders only. Today, it's only the small business that the elders handle. . . . But the government is not bad. [The elders] work with the government to plan [for] water and grazing. And we get help, we get support/services easier because assistance [Swahili: *msaada*] is distributed by the government. . . . And the government can't do anything without first talking with the elders (Elder2, Esilalei; Seuri age-set).

Across Maasailand, boundary overlaps reflect the historic introduction and manipulation of boundaries by colonial administrators, conservation agencies, and representatives of the independent Tanzanian state. Colonial officials solidified and stretched, but also disrupted and severed, some of the long-distance social and spatial relations that Maasai customary land use relied on. Later boundary-drawing practices by the independent Tanzanian state built on preexisting Maasai boundaries (i.e., *inku-tot*) to enact official administrative categories of control that didn't always match onto Maasai customary management processes. And Maasai have adopted some of these new boundaries, with customary leaders strategically utilizing Tanzanian governance categories to strengthen their own legitimacy. For instance, while there used to be *ilaigwenak* (traditional leaders) at the *enkutoto* and *olosho* levels, today there is a pro-liferation of village-level *ilaigwenak*, particularly for clans, as well as district-based *ilaigwenak* councils (Goldman, forthcoming).

An Administrative View: The Tanzanian Village

Villages were promoted across Tanzania through the official villagization program of Julius Nyere's Ujamaa policy in 1974. They represent the smallest unit of the decen-tralized system of governance, which in descending order are region (*mkoa*), district (*ulaia*), ward (*kata*), division (*tarafa*), village (*kijiji*), and then, when needed, subvil-lage (*kitongoji*). In Maasai areas, the customary boundaries of *iloshon* and *inkutot* were utilized to demarcate some of these categories.[17] And while Maasai continue to utilize both sets of boundaries, they have drawn strategically over time on the village as an official state-recognized unit of production, a site where development assistance such as food aid and schools could be requested, and a legal entity, which can sign contracts with outside investors (Gardner 2016a). Customary leadership, too, has shifted over time to meet the increasing centrality of the village, with age-set *ilaigwenak* having "helpers" in each village and clan *ilaigwenak* being enacted at village levels.

As the primary unit for development assistance and local politics, villages have been dividing into smaller and smaller units, making common-property management within village boundaries more difficult. Oltukai and Esilalei began as one village. Together with Losirwa, they made up the village of Esilalei inside Monduli District, Arusha Region. In 1975, Losirwa officially broke off as its own village. In 1999, the village divided again into Oltukai and Esilalei, with a boundary drawn along the seasonal Makuyuni River (*Olkeju Loorg'abolo*) on maps in the district capital. Yet a different boundary was pro-posed and used by villagers. As of the time of writing, both villages had formalized legal boundaries, land-use planning, and grazing areas, with the help of a community-based organization, the Ujamaa Community Resource Trust (UCRT), which has been working to help Indigenous resource-based communities create legal land-use plans to protect communal pastures.[18] While these two villages remain inside Monduli District, Arusha Region, a new administrative region, Manyara, has been formed, which contains all land north of the Oltukai River, including many places discussed above.

Despite that it is against Tanzanian law for villages to be defined along ethnic lines, Oltukai and Esilalei identify as Maasai, with many inhabitants descending from a few founding families. Others moved into the villages from nearby areas, which had become dominated by the related Waarusha tribe.[19] As a result, there was an unspoken rule that Waarusha families in bordering Minjingu Village were not to cross the Oltukai River to access resources (pasture, water) or to set up an *enkang'*. Other non-Maasai residents were either considered to have "become Maasai" through marriage or assimilation[20] or were laborers who maintained homes elsewhere and did not participate in village politics or attend meetings.[21] Now to provide some details from the time of research on these two primary villages. First a story told to me to explain "how the neighbors in Esilalei got so rich" that also touches on the importance of clan loyalty and generosity, so valued in the community.

A Story of Clan Loyalty–or How the Neighbors in Esilalei Got So Rich

Two *ilmurran* were returning home from traveling. On their way walking home, one of the *olmurrani* told the other that he needed to stop to relieve himself by a nearby tree, and for the other to wait for him up ahead. So, the other warrior went ahead and waited—and waited. But the second *olmurrani* never came. "Perhaps he was lying and had gone off to do something else," thought the friend, who decided to continue home on his own. Meanwhile, the *olmurrani* who had gone to relieve himself by the tree had been bitten by a snake. He died alone by the tree from the snakebite as his fellow *olmurrani* went home, also alone.

When the *olmurrani* arrived at home, people asked where his age-mate was. Why had they not returned together when they had left together? He told them that he did not know; he had strayed off the path but should be coming back any minute. The second *olmurrani*, of course, never did make it home. His family blamed his age-mate, who had made it home safely but alone, of killing their son. The *olmurrani* denied the allegation, and the case made it to the council of elders and meetings were held. The local *olaigwenani* agreed that the *olmurrani* should be blamed for the death of his fellow *olmurrani*, because they were on the path together and he returned home alone while his fellow warrior died. He was fined the forty-nine "blood cattle" of a murder, to be delivered to the family of the bereaved. The *olmurrani* had no option but to agree to the fine, because it is true that he returned home while his age-mate died along the way, but he continued to deny the allegations of murder.

As per the normal procedure, the warrior needed to collect the payment of his fine from his clan members. The warrior's father began circling around from *enkang'* to *enkang'* to get donations of cattle from fellow clan members. There was one elder of the clan in the area who had only one cow. Upon hearing that his clan mates were working to collect enough cattle to pay the fine of a fellow clan member, he volunteered up his one cow. Those doing the collection were ready to pass by this man's *enkang'*, knowing that he had only one cow and therefore nothing to contribute. Yet, the elder insisted on contributing his one cow. He said that he could not put himself before his clan. His clan was looking for cattle, so why should he not contribute what he could, which was just one cow. The elder had a wife and kids who were dependent on the cow for milk, but the man contributed it anyway. Those doing the collection tried to refuse, but he insisted they take his one cow, and so they did.

Finally, the forty-nine cows were collected, and the clan was ready to make its payment. The *ilmurran* set off to drive the cattle to the *enkang'* of the bereaved. They failed, however, to reach the *enkang'*. On the way, a huge black snake appeared in the path and set up to attack the *ilmurran* and the cattle to stop them from passing. The *ilmurran* would push the cattle aside and try to fight off the snake, but every time they did so, the snake would disappear. They would then start on their way again, and the snake would reappear. Finally, the *ilmurran* were forced to go home with the forty-nine cattle and try again another day. The next time they tried, however, the same thing happened. The snake stopped them in their path, and whenever the warriors would push the cattle aside to fight off the snake, the snake would disappear. The *ilmurran* returned home again, unable to reach the *enkang'* of the bereaved. Another meeting was held. The *ilmurran* explained the situation to the elders. The elders decided that the snake was trying to tell them something. The *olmurrani* who was blamed for the death of his age-mate was innocent, as he had been claiming all along. The lost *olmurrani* was killed by a snake. The snake was trying to tell them that it was he who was responsible for killing the *olmurrani*, so this other *olmurrani* should not be fined for the death. The cattle should be returned to the clan members.

The clan of the originally accused *olmurrani* held their own meeting to decide what to do with the cattle they had collected. The cattle had already been donated, but now there was no payment to be made. What should be done? They discussed the option of just returning the cattle as they were donated or of using the donation for the clan. Then the man who had done the initial collection of cattle stood up to speak. He explained how there was one elder who had only one cow. He was a man with a family to support and nonetheless had donated that one cow to the clan. Imagine if he had twenty cows? He would likely have donated five to the clan. That elder, he continued, showed a kind of selflessness and loyalty to his clan that is unusual. He should be rewarded. Why not give that man, who now has no cattle at all and a family to support, all forty-nine cattle? The cattle were all donated for the purpose of the clan, and so people did not expect to get their cattle back. Why not use this donation to help this elder who has shown such loyalty to the clan? And in the future, if we need donations, he will have the cattle to donate as he did today. The elders all agreed that the forty-nine cattle should be given to this elder alone.

The *ilmurran* went to drive the cattle to the elder's *enkang'*. The elder was shocked at the turn of events and extremely grateful to his clan members as he received the forty-nine cattle. That elder went on to be the wealthiest Maasai in Esilalei Village.

VILLAGE DEMOGRAPHICS

Oltukai is dwarfed by Esilalei in size, population, and wealth. According to 2002 estimates, when this research began, Oltukai had a population of 1,071[22] across fifty-four *inkang'itie* and Esilalei 2,203[23] across eighty-six *inkang'itie*.[24] By 2012, the last official census, Oltukai had a reported population of 1,551 and Esilalei 3,687.[25] In 2002, Oltukai had a total of 5,923 livestock (3,991 cattle), with an average of 73 per *enkang'* (ranging 0–700). Esilalei, in contrast, had a total of 20,423 livestock in 2002, (11,840 cattle), with an average of 138 per *enkang'* (ranging 0–1,788). By 2005, the wealthiest herd owner in Esilalei had a total of 3,067 cattle, while the wealthiest *enkang'* in Oltukai had dropped to 520. While livestock wealth quantifications at the *enkang'* level have limited analytical power regarding poverty and wealth definitions, they do provide a basic picture of the livestock populations within the study area.[26]

Over time, of course, livestock numbers have fluctuated, particularly related to periodic droughts (2005, 2009, 2011). For instance, while average household cattle holdings across *Emanyara* (Oltukai, Esilalei, Elasiti, and Minjingu Villages) before the 2009 drought was 208.5 (min. 5, max. 1,354), the drought resulted in an average loss of 31.5 cattle per *enkang'* or 10 percent of the household herd (max. 36 percent) (Goldman and Riosmena 2013). This highlights the vacillation in cattle holdings that have occurred in Maasailand over the years, reflecting a common trend for semiarid sub-Saharan Africa (Behnke, Scoones, and Kerven 1993; Scoones 1995). But Maasai in *Emanyara*, and elsewhere, do not survive on livestock alone and have steadily been engaging in various pursuits to diversify their livelihoods and accumulate wealth (McCabe, Leslie, and DeLuca 2010). This includes participation in the gemstone mining industry. Nearly half (40 percent) of sampled homesteads in *Emanyara* in 2003 named at least one person from their *enkang'* working in the mining town of Merrerani, in Simanjrio. Yet the "gemstone business" had not brought as much wealth to this area as it had to those in Simanjiro District where the mines are located (Smith 2016).[27] Other income-generation pursuits included working as a guard in Arusha town, going to the Manyara Ranch for a range of jobs (game scout, herder, store-keeper, guard, driver, radio controller, and tree-nursery attendant); and participation in petty trade at local markets—men selling beads and skins and women selling milk, eggs, tobacco products, tea, sugar, and soda. All these various activities helped people obtain cash to meet household needs, especially the purchase of food (maize), when farm outputs were insufficient. However, all homesteads in the study area engaged in livestock rearing as the dominant livelihood practice, supplemented by farming, with cash needs usually met through the sale of livestock. Every *enkang'* in Oltukai and Esilalei had at least one small farm (*shamba*), and many had a *shamba* for every adult male and older wife (ranging in size from one to fifty acres). Most farmed maize for subsistence and beans (and extra maize) for sale. However, in my time living in Oltukai (2002–4), the sporadic rains contributed to low farm outputs, exacerbated by crop raiding by elephants, which grew in number with the conversion of Manyara Ranch into a conservation area. In 2003, very few people planted crops; even fewer planted in 2004. Yet as of writing this book (2020), nearly everyone is still farming every year, and much of *Engusero* has been turned into small *shambas*.

Formal education levels in the study site were quite low when field work began in 2002, despite both villages having their own primary school. The Oltukai school was new at that time, built only after it split from Esilalei. Men of the Landis age-set were the first to be educated in the Esilalei Village school, which initially met under a tree for several years, before school rooms were built. The only member of Oltukai at that time who had received a high school education left the village to work and live in Simanjiro. Much has changed since. In 2004, Oltukai sent its first group of students to secondary school. In 2017, the first group of girls entered secondary school, and there were three college-educated men in Oltukai, one working as a professor at the University of Dodoma.

A View from the Conservation "Heartland"

Heartlands are large, cohesive conservation landscapes which are biologically import-ant and have the scope to maintain healthy populations of wild species and natural processes well into the future.

—AWF WEBSITE, NOVEMBER 2005

Conservation boundaries also crisscross this space with associated ideas of what it should look like and how it should be managed. The largest boundary is what AWF calls the Maasai Steppe Heartland but is also referred to as the Tarangire-Manyara Eco-system, the name I use throughout (Borner 1985; Tarangire-Manyara Conservation Project [TMCP] 2002a), which covers an estimated 20,000–35,000 km² (Borner 1985; Prins 1987).[28]

Despite ongoing attempts to naturalize and solidify the boundaries around the TME, the boundaries of the ecosystem, like its name, remain multiple. Central to all definitions is an attempt to define the ecological and social systems integral to the functioning of the Lake Manyara and Tarangire National Parks, often in accor-dance with the migratory patterns of wildlife. The two parks comprise only a small fraction (2,700 km²) of the larger ecosystem, with the remainder stretching over two administrative regions (Arusha and Manyara), five districts (Babati, Kiteto, Simanjiro, Monduli, and Ngorongoro), and 263 villages, where Maasai of the *Kisongo* section constitute roughly 80 percent of the population.[29] Maasai are not the only inhabitants; there are also agropastoral Waarusha, Mbugwe, and Iraqw, and pastoral Barabaig.

The TME encompasses topographic variation ranging from the Ngorongooro highlands (3,650 m) and the Mbulu plateau (2,135 m) on the western boundary to the low-laying plains of the Lake Manyara Basin (920 m) and back up to the peaks of the Losimingori and Monduli Mountains in the northeast (2,130 m to 2,660 m) (Mwaly-osi 1990, 1). At the broadest level, the TME is characterized as *Acacia-Commiphora* deciduous bushland and edaphic grasslands. Rainfall increases with topography, with Ngorongoro highlands averaging 1,000 mm per year, Manyara and Tarangire National Parks below 700 mm per year (ranging from 400–800) (Mwalyosi 1990, Bevenger 2004) and Simanjiro averaging 600–650 mm (Voeten 1999). Rohde and Hilhorst (2001) suggest that the "pastoral Maasai plains," which includes the study villages, averages 200–600 mm per year. The entire area is characterized by a great deal of variability in rainfall across time and space (Prins and Loth 1988; Gereta et al. 2004).

Within the TME, conservation actors have focused on different areas seen as vital to the health of the larger ecosystem, such as the Kwa Kuchinja corridor, which includes much of the *Emanyara enkutoto* and refers both broadly to the entire area between TNP and LMNP and to a specific place next to the turnoff for Oltukai Vil-lage, along the tarmac Arusha-Dodoma road. The place where the name appears on maps was supposed to be a market during villagization in the 1970s. People moved out and set up stores, but Maasai did not settle down, so the storekeepers packed up and left. All that remains is a small handwritten sign with the name "Kwa Kuchinja," Swahili for "to slaughter," referencing a business attempt by a non-Maasai man who used to hunt wildlife and sell the meat—an unfortunate name for an area designated as a wildlife conservation corridor.

The name Kwa Kuchinja is used by AWF to refer to the entire area between the two parks. AWF was instrumental in establishing the Vilima Vitatu WMA (Davis 2011; Igoe and Croucher 2007) and securing Manyara Ranch as a conservation area in 2001 to protect a critical part of this "corridor," as seen in the following statement taken from a press release:

> Tarangire, with its characteristic baobab trees and numerous elephants, and Lake Manyara National Park, famous for its tree-climbing lions, are linked by the Kwa Kuchinja wildlife corridor, which passes through Manyara Ranch. Now, the animals can continue to freely travel the corridor between the two parks.[30]

The 17,807 ha Manyara Ranch used to belong to the village of Esilalei before it was ever an official village. When the ranch went up for sale as a part of the country's economic liberalization in 1999, Maasai from both villages went to the president of Tanzania to request the land be returned to them. Yet the importance of the area as a wildlife corridor resulted in heavy lobbying by conservation agencies, and in 2001, a ninety-nine-year lease was granted to the Tanzanian Land Conservation Trust (TLCT, established by AWF), to run the Manyara Ranch for the "joint benefit of local communities and migratory wildlife" (Sumba, Bergin, and Jones 2005). Sumba, Bergin, and Jones (2005) describe the creation of TLCT as a joint effort by AWF, local politicians, and community representatives. Yet villagers were under the impression that the area was being returned to them. As many people explained to me in 2002, they agreed to have AWF *manage* the area for wildlife for a short while but thought that the *land* was theirs. They were surprised to discover that a lease was granted to TLCT for ninety-nine years. In their eyes, TLCT *was* AWF, and for most purposes, it was quite difficult to discern the difference between the two. TLCT was established with a board of trustees chaired by the local member of parliament, with representatives from AWF, WWF, TANAPA, United Nations Development Program (UNDP), the private sector, and a local Maasai *oloiboni*, as the community representative, although he neither spoke nor understood Swahili, the language used in meetings. Maasai involvement in management was limited to a "steering committee," comprised of the village chairman and three additional men and one woman from each village. The steering committee had limited power, which members learned quickly. A new manager was hired by TLCT (an *mzungu*: white man/European), without their input or consent, and then this manager hired a "community liaison officer" without their input, who happened to be from the Waarusha tribe, which many found troubling. After much complaining and an outside inquiry, members found that their capacity was only as an "advisory" and not a "steering" committee. This became abundantly clear in meetings, which were always directed by the manager, *not* run in the open Maasai *enkiguena* style, and dismissive of Maasai ways of knowing the land, wildlife, and even livestock. Maasai steering committee members had to fight for their knowledge to be taken seriously—even regarding cattle management (see interlude 1).[31]

Knowing Wildlife Within the Study "Site"

The different geographies presented above draw on and produce different ways of knowing and being in the world, including different boundary drawing practices not only in space but also between what is considered natural versus social, and how wildlife are known and understood. For Maasai, knowledge about wildlife is closely connected to the ways in which they move through space on paths, to and from named places, and the observations and expectations they have based on seasonal changes and place-names. Conservation scientists and practitioners often begin knowing a place by starting with maps and then delineating formal boundaries within which to count wildlife and measure their movements along demarcated spaces (transects) that are meant to represent larger landscapes of value to conservation (i.e., national parks, corridor areas). Not all ways of knowing always come to matter in the same way, as illustrated in the following story.

> **No, I Am Not an Expert**
>
> Landis M mentions, with some envy, that his age-mate Landis Taeto is going to the state-run institute in Mwanza to study wildlife conservation for a month and will become more employable because he will be an "expert" (Swahili: *mtaalamu*) on wildlife.[32] This training makes you an expert, he told me.
>
> Me: An expert? Is it not only a one-month course?
>
> Yes, but he will know more than someone who does not go. They are experts there, at that school.
>
> Me: And someone who does not attend this training?
>
> They do not know. They are not experts, *he says flatly.*
>
> Me: So you don't know about wildlife? *(Mind you, he has only been helping me with the transect work for the last six months, pointing out wildlife, wildlife footprints, dung, and always explaining what we saw in great detail.)*

I know only from what I learned from the elders, from what they tell us is true. That is only what we hear though.

Me: So the elders are not experts?

No, they are not experts.

He continues to explain to me his lack of knowledge about wildlife.

I only know a little about this and that. I do not have expertise. I am not an expert.

Me: So could you tell me about wildlife if I ask, like could you tell me about the birthing patterns of different wildlife? Wildebeest for instance, can you tell me about them, about their birthing patterns?

OK, he says, I could tell you that.

When I pause to go get my notebook, he stops me, saying if I was going to write it down he wouldn't tell me. So I just listen. And he explains to me in great detail the social structure, behavior, and reproductive cycle of wildebeest. Then, with his permission, I go to retrieve my book The Behavior Guide to African Mammals *(Estes 1991). I read to him the section on wildebeest (translating into Swahili). He grins. It is nearly verbatim what he has just described.*

Me: And so do you still believe you are not an expert?

We are interrupted by the village chairman who happens to be one of his age-mates. I ask his thoughts about the training. He agrees that it is a good course and that people come back knowledgeable because they study every day. They learn how to use a gun and how to recognize different forms of poaching. They also learn how to capture animals. But when questioned, he says that a Maasai who grew up here would know more about wildlife, where they go, their behavior, than a non-Maasai who just went to the training and did not grow up here.

Me (to the chairman): If there was a position open in the Manyara Ranch for a new game scout, who would be best for the position? Someone who grew up here and did not go to Mwanza for training or someone who went to Mwanza but did not grow up here or have "Maasai training?"

Chairman: I would have to look at what they know ("their knowledge," Swahili: *ujuzi*), as well as their working abilities, their ability to work with others, their enthusiasm to work and to learn, their honesty. If someone did not go to school but speaks Swahili, then that is not a problem; he could be recommended to work alongside someone that knows how to read and write. And he will be a good worker.

The above interaction highlights the ongoing contestations over what counts as valid knowledge, particularly regarding wildlife, where knowledge labeled "Western scientific" has long held the hierarchal reins. Yet knowledge is not a static object. It is multiple, enacted, always becoming, and transforming. I therefore hesitate to describe something "out there," called "Maasai knowledge," as opposed to "Western scientific knowledge." However, there are specific (and multiple) knowledge-generation practices that Maasai engage in and respect, just as there are epistemological framings that conservation scientists and practitioners regularly use and accept as valid. In this section, I briefly outline these ways of knowing wildlife that are enacted in the *enkiguena* chapters.[33]

MAASAI KNOWING WILDLIFE

What combines something from all four things: a person, bird, lion, and a snake? An ostrich. It makes a sound like a lion. It leaves footprints like a person. If it is sitting in the grass with its head up, it is like a snake. And it has wings like a bird.

—MAASAI RIDDLE[34]

Place-names illustrate one way in which Maasai know, talk about, and live within their landscape.[35] There are multiple knowledge-generation and transfer practices that Maasai employ, including riddles, stories, myths, legends, songs, direct teaching with practice, and, more recently, attendance at school, to impart knowledge and moral lessons of various kinds. This is of course not unusual and has been illustrated by scholars of Indigenous knowledge around the world. Riddles, stories, and songs teach lessons of morality, behavior expectations, and societal norms (Kipury 1983). Many stories teach the behavior and personality traits of certain animals. Others tell the challenges brought by colonialists, as predicted by the spiritual leaders, or the need to respect clan and age-set relations. Stories are told in various contexts, modified to fit a specific situation, or to include local names (of people, clans, and places). Stories are utilized not only to teach the young but also to explain phenomena in relation to "the way things are" or "were." They are world-making practices that also communicate expectations of practice.[36]

Young Maasai boys and girls also learn by accompanying their elders—herding, going for water, collecting firewood and grass, collecting and using medicinal plants, and treating and slaughtering animals. As they do so, they are taught to watch, listen, touch, and repeat. They will be tested, retaught, retold, and eventually entrusted with small tasks. A junior elder explained the process as such:

Every day they go a little further, a little further, see a little more, learn a little more, until they know. And then when they are ready, they go out with the calves and they learn from the larger boys who have already been herding with the calves, until they are big enough to go with the cattle, where they will also learn from others older than them. It is a long process of seeing, doing, and hearing.[37]

In this way, Maasai men and women learn the names of places, as well as the names of grasses and trees, how to care for livestock, and even the names and behaviors of wildlife.[38]

Of course, as in all societies, some Maasai men and women are respected as more knowledgeable, smarter, or more skilled than others, and these are not all the same qualities, though they are deeply interconnected. In discussions with various Maasai individuals, people differentiated between *arriya* (skill, expertise), *eng'eno* (intelligence, wisdom), and *o-le-ngeno* (experience), which can literally be translated as "the one of wisdom."[39] Someone who is expert or particularly skilled at something (e.g., helping with cattle births, midwifery, beadwork) is respected as *arriya*. *Eng'eno* is more difficult to describe and seems closest to the English word "intelligence" or "wisdom" and can loosely be understood as the ability to pick up new knowledge quickly and see the larger picture clearly.[40] *Eng'eno* was often explained to me with the Swahili words "ujuzi" (knowledge) and "akili" (intelligence). One *ilmurran* explained, "If a person has *akili*, then they will have *ujuzi*, but if they don't have *akili*, then they will fail to get *ujuzi* [to learn]," similar to how we conceptualize intelligence in English. But *Eng'eno* is also associated with intuition, with just *knowing from within*. As one junior elder explained:

> Maasai of long ago would call together all their youth and talk to them for example about people who have *eng'eno* [*ol-tungunak ng'engi*]. Someone can't know himself if he is smart. So for me, myself, I cannot say if I am [smart]. But when I hear that someone wants to talk to me, I will think about it. I will think about what I want to say, what I want to get across, and then when we talk, it [the topic of conversation] will be about that [which I was thinking about].

This description highlights the value of *communication and intuition* as related to *eng'eno*. Intuition is often described as coming in dreams, with some elders respected for their ability to know the location of lost cattle from a dream. *Eng'eno* can also have a slightly negative connotation, like the Swahili word *ujanja*, which implies cleverness but also shrewdness, slyness. A smart elder, for instance, can combine his intelligence and oratory skills to shift the tide of a meeting in his favor—viewed as clever, sneaky behavior, that is nonetheless respected for its craftiness and success.

Over the last two decades, many young Maasai men and women have started to attend school, where those with *eng'eno* (intelligence) learn quickly and bring new knowledge home to share with others. Those without this education often put themselves down, even at times referring to themselves as *emodai* (stupid) (Hodgson 2001; Igoe 2000). Yet at the same time, some Maasai I spoke with continued to value knowledge gained from experience (*ole-ngeno*), and what they call knowledge from "home." The difference between "schooled" and "Maasai" knowledge was explained by an educated junior elder regarding the knowledge he used during his work as a game scout in the Manyara Ranch:

> We know about the forest, we know because we come from the bush, so we know the forest. I learned from my parents who had an education more than that of the classroom. They know because they are used to it. But they don't know how to write. I knew all the trees because it is something I *am inside of, all the time*. I can tell you about this tree—its name in Maasai, but its Latin name, I won't know that until I write it down and look at it. (Game Scout 1, September 30, 2003)

For most Maasai, wildlife, like trees and grass, are not an external "nature," something "out there" to be studied and counted. They are, rather, "in here"—followed around, avoided, hunted, ignored, chased away, admired, or feared as they carry on with their lives—farming, herding, moving, gathering plants, attending ceremonies, and so on. This does not preclude a general interest by many Maasai in different animals as beautiful and "good to look at," but rather suggests different opportunities to see and notice animals around them (Roque de Pinho et al. 2014), with certain animals such as the ostrich, called *esidai* in Maa, meaning "the good beautiful one," followed for their feathers, and others, such as wildebeest and lions, either followed or avoided. Here, I temporarily abstract these complex interactions to suggest three overlapping methods/processes by which Maasai know the whereabouts of wildlife: direct observations, word of mouth, and reference to trusted sources.

Direct observations of wildlife movements come from living and herding in surrounding lands, as reflected in some of the place-names. Their own activities take Maasai to different places for grazing, water, firewood, medicinals, meetings, and so forth, where they observe the state of the pasture and the presence (or absence) of different animals. They also see animals at home that come to graze nearby, raid their farms, or seek protection from predators at night. Observations include direct sightings of animals, signs of wildlife presence or passage through an area (dung, footprints, tree or crop damage, heavy grazing), and the clearly visible paths created by wildebeest, zebra, and elephants, moving from place to place. Since wildlife and cattle are often in search of the same resources (e.g., water, pasture, salt) herders often see wildlife while out with their cattle, with a total of twenty-five different species named by interviewees as seen while herding (see table 6, listed in order of frequency across responses). Observations of wildlife whereabouts often include discussions of wildlife behaviors, personalities, and the plants they like to eat.

Maasai observations provide snapshots in time of places they pass through and reside, but since most herders frequent the same areas over the years, their observations can be discussed in terms of longitudinal trends. Many Maasai will also speak with confidence about wildlife movements to places they had not visited in a while or had never been to, drawing from stored knowledge of what the elders had taught them. The elders' words become a trusted source, repeated through stories, comparable to the early scientific articles that are continuously called upon by scientists and conservationists regarding wildlife patterns in the TME. However, the stories and knowledge of the elders do not always reflect current movement patterns, which may have changed. Here, word of mouth is an important methodological tool. From a visitor passing through or a local resident returning from an excursion, people know where it is raining and where it is not, and the whereabouts of wildlife from someone who saw them directly. In the absence of direct observations, Maasai often deduce the location of animals based on other information received (i.e., recent rainfall and/or grass growth, water in a dam) and known behavior patterns of wildlife.

CONSERVATION SCIENCE

Conservation boundary drawing begins with an assumption that there is a preexisting nature "out there," fixed in time and space, which scientific instruments can objectively and accurately measure and report on from afar, including wildlife. The boundaries of the TME are drawn to include wildlife movements and habitat. For this reason, most discussions of wildlife conservation planning begin with locating animals in representative time-space units (i.e., seasons, transects) (Caughley and Sinclair 1994; Jachmann 1999; cf. Sinclair and Arcese 1995). This is far from a simple undertaking, especially when wildlife are migratory, the area of concern is large and covers human-occupied spaces, and forage quality and quantity vary with rainfall patterns that are irregular from year to year (Gereta et al. 2004; Prins and Loth 1988).[41]

Table 6 Wildlife reported to be seen while herding livestock, listed in order of frequency, named and filled with additional observations, including degree of "troublesomeness"

Species with Maasai name	General observation and significance of presence	Troublesome behaviors?
Gazelle (Thompson's: *enkoilii [ingoilin] minimin*) (Grant's: *Olwargas; Iriwargasi*)	Are not afraid of people; Hunted with dogs	No: but transfer a disease to goats
Zebra (*Oloitikoshi; Oloitiko*)	Always hungry; not afraid; have good ears for predators; Eat corn crops, graze peacefully with cattle, just like donkeys; but often chased away by herd boys	Very high: crop raiding*
Wildebeest (*Oingati; engati*)	Smart but easily scared; need water; Avoid during calving when spread a disease to cattle; Follow to access early rains	Low: but spread disease to cattle
Ostrich (*Sidaan; Esidai*)	Admired; in a class by themselves (i.e, not with birds or with animals); collect feathers for new *ilmurran* initiates	Low: but eat bean crops
Giraffe (*Oramaut; ilmeuti*)	Admired animal; slow, mellow, smart, peaceful	No
Reedbuck (*Olpua; ilpuai*)	Quick and smart; can't run well but can jump high, they hide in valleys, in tall grass areas with a lot of shade	Very low: but does eat crops
Warthog (*Ol-bitir; il-birito*)	Can bring good luck if they pass in front of your path; Digs wells (which can be enhanced by people)	High: crop raiding and hard to catch
Impala (*Ololubo; ilpoolubo*)	Can jump! Has a lot of anger when males compete; Likes bushed areas, afraid of sun	None
Jackal (*enderai; interrahin*)	Sneaky; Prey on small goats and sheep	High: prey on young small stock
Elephant (*Olkancaoi; ilkancaoni*)	Very destructive—destroys woodland and crops; Dangerous—to people and farms; Useful for grazing—"opens up the bush"	Very high: crop raiding; cannot be chased away

Animal	Description	Pest status
Buffalo (*Ilarroi/olarro*) *Olosowuan / inkosowuani*	Dangerous and tricky; eat a lot of grass; like the bush; Historically hunted to make shields	No
Dikdik (*Erongo; irongon*)	Travel in pairs and always defecate in the same place	No
Rabbit	Smart; blood used as medicine, but hard to catch	No
Hyena (*Ohng'ojine; ilng'ojiniaa*); one with a limp	Despised, stupid, sneaky, gluttonous, thieves; No other animal as bad as the hyena	Very high: prey on livestock
Lion (*ohng'atuny; ilgn'atunyo*) *Ohng'aririma—Oldiamingi*	**2 types:** *Ohng'arurumi* (large, tan, with a large mane): very mellow; cannot kill easily *Oldiamingi* (small, no mane, redder with white in back): very fierce; can easily kill an *ilmurran* and will chase people; hunted by *ilmurran*	Medium: prey on livestock (donkeys and cattle)
Eland (*Osirua; isirua*)*	Does not like places with a lot of people; have been heavily hunted; similar to cattle	None TZ (ky: yes crop raiding)
Porcupine (*Esasa*)	Hard to keep off the farm; can injure people	High: crop raiding
Leopard (*Olowaru keri* [the spotted predator])	Likes forested places; Preys on stock but not at the same level as lions or hyena	Low: but does prey on livestock
Hartebeest (*Olkonde, ilkondin*)		No
Monkey (vervet) (*Endere*)	They can steal corn by tying it together and swinging it over their back!	Low: discussed by women as crop raiding
Lesser kudu (*Ostram; isirami*)	Can stay in dry country (doesn't need water)	None
Mongoose (*Orljuki*)		Low: preys on goat kids
Gerenuk		No
Fox (*Esiro; isiron*)		No

Information obtained through interviews and informal conversations. This does not draw on the ways that animals are discussed in oral literature.

*In Tanzania zebra are seen as a pest on farms, whereas in Kenya eland are. Both of these observations are relatively recent with the rise in farming.

The first scientific survey of wildlife in and around TNP was conducted in the early 1960s when it was still a British-controlled game reserve, providing detailed data on large mammal migratory movements outside the park (Lamprey 1963, 1964). Lamprey's original map continues to be used today by conservation scientists and practitioners as baseline data. While he used a large African labor force to conduct walking transects, the most common method today in Northern Tanzania is the standard reconnaissance flight (SRF), which has been used in the TME by the Frankfort Zoological Society since October 1987 (in different time intervals, not every year) (Tarangire-Manyara Conservation Project [TMCP] 2000; Norton-Griffiths 1978).[42] The procedure involves counting animals from the air along evenly spaced parallel transects over a defined area and then utilizing a model to calculate animal abundance estimates for the remainder of the area (Norton-Griffiths 1978). SRF counts are subject to high standard errors and rely on an assumption that the density and distribution of animals is constant between transects and across years for discrete "seasons" (that are assumed to stay put).

Ideally, large-scale SRF distribution maps are combined with smaller-scale data and focused studies of wildlife movements (Msoffe et al. 2007). TMCP began doing just that in the late 1990s in the TME in response to growing concerns over threats to wildlife migratory pathways (Borner 1985) (covered in the *enkiguena* chapters).[43] Even with the expanded methods, animals were counted in places where "nature" is meant to exist (inside MR, in proposed corridors) in what are considered discrete/ well-defined "wet" and "dry" season categories.

MY HYBRID WAY OF KNOWING

I began my fieldwork with the assumption that I too could study wildlife "out there" on the landscape, using standard ecological methods. I initially planned to place transects randomly and systematically across the study area to collect representative data for the whole area. I soon learned that knowing the landscape through Maasai placenames was essential to talk about wildlife and livestock use patterns with Maasai, as well as for understanding the complex ecological and social histories of the area. I thus did not conduct transects until the second year in the field and then did it together with Maasai to better reflect a "Maasai view" of important areas for wildlife and livestock. I conducted transects with two Maasai men the first year, who then conducted them without me for an additional two years.

The transect methodology provides reliable and comparable data across time, but only a snapshot view. For this reason, we also recorded "opportunistic" sightings of wildlife with precise location and timing noted (with GPS if possible). These data were mapped in a GIS to reflect wildlife presence in village lands as observed by myself and Maasai interlocutors.

Conclusion

My goal in this chapter was to introduce the specific geographies of the study site from differently situated perspectives: "Maasai," "administrative," and "conservation." Yet these are not isolated, mutually exclusive categories. They are partially connected and overlap in many ways. Maasai in the study site use all sets of boundaries to negotiate land use and make management decisions. Yet rarely are their own boundary-making processes acknowledged or taken seriously by conservation agencies and land-use planners—even when "participatory" land-use planning is pursued. Part of this is due to the hegemony of Western mapping technologies (Lovell 2018), and assumptions of epistemological hierarchy. Maasai ways of knowing and being in the world do not easily match up to Western cadastral traditions and seasonal land-use maps. I argue that in order to move beyond the rhetoric of "participatory" processes, we need to change the language, context, and ways in which we bring different "stakeholders" to the table. This is particularly true for wildlife management, which has historically been dominated by Western ontologies and epistemologies. Why not use Maasai place-names to talk about wildlife presence on Maasai lands? Why not use Maasai sociospatial management frames for land-use planning? The landscape described in this chapter is used by people and wildlife across village boundaries, for grazing, farming, living, and passing through. Yet, there is little agreement on what this means ecologically, or ontologically, or even how to talk about it, as explored in the next *enkiguena* chapter.

| Interlude I |

Parsing Knowledge, Closing off Dialogue

Members of the steering committee (SC) of the Manyara Ranch (MR) sit around the Oltu-kai village school grounds, waiting patiently for the car to arrive to transport them to the MR for their monthly meeting. Today the SC members are angry. They feel marginalized from the actual work and decision-making that occurs on the MR. Today they are going to speak up to the manager. They are particularly upset about all the news they keep hearing about cattle on the ranch dying. I am tagging along to observe. The meeting lasts several hours; I present parts of it here.[1]

SCHOOL BENCHES are arranged in a semicircle in a clearing, partially shaded by tall acacia trees. The SC members find seats, separated out by different social groupings of age-set and clan, with the women clustered on one side. At the opening of the semicircle is a table with two chairs and a large pad. The chairs remain empty as the MR manager, who is a British expat, sits on top of the table with the community liaison officer, who is from the neighboring Waarusha tribe and will translate for him. Maasai meetings always begin with a blessing, usually by the eldest man present, who in this case happens to be the local *oloiboni*. A large man, he stands slowly and speaks in a melodic tone, blessing all those present, our children, cattle, the grass, and asks god for rain. He sits down, signaling that the meeting is ready to begin. The meeting is then officially opened by the chairman of the steering committee, who is also the village chairman for Esilalei. He merely opens the meeting but says, "As usual, the ranch manager will begin."

The manager begins by reading the agenda items for the meeting, which include the following:

1. To prepare for the upcoming board meeting
2. To report on the state of the ranch livestock (cattle and sheep)
3. To report on money from livestock sales

Agenda 1: Preparing for the Board Meeting

The manager explains that he has written a summary of what has been happening on the ranch to present at the board meeting but hasn't had time to have it translated into Swahili. He asks if any of the steering committee members have an agenda item they would like to add to the report.

Chairman: This would be very difficult because we don't have the report. So maybe after you translate it then we will get ideas. Because we know that we will have to talk about what is happening on the ranch.

Manager: But do you have any issues that you would like to have raised at the board meeting that I can help to generate information on?

Senior Elder LL: From what I recall, we had discussed the need to go back to the communities to gather information, to know what to bring to the board.

Chairman: There are many things that we have discussed with the communities, like dams [inside the ranch] for the communities to bring cattle to for water. Maybe we could talk about that at the meeting?

Manager: First we need to talk about the school, and then we can also talk about the issue of water.

They exchange brief words about the new school and move on to the issue of water . . . which shows the lack of involvement of the SC in planning and the precedence placed on Western expertise and the priorities of the manager. SC members push for assistance on projects they have already begun, and for all work to start before the rains. The manager then announces the next agenda item.

Agenda 2: The State of Ranch Livestock

Manager: I don't have exact numbers, but this is mostly because there have been sales, and because this month we had problems with fatalities. More than we are used to. But the reasons are well understood, so there is no alarm. It was mostly with mature stock, and from ECF [East Coast fever; Maa: *Oldikana kali*] and anaplasmosis [Maa: *orkipul*]. The reason is that we dipped late. Because the dip was being repaired and it wasn't finished in time. So, the tick load was too high on the cattle. Also, when they were dipped, many didn't go under the water, and ECF comes from ticks by the ears. ECF only comes through the ears into the brain. So, we lost a lot of mature stock. But we didn't lose any young stock because they were all vaccinated. But it is still not a crisis compared to how many cattle we have. Twenty-four cattle died [in a month]. Normally we lose eight to ten cattle a month in the dry season. And in the village?

Elder: only small calves die in the village, not large cattle. That is because the calves that survive ECF become immune.

Manager: On the ranch, they are dipped regularly, so they are not exposed to ECF. But now I want to open the dipping and slightly expose the cattle to ECF. We will lose some, but it will lower cases [overall]. We are treating cattle as well, and we are vaccinating the calves, so we should eventually have good resistance.

Senior Elder: For this time, during the dry season in the hot sun, ECF is very dangerous. So, continue to dip regularly. In the rainy season, make the break from dipping.

Manager: *Frustrated.* Yes, but in the dry season is when ECF ticks are around, and we need to expose the cattle to some extent.

Senior Elder: From what I know, in the dry season, the *Oldikana* [ECF] is very *kali* [hot, severe]. But in the wet season it is still here, but it is not as bad, the Maasai call it *Oldikana baridi* [cold, mild]. It can still help the cattle, but in the dry season it is too harsh. The ECF likes the hot sun, so it would not be a good idea to stop dipping then.

Manager: We just dipped yesterday.

Clear signs of relief from the Oloiboni and others.

Chairman: Maybe also with the cattle . . . *he pauses and looks around* . . . maybe . . . *his voice gets a bit stronger as he tries to look directly at the manager* . . . you should involve the committee, because Maasai are very knowledgeable about cattle. Most of us were born here. And even the first white man [on the ranch] involved Maasai in the cattle issues. When something happened, he would come and talk to the elders and ask them what was happening. For example, do you know about the disease of the wildebeest?

Manager: *Seems confused. I translate for him that they are referring to MCF (malignant catarrhal fever).* Yes, I know.

Chairman: What is it? How does it work?

Manager: *Seems startled, taken aback that he is being quizzed by these Maasai.* Yes, I know, it is transferred from birthing wildebeest calves. You all think it comes from the placenta, but it doesn't. It comes from somewhere else. *Then he seems to second-guess the reasoning for going into this detail, or in questioning Maasai knowledge because he interrupts himself.* So yes, I know.

Chairman: Because that disease gave George Dam [the earlier European manager] a lot of trouble. He went all the way to Europe looking for medicine, but there was nothing. Until he went to the Maasai to ask what was happening. They told him it was easy. The wildebeest come and give birth in January and February, and it is during those months [that they spread the disease]. If you see the wildebeest go to a place for water, you move your cattle to the side where there are no wildebeest. It is that easy. Because if they get sick, there is no treatment. They will die. So it is good for you to talk with the elders. They even give advice to Lowasa [MP, minister of livestock and water, and chairman of the board of TLCT] about what to do with cattle.[2]

Manager: Yes, I agree that you have a lot of expertise in this area. If we have problems, we will bring them in. Right now, I am not so worried because I know why it has happened. Because we were late in dipping, and they have now been dipped. And the death toll is not too high. So after another few days, which will make it twenty-four days since they have been dipped, the life span of ECF, the deaths should stop. If they don't, well, then I will call you in. We have also brought in [people from a] veterinary center in Arusha who are taking blood samples of the cattle. We also brought an Italian vet in who has worked in Tanzania, Kenya, Somalia for twenty years.

Junior Elder: Are you trying to treat the cattle?

Manager: Yes, and most get better. Some die. If you see the symptoms and you are just one hour late, you lose the cattle. And Alex [the veterinary doctor on the ranch] didn't do inspections one day because of the theft, and so cattle died that day.

Junior Elder: Maybe this is good. Good to get this information today; because we keep hearing that cattle are dying on the ranch, without knowing why. I have seen cattle grazing and I have seen sick cattle, and I asked Alex what was happening, if he was treating the cattle with *Oldikana*. And I join hands with the chairman for us to be more informed about the cattle. Because we know a lot about cattle, even if we did not go to school. For instance, it is my experience that from April to July you don't let the cattle go to graze by the river because it will bring trouble for cattle. Because when children take cattle to the river and come back, you know because the cattle have diarrhea. And with *Oldikana* [ECF] you inject [the sick cattle with medicine], and they don't go out [long distance] with the other cattle; they stay back in the shade. Because if cattle with ECF walk even a very short distance, it can bring them problems; they can die. Maybe my advice would be if you see cattle with ECF, don't let them follow the others. Choose one person to graze them around the boma (cattle enclosure). Because I was surprised one day when Masuni called me and asked, "What is going on with all the cattle on the ranch? I heard they are all dying." So, let's work together with the cattle.

Manager: You already have an early warning system of Indigenous knowledge. The herders are all Maasai from these two villages. We rely on them to report sick cows and to not go to the river. Regarding the sick cows not going with the main herd, now they are going, and I expressed concern to Alex when I saw this. He said that it was difficult to bring cattle from different groups together and to keep them from going with the others. It is hard to do with our [limited] staff now. They run around and try to reenter their group. In the end, you end up tiring them out just as much as if they had gone herding. Any advice? I already asked the herders, but we have no solution.

Me: Why don't you use the herders to hold the sick cattle back? It is my experience that Maasai are particularly good at this; one holds a leg, the other the tail, the other the ears, and so on, until it is placed aside. They are not tired out by running around.

The elders nod their heads in excited agreement. They also explain that the cattle should be put aside from the moment they are given treatment and not allowed to mix again. Other ideas come forward about how to separate out the sick cattle, or the cattle will keep dying. The manager again states that they have herders who should be sharing ideas with the vet.

Me: *I question if the herders would really feel free, themselves, to go to Alex with information, or to question his way of doing things, since he is in a way their boss and their elder, so they would likely be held back by respect [enkanyit].*

Junior Elder: *Nodding his head in agreement with me.* No, they would be scared. Of course they are scared. They cannot go to Alex like that.

The others agree, saying out loud, "Of course they would be scared. They could not go."

Manager: *Shrugs, disbelieving.* Well, that is the job of the headman. He is supposed to look after the younger herders and help them.

Me: *I am fully aware that the man in the current position of headman is not capable of this job, nor is he respected by the herders as their boss. He is too young. The manager had given him the job because he had shown himself loyal by turning in the former*

*headman, who was stealing. Maasai are not pleased with this choice—he should
have been rewarded, yes, but he is too young and not knowledgeable enough for this
job.* Well, maybe there needs to be more pressure placed on the headman to
gather this information from the herders.

*The elders agree. The manager needs to push the headman to get the information from
his workers and then deliver it to Alex.*

Manager: OK, on to the sheep. The problem with the sheep is that they have
trouble walking. Alex is a good vet, but he doesn't have much field experience.
The Italian vet came. He said the problem was heart water. He said it happens
to sheep, but not often. So, we listened to him and treated the problem, and
it is going away. He also noticed they were in bad shape, not getting enough
nourishment. So we are feeding them *pumba* [supplemental feed] and *chumvi*
[salt]. And we also sent off [blood] samples to be tested in very good labs in
Nairobi. We also took some soil samples and sent them to the UK to see if there
are mineral deficiencies in the soil.

Junior Elder: *Laughs.* This problem with sheep is just the problem with the dry
season.

Senior Elder: Do they drink water every day?

Manager: Yes.

Senior Elder: Well, that is the death of sheep! They should not get much water.

Chairman: So perhaps you shouldn't be looking at the blood. The problem is water.

*There is much commotion, and the manager suggests that perhaps this is a disease they
do not know about, and they would learn from the blood samples.*

Chairman: Maybe you are right because there are a lot of diseases that we do not
know. But those who don't let their sheep give birth in the dry season, they
are fine. Try having the ranch [not have sheep give birth] in July. If you have
problems, let us know.

Manager: Even us, we want birthing to happen when there is plenty of grass, but
this year we inherited sheep, and obviously we did not manage them well. The
rams were let in early.

Elder: Don't let rams in with the females.

Manager: *Contemplating this idea that birthing in the dry season can be the problem.*
It makes sense that the milking sheep will be more stressed, but I haven't seen
statistics that it is nursing sheep that are dying.

Elder: But don't let them drink water every day. They need to skip at least a day.

Junior Elder: Maybe you need to push the headman to get more information from
the Maasai herders.

Chairman: If you get the steering committee together one day, we can give you advice on where livestock should go. For instance, the *embolelo* [kids] like it here, close by. They don't like to go far, and they don't like tall grass.

Agenda 3: Cattle Sales

This proves even more difficult a conversation. There is a great deal of misunderstanding between what the manager means and what the Maasai hear, what the manager thinks Maasai know about cattle sales and what Maasai think they know, how money is calculated (Maasai do not think in terms of percentage, insisted one Maasai elder), and how trust and respect is expressed. In sum, the manager has in mind that Maasai would benefit from selling ranch cattle to high-end beef markets in Arusha, receiving a percentage of the sale. But the manager has already negotiated prices with the buyers. From the Maasai perspective, the manager is asking them to transport his cattle and get paid for it. A wealthy Maasai won't even transport his own cattle to market but will pay a poorer Maasai or a man of another [thought lesser] tribe to do so. The Maasai men present are angry and frustrated. They say it doesn't matter how much money is involved, they want to have nothing to do with the plan—to transport the manager's cattle? Who does he think they are? Respect is more important in this case than money.

| Chapter 3 |

Enkiguena Agenda II

Managing the Range for Wildlife and Livestock

The Setting

The gathering for today's *enkiguena* is in the dry riverbed (*korongo*), under the shade of an old ficus tree. The preferred location for an *enkiguena* in Oltukai is under the large baobab (*olmesera*) tree that stands at the administrative center of the village, near the school and the new village office. But it is now the end of a long dry season with most trees bare. Shade is hard to come by. The large ficus tree, nestled among smaller trees and tall grass along the walls of the *korongo*, provides the rare escape from the hot October sun. Men flank both slopes of the riverbed: several crammed on the limited space provided by the roots of the trees, many outstretched leisurely on the sloping walls of the *korongo*, others squatting on rocks they gathered for this purpose on the *korongo* floor. Women gather as a group in the tall grass at the very top of the *korongo*, out of direct sight of the men. There are no chairs nearby that can be brought in for guests, who either sit among the Maasai or lean against their cars, parked where the road passes through the *korongo* floor.

Since the meeting concerns a government decision—the granting of a contract to a tour company and planning for dam construction—it is chaired by the Oltukai village chairman. Yet it is started, as always, with a blessing by the oldest elder present. He stands in the *korongo* floor, which is the center of the meeting site and will act as the speaking "stage" for those who will address the crowd. He blesses all those present for rain, health, and fertility, but particularly for rain and for the cattle to survive until the rain arrives. The meeting is then opened by the village chairman.[1]

Chairman O: *He stands in the center of the* korongo *floor, turning around proudly, grinning a bit nervously at the crowd that has gathered, which is not as large as he had hoped for. He is young, a member of the Landis age-set, with basic (primary school) education and an easygoing, friendly personality. He is still naïve and excited about the possibilities of a new conservation-related company in the village yet seemingly unaware of the changes and challenges it might bring. Along with his fellow village government members, he has sought to gain personally from the new tour company. He has not, therefore, been as forthcoming and open with his constituents as he should have been. Many are present at this meeting to call some of his judgments into question. Others would just like to know more about what is really happening. He speaks loudly and confidently.* Today we are all here at this meeting to receive our guest and to talk about the work he would like to do in the village—put in a campsite and a dam. So please find a place to sit in the shade and let's welcome our guest. *He turns to Corbett (the honored guest) and says (in Swahili),* The meeting has been opened with the elder's blessing, and I have explained why we are here, but maybe it is best, because maybe there are some people who don't know you, for your to introduce yourself and your guests.[2] These people gathered here in front of you are the people of this village, except they are just a few. This is because it is the dry season—some are off watering their cattle. And, well, you know how the situation here is very bad right now; it is a drought. So there are many people who have moved and are unable to be here today. But I think that those who are here should be able to participate in the meeting, and they will also be able to explain to others, those who were not able to make it, what transpires. There are elders here and *ilaigwenak wa mila* [traditional leaders] and government representatives of various types. So perhaps it is best for you to introduce yourself and your guests for those who may not know you. Please, welcome.[3] *He motions for Corbett to take the floor, and he retreats a bit but remains standing. He will translate for a while.*

Corbett: *He had been sitting in the crowd with the younger elders, with whom he is friendly, all Landis mostly from the Ilaiser clan. He is an easygoing and friendly guy most of the time, though he also has a very hot temper and can erupt into uncontrolled violence quickly. He sits on the ground among Maasai at meetings, chewing tobacco and participating as the others. He is originally from Texas and came to East Africa as a guide on treks up Mount Kilimanjaro. He sees himself as a business-*

man, a conservationist, and a hunter. These three roles do not necessarily contradict one another—conserving high wildlife numbers is important for tourism ventures to succeed, and for hunting. He stands up and wipes the dirt off his pants before he speaks. Thank you, chairman, and greetings to everyone (men and women). My name is Corbett. I think most of you know that I am interested in starting a tourist business here in your village. I am here today with two *fundi* (Swahili, *mafundi* pl.: technicians/workers). *He points out the two men who are standing to the side of the meeting.* They will help with the dam building. *Looking over at the chairman, he asks,* Are there any other agendas, or is it just our business today?[4]

Chairman O: We will be continuing with another agenda item but continue for now. *Corbett returns to his seat but motions the two* mafundi *to come to the center and introduce themselves, which they do in Swahili. The chairman then thanks Corbett and the* mafundi *and then addresses the crowd. He does so in Maa and then turns and explains what he has said to Corbett, in Swahili.* We have two agenda items to cover today. There is first the agenda concerning Corbett (the work that he has already discussed), and then there is the agenda concerning wildlife-livestock relations.[5] After these two agendas, if there is something that we missed or something that someone needs to add, then we will address that. We have decided to start with this agenda concerning Corbett.

We have already received the news that this person, Corbett, wants to start a tourism business here, and he has left us with all the papers regarding his plans. They are all here, but because of a lack of time, or rather because of the dry season itself, we have not had the time to read them to everyone. There is a lot there, and it would take a very long time to explain to everyone all the different issues, but [the important point is] that we agreed in that [first] meeting that we understand the plans and we agree with them. After this, some of the village leaders and some of the elders went to look for a place to put the dam and for a place to put the campsite. Regarding places to put the dam, the first suggested location is a place called *Endarpo*, second is over there with the palm trees in a place called *Kimoridaki*, and lastly a place called *Embarimbali* up there, at the top of *Lera*. We have decided that the best place is probably *Endarpo* because the water there is good. Today we wanted to look at our first choice, at *Endarpo*, together with the location to put the camp, in a place called *Enkung'u Olduka*. Now it is important that [we are having] a meeting like this, a full assembly meeting. When I called this meeting, it was because it is important to explain everything so that everyone is aware of all that is going on and how things are proceeding so that the work can get started. This way we can know if there is a person that has an opinion or if there is a person who has another issue to raise. This way it will all be open. Also, if someone has a particular preference, it is important that they are able to say it now in front of everyone so that everyone knows, rather than there being elders that do not know what is going on. There are some elders here who went [on those prior trips] to see these places that we are recommending for the dam and the campsite. They were a part of picking out these locations, so perhaps they could speak about this in more detail. *He asks two of the elders that had been a part of the process to stand up, but before they can come down to speak, a young man grabs the stage.*

Landis R: *A young, thin man, he is also a representative of the village government. He is respected beyond what his age, social status, or wisdom would suggest. This is because he is a very good speaker. He always speaks at meetings, concisely and clearly, and people listen to him. Yet he is also very strategic and political, encompassing what Maasai refer to as* siasa, *which often translates as "deceitful." He is often behind village disputes, always looking to personally gain (usually financially). He is from the Ilaiser clan, though some of his closest friends are Ilmamasita, including the village chairman, whom he tries to push around. He has become very close with Corbett and is trying to push his agenda through. Today he speaks quickly yet authoritatively.* The chairman has explained things at length, and we already understand the situation, so maybe if there are those who do not understand or who do not agree with the places that have been named, then they should speak, because we already understand completely, and we already agreed [on everything] that day in the church [a prior meeting] when we heard the details. Therefore, rather than talking further about this, if there is someone who does not agree with the places we have suggested or does not completely understand, then they should speak out.

Corbett: *Without standing he speaks from where he is sitting.* This is very important [for people to voice their concerns or disagreements].

Landis T: *A healthy and strong man of the Ilmamasita clan and Landis age-set, he is one of the most trusted and liked men in the village, seen as honest and generous. He is not around much these days, as he works as a game scout in the Manyara Ranch. He came today for this meeting. He is very smart and is concerned about the lack of attention that has been given to campsite and dam issue by the current village government, but he is also diplomatic. He speaks quickly and sharply.* This is all good, because we already understand what it is that needs to be done, and the reason for calling this meeting was to make sure that everyone understands what is happening. If there are people that don't understand, they have an opportunity to talk so that we can continue with the work at hand (the work can get started). Is this the reason why the meeting was called or not? *He pauses and looks over at the chairman and his fellow government representatives. "Yes," they say in unison. He continues.* OK. Aren't there only a very few that might not fully understand the issue that we are discussing? Does everyone understand? *Murmurs across the crowd: "Yes, yes we know, yes we understand."* So we all know? OK. Then since we all know, let's not take a long time again to talk about this. Let us say that the person who has something to add or ideas that are different than those that have been said or a different recommendation, then they say so. If it is time to start the dam, we should get started on it. Let us not start with a meeting from scratch again but let everyone give his or her opinion.[6]

Makaa MT: *A slight man, he is poor, but also an* oloiboni, *from the respected (and feared) Inkidong'i clan, and on the village government. He holds on to an* olkuma *while he speaks.* We remember that Corbett came to the village two times. The first time was to tell us he wanted to do work in the village, and the second time we went together to look at all the different places to put the dam and we agreed together on the places, like *Endarpo*. If he is ready, then he should start now. Because we don't have any changes to introduce.

Corbett: *Looking at the chairman, he asks,* Can I have a chance to talk? I'd like to speak for a bit. *He takes the stage, grinning but serious.* Good, thanks. This is all good. I am no longer very concerned about things. There is one thing, though: I cannot continue without a letter from the village, which nearly everyone signs, or some sign for those who do not know how to read and write, to demonstrate that they agree with what is planned. This is because the contract itself will only be between me and the village chairman. And this letter will be like our agreement. Do you understand? *People respond, "Yes." He continues, a bit more strongly now.* OK, so can you agree to write this letter quickly? Are you ready to write it now, or do we need to wait an entire month? Because I have paper and pen here today if you are ready.

The village chairman speaks from his seat: This is easy, no problem.

Corbett continues speaking. Good, because I want to be on time with this. And another thing . . . is the land committee here? Are they here? Can I see them; can you put your arms up? *After a few men raise their arms, he continues.* Do you all agree with what we are saying? I would also like to have a letter from the land committee. After getting both of these letters, then we will start work. I don't know if everyone knows this, but I have three tourists coming on the twenty-second, and the camp will start up on the twentieth to twenty-first of this month. So business is starting. And on the eleventh we will also have guests. I see that the tourists are already starting to want to run this way. I have another idea as well that I'd like to share. Out in Loliondo, in Ololosokwan, we did a plan regarding money that came from this business. This is a big deal, how will the money be used? Because I want everyone to know where the money goes. Do you understand? Is there an environment committee in this village? Is there a woman on it? *Laughter from the crowd as he mixes up his Swahili words.* This is important. You are all laughing, but the knowledge of women is different than our knowledge and can help out.[7] Because the first thing to know is that the first money to come in will be contributed to help build this dam. It will be about 700,000 TSH [approximately 700 U.S. dollars] for this month, November. But what I want is for the environment committee or the land committee together to write a list of the things that the villagers want to use the money for. And then we will use the money to do the things on the list. And put the things on top that are the most important down toward the least important. Does everyone understand? OK. Another thing is that it is important to start a receipt book. Because when you get this money, we need to have a record, and I'm not sure if it will be a bank account or what, but that is something to talk about later, another day. But the important thing is that money is given to the village to do the things that are on the list. So I see that if everything is fine and the elders agree to this work, then on the twentieth to the twenty-second we start the dam.[8] OK? *One of the village government members tells people to clap hands for him, and they do. Corbet smiles and responds with* Ashe Naleng [Maa: thank you very much]. I request you get those papers ready so that I can go home with them today. *He then starts to walk out of the meeting.*

Chairman O: *To Corbett,* Wait first and listen to the elders a little bit [*as an elder stands to speak*].

Landis R: I have stood to ask that we not take yet another long time to get these two papers—the one from the whole village and the one from the land committee. Since work is already starting, let's take the minutes of the meeting. It will help to draft the letter from the village government, and those representatives of the land committee, they should start to write their letter right now. If it needs to wait a little bit, OK, but let's get the letter from the village. *There are murmurs throughout the crowd. Some express relief that the meeting will be over and things will get started. Others, however, are not happy and are grumbling and asking questions of one another. Landis T stands to speak again.*

Landis T: *He speaks loudly to be heard over the noise.* I would like to say before we finish the meeting, I have an issue to raise that I think we need to discuss. What I would like to talk about is that this dam, to be built in *Endarpo*, won't it also be used by wildlife? You all know as I do that if there is water, all the wildlife will come. They will all come from the MR. All the animals from the MR will come. And what will happen when all of the wildlife fill this space? What will we talk about then? I am very thankful to our guests for the help they bring. It is very good to have this dam, but we need to talk with the MR so that they know that the wildlife will all come to this area, and if they come to eat the grass, when the grass finishes, what will the cattle eat? Will we be able to negotiate use of the MR for grazing? These are important questions. Also, what is the size of the campsite? And is grazing prohibited there? These are all very important questions that we should discuss before we agree officially to anything.[9] *Others stand up and talk about this, other men of the Landis age-set, but some of the more senior elders also back up Landis T on the importance of the questions he raised. Others (village government members and Corbett) are clearly getting angry.*

Makaa Ntoipo: *An easygoing man, he is often at odds with the village government, as he is not afraid to say what he thinks but he has also been seen as playing the clan card to fuel conflicts when needed. He is poor and has no position of authority, but he is respected for his intelligence and honesty, most of the time.* What Landis T says is very true. In a short while in the future, there will be nothing left for the cattle. The area will be full of wildlife, and they will finish the grass and make the ground bare. This is not a light matter, and we have not had enough discussion about this. We need to discuss this more. As a member of the land committee, I can say that we discussed these issues when we were looking for the best place to build the dam. For instance, we decided that even though there are places in *Lera* that would work well to capture water, it would not be good to put the dam in *Lera*. This is a very important grazing area. If we put a dam there, the grass will be quickly finished by cattle and wildlife, especially wildebeest. They are particularly damaging (*maharabifu sana*). They will finish all the grass. *Sounds of "oosho" from the men and women around the circle, attesting to how the wildebeest will "finish the grass."* Better to put the dam [...] near *inkang'itie*. This way the cattle will go to drink water there and go elsewhere for grazing.[10]

Landis Z:[11] This is true that we need to look carefully before we build a dam. What this elder says is true. If a dam is built, and there is water year-round? *Oosho*, all the animals in the Mara Ranch will come to the village lands, especially to *Lera* and *Oloyeti*. They will also come near to the *inkang'itie'*. Even guinea fowl and francolins will come because there is a certain kind of grass that they like to eat that there is a lot of here [in the village]. Only elephants will stay in the ranch because of the trees there.

Corbett: I am happy that you are asking all these questions. These are good questions. First, someone asked the size of the campsite. It is five hundred meters by five hundred meters. But this question about wildlife eating all the grass raises a big issue. I also talked to the lawyer for the Manyara Ranch. I asked why it is so difficult for you all to enter with cattle. We will build a dam and wildlife will come. I am on your side. The south side of the Manyara Ranch [near to the villages] is not so important for animals, but animals pass here [through the village] from everywhere, more so than in the ranch. However, today is your last chance to approve the campsite. I have been asking for this paper for a long time. This is business; this is not aide/assistance [*msaada*].[12]

Chairman O: Corbett is right. We need to decide today. I want the land committee to decide today and give him the paper he needs.

Corbett: Thank you chairman. I really want to get this paper today.

Makaa Ntoipo: We cannot write the paper today because the female members of the committee are not here. There are nine people in the land committee and seven people in the *baraza* [assembly]. By law, if the women members are not present, no decisions can be made.

Senior Elder: *Despite the shift in subject and attempts to close the meeting so that Corbett can go, he stands to speak, holding tightly on to a tall, thin walking stick.* Really it is true. If all these dams are built—this one Corbett is planning to build us, the one in Esilalei [ranch dam] which is being fixed—then this will all just be conservation [*hifadhi tu*]. And there, there, and there [*he points with his free hand in the direction of the Manyara Ranch, TNP and LMNP*] it is conservation [*hifadhi*] already![13]

There is commotion from Corbett and members of the village government, the latter who are conversing among themselves. "What are these people doing?" they ask. "Stirring up trouble," they mutter. "Everything was already decided on."

Landis M: *A natural arbitrator, he tries to reconcile the views, or at least calm down Corbett and his allies. The chairman quiets down the crowd so he can speak.* Nobody disagrees [to the campsite or the dam], but we need to have a good system for planning. The village will become full of wildlife, yes. But isn't this better than not having water? This is a big question. It is a big issue.[14]

This is the end of the transcriptions from that original meeting, with the remainder of the chapter drawing from a variety of sources.

Corbett: Landis M is right, this is a big question, and it is important for you to all think about more than just your cattle. Wildlife will bring you money! Wildlife will bring you development! And it would probably be best to set aside certain areas of the village to be left without livestock grazing for certain times of the year, to leave them open for wildlife. This works in Ololosokwan, where I know some of you visited, and where Maasai are profiting from wildlife conservation.[15] They are learning that having a lot of wildlife is much more profitable than having a lot of cattle. For now, in the area nearby the campsite, we will need fifty acres where no livestock will be allowed. We don't want cattle near the campsite; they will scare away the wildlife and maybe the tourists![16] *He laughs at this final point. Maasai laugh with him.*

MG: *Without standing, she tentatively speaks from where she is sitting, less to the meeting than to Corbett himself and to the elders who had been involved in the process, and the chairman.* And where is the exact location of the campsite? I have heard it is in *Enkung'u Olduka.* Isn't that an important grazing area for livestock in the dry season? *With this last statement, she looks around at the men she is sitting with.*

> **Note:** This statement reflects my attempts to make sure that planning was well understood and transparent to all. Corbet often communicated only with a few individuals associated with government leadership (all of the Ilaiser clan). Many of them claimed that I was associated more strongly with the Ilmamasita clan, and thus it was "their turn" to control and benefit this new outsider. I continued to talk to Corbett as well as to villagers throughout the negotiations.

Makaa MN:[17] *He doesn't usually speak at meetings, but he was one of the elders who was involved in the negotiations on the dam and camp placement, as he is one of the most knowledgeable and respected in the village. He stands to speak, using only a small walking stick and speaking in a soft and comfortable tone.* MG has learned a lot staying with us! It is true that *Enkung'u Olduka* is important for dry season grazing, but only for those who live in *Engusero*, not for everyone. And the place that we picked for the campsite is small, and it is not the most important place; it is not in an area used very much by cattle. It is OK. Really, if it was in an important grazing area we, the elders, would not have allowed it. But the dam is another story. We cannot put the dam down there because then it will attract wildlife from all over to finish the grass in *Lera* phew [*he moves his hand across his mouth to demonstrate*] . . . all the way through to *Kiripaa* . . . and the cattle will be left with nothing. So that is why we proposed *Endarpo*: it is not in a grazing area.

Yeiyo N: *The women are talking loudly among themselves, and they are called on by the chairman to speak. An older woman, wife to a wealthy agreeable elder, speaks quickly but concisely.* We agree the dam be built in *Endarpo*. This is good because it is far from grazing areas and so cattle coming will not destroy pasture. It has clean water. There are places for the dam that we know the elders were discussing, like *Embarimbali*, but this is not good. The water there is salty [*magadi*].[18] It will be fine for wildlife and for birds; they don't care if it is *magadi*, but it won't be good for people. *She trails off and is quiet while other women whisper to her. An elder begins to stand up to speak, and just then she continues to speak, loudly this time.* All this talk about wildlife is fine. But like Landis M said, even if the village is full of wildlife, won't it be better to have water? We say **yes!** *She says this last word with extra emphasis, and the other women laugh.* We struggle to find water here every day to drink and cook with. In the dry season, we have to go all the way to Mswakini for water.[19] That is very far! Maybe the government can arrange something with Manyara Ranch, as has been brought up. But don't give up this dam![20]

Koko B: *As the elders try to speak, another woman speaks up, in a loud coarse voice, weathered with age.* It is true. When the dam is built, all the animals will come. All of them [*using her hands, she gestures in a coming motion*], the whole area will be full of wildlife, they will all come. Oh, and these animals will be very happy because this was their area, it is open plains [*mbuga wazi*], they like it here. They will be happy because they will get water and they won't be thirsty again. And the people too. All those Maasai that moved to Mto wa Mbu to look for water? They will come back, together with the wildebeest! *The women all laugh.* If there is water, *basi* [that's it], all the people will come back and the wildebeest, the gazelle, all of them will come.[21]

Peter:[22] *The microenterprise development specialist for AWF, he has been actively involved in management questions on the Manyara Ranch and in the surrounding village lands. He has been leaning on his car and chatting with the driver on and off through the meeting so far. He has been listening, waiting for the village to finish their discussions with Corbett on their own. He now enters the center of the meeting in a very confident manner. He is a non-Maasai, Tanzanian man. He is not very tall, but with a large midsection, which makes him seem larger than he is. Standing in* *the center, he turns and looks at everyone before speaking in a condescending tone.* "Do you want the dam or not? It sounds like you want it, but then only if you can get something from someone else [i.e., the Manyara Ranch]. You just want access to the ranch and now see an opportunity to pull [your] arguments in just such a way to gain access. The Manyara Ranch is an island. The rest of this area is all overgrazed, badly overgrazed. If we want to look at the big picture, then you need to use [the land] within its capacity and not have more animals then the land can take." So, is it possible for you to access the ranch if wildlife use of village lands increases? I'd have to say "yes and no. Yes, if [you] learn to keep livestock in a sustainable way. What [you] do now is not sustainable; it is not a good match of livestock numbers with the resource base. There is an optimal number of livestock, **the carrying capacity**, given the resource base. *He stresses this word* carrying capacity *in English.* Right now, there is a big mismatch. So, no [in that sense, you should not be able to graze in the MR], or five years from now the ranch will be like it is in the village lands [*he looks around and swings his arm at the nearly bare shortgrass plains behind him (just northeast of the* korongo, *toward the MR)*], where there is no grass. So the time is not right. Not until you agree to keep livestock numbers at a sustainable level. The ranch is a training ground to see how to use land in a sustainable manner."

There is a great deal of commotion in the crowd until a highly respected elder stands to speak.

> **Note:** Carrying capacity, as Nathan Sayre contends, "may be the most versatile and widely popularized concept in environmental politics today" (2008, 120). It is commonly used by rangeland ecologists and conservationists to argue that there are more livestock than the range can support, "with the advantage of conveying a sense of calculability and precision" (Sayre 2008, 120). Yet it is an incredibly contested term, particularly in semiarid rangelands where pasture quality has been shown to be linked to complex and multiple stressors, including rainfall and land-use histories (Turner 1993).

Seuri K: *Chuckling to himself, he puts on a serious face as he addresses his words at Mr. Peter in particular.* First of all, this area that you point to as being "overgrazed," that is what we call *olpura alamunyani*! I have lived in this area all my life, and it has always been like that, "even before they drew the boundary for the Manyara Ranch, it was like this." You see *olpura* means a place that is bare and no grass grows, and *alamunyani* refers to a different kind of soil [see chapter 2].[23] "The soil is *magadi* [salty]; if you dig there you will get water, but it will be salty." You see, *alamunyani* is a "place that above it has grass, but if you dig about like a foot below, you will get *magadi*, which causes all these changes in the grass." Throughout the village there are places we call *alamunyani*, like just before entering *Lera*, and then there is *Alamunyani* near *Endarpo*, near to this place where the dam will be built [see map 3]. Grass grows in some of these places, but it is a short, light grass that finishes fast [annuals]. In other places only *imbenek*[24] [forbs] grow, which also finish fast. That is why the area is bare now; it is the end of a long and hot dry season. *He pauses, looking around at the dusty landscape.* It is complex. There are different types of *alamunyani* — "where grass grows, the *magadi* is deep down in the soil. In this area you point to, grass doesn't grow, because the *magadi* is very close to the surface. Even long ago it was like this. No grass [*he shakes his head*], just *imbenek*." Of course there **are** also places that have become filled with *imbenek* because of grazing. That can happen, because if cattle are many in one area, they can finish that grass completely until it changes, and *imbenek* will come to dominate. Even trees will increase because you can't burn since there is no grass to burn, so the trees will continue to grow. But there is no place here in these villages that I have seen this happen.[25]

Game scout 1: *A junior elder of the Landis age-set, he is from the wealthiest enkang'* *in the area, where the Oloiboni lives, and where cattle regularly enter the Manyara* *Ranch to graze, though he is not from that family. His game scout training gives him* *an added air of confidence.* I am sure what the elder has said is true; he knows this land better than I do. But I understand what Peter is saying, and I know that it is something that is hard for Maasai to see. There is a lot of grass in the Manyara Ranch, plenty for livestock and wildlife. So if the cattle from Esilalei and Oltukai all start coming into the ranch, they cannot finish the grass. But they will ruin the environment because they will come in on one path — more than eleven thousand cattle from Esilalei; they will bring a *korongo* [create a ditch for water to pass, gully erosion] if too many cattle pass in one place. And then no grass will grow again. I have seen this and learned this in Mwanza, where I studied wildlife conservation.[26] Also, if cattle eat all in one place, they can finish the grass until it is taken by the wind and the land becomes tired [wind erosion]. Maasai don't see this. And they don't account for the difference between now and long ago. For example, at our *enkang'* long ago there were only six men of the Makaa age-set, now there are seventeen Landis, and the Korianga will be fifty! Where will we all go with all the cattle? In 1989, there were only 150 cattle at our *enkang'*. Today, there are close to 3,000. If we want to conserve the environment and wildlife, we need to get rid of cattle [in Manyara Ranch]. This is because, like I said, they can "ruin the environment" and also because wildlife are scared away by cattle and by people who make noise.[27] *People start to make noise . . . upset with what he is saying. The* Oloiboni, *the owner of the 3,000 cattle, tells him to sit down as he stands up to speak.*

Meshuki L: *He is one of the most respected and powerful elders in the area, and by far the wealthiest. His love of cattle is notorious. Despite the respect he knows he demands, he speaks in a gentle, melodic tone.* Youth these days! *he says as he waves his* olkuma *in the direction of the young man who just spoke, laughing as he does so. Others laugh along with him.* They forget what their elders taught them and brag about what they learn in school. It is good for them to study to know how to bring profit from wildlife. We need to know how to gain from the milk of wildlife like we do from cattle. But we mustn't forget the importance of cattle—from which we gain our sustenance and even the money to pay for school fees! Also, if the young men spent more time at home and less at school, they would know that "cattle can't ruin the environment by finishing the grass, [not] if it rains." But he was correct in talking about the damaging effects of pathways, where grass cannot grow, because cattle walk there every day. This can be seen for example when the cows come home. Grass fails to grow there, but next to [the path] grass will grow as usual. So there can be a problem with too many paths. But we have rules about where the cattle can go at different times to prevent this and we have pasture reserves [*alalili*]. We, the elders, try to prevent large paths from forming. If a lot of cattle pass in one area, if they like this one area until a lot of paths [are created], then we make sure they get taken to a different area next. We can tell our sons to not take the cattle to that place again today, you will finish the grass. *He laughs.* So yes, sometimes I guess cattle can finish the grass. If they do so, then sometimes when it rains, *imbenek* will grow instead of grass and then the cows don't get enough to eat. But an area can fluctuate between grass and *imbenek* depending on the rains. It is really the rainfall that determines these things [little or sporadic rain will result in *imbenek* instead of grass growth]. But an area can start to become *osero* [bush, scrub] if it is grazed too heavily. But if we burn, then it will be OK again for grazing. And it is not just cattle that can finish grass. As we have been talking about today, even wildlife can finish grass—in the village or anywhere. **They are all animals**. Goats and sheep, for instance, can finish the grass of an area. So can donkeys, together with zebra. But wildebeest really ruin an area because wildebeest don't leave an area until they finish the grass completely, leaving only dust behind.

But they are all animals, and grass is the food for them all—the wild ones and livestock, it is food for them all, so they cannot be separated, Enkai! *he says, looking up at the sky.*[28]

Makaa MN:[29] The elder has spoken truthfully. What I think/say is that there are two things that can ruin pasture. Cattle can go to one place every day, where they mix up/trample [Swahili: *kuvuruga*] the grass. It is not just grazing; it is that they step on the grass every day and the grass gets tired. Second, wildebeest can come to one place and stay only one week, and they can finish the grass. They eat it until the bottom. Only wildebeest, no other animal does this. *In his joking way, he nods his head in imitation of a wildebeest feeding, and then, laughing, he swings up his stick to motion that he is done. He starts to walk away and then stops, addressing the crowd.* And farms. Farms can ruin the land. Like out by Kisongo and Duka Mbovu?[30] All that gully erosion? That is because of all the farms. The land is tired. There are no cattle there anymore; they all moved.

Seuri LL:[31] Really it is true what is being said about wildebeest. Cattle and wildebeest both like short grass so they like "a pasture after it has been eaten by donkeys or other wildlife." But, wildebeest and zebra can eat until [the grass] is done. They know how to cut [the grass] like a saw, and can cut until there is nothing left, even for goats! Wildebeest really like grass that is short. Wildebeest really ruin an area. They go in groups and they can create an *empoor* (a place where no grass grows). They don't like to move until they finish all the grass. They eat like a machine grinds maize! Even if there is only a little grass left. Cattle are [also] capable of this, but cattle are led (by people), so it is not common, because if we see grass starting to finish, we move the cattle.

Makaa KAL:[32] Yes, a lot of cattle can ruin a pasture and so can a lot of wildlife. They are the same as cattle. The same. Because the places where wildlife stay, they finish the grass. The difference is that the wildlife usually move, and in this sense they are different than cattle. But if there is water here year-round [i.e., with a dam built], the animals won't move. In fact, in some years, when the lake is not too salty (from low water level), then wildlife stay around the village. So if there is a dam, they will not leave.

Dr. Robin Reid:[33] *A tall thin woman, she is American, but has been living and working in Kenya for nearly two decades. She is based at the International Livestock Research Institute in Nairobi, where she directs a research team that is addressing wildlife and pastoralist co-use of rangelands across Maasailand.*[34] *Despite her wealth of knowledge and position of authority, she is modest and respectful of the views of others. She has been paying very close attention to the meeting, sitting with Landis*

MI, who has been translating for her. He is from Simanjiro and represents the TME in the larger project (Reid et al. 2009). She looks at the chairman and motions that she would like to speak. In doing so, she pulls out her elaborately beaded olkuma *and shows it to him, while laughing and slouching a bit so as not to appear tall and imposing. She giggles and holds out the* olkuma *again. She speaks clearly, turning to all present as she does.* So, I was told that this is a very special club that will help bring me respect when I speak at meetings! And [*she pauses for effect*] that it is usually only given to men. *MI translates and elaborates a bit while doing so, since he was part of the group of men that gave her the* olkuma. *She laughs and then continues.* Well, it was given to me by my amazing team of Maasai men, whom I have worked with over the past three years, and for me it says that I succeeded at least in gaining their respect, which matters a lot to me. I use it here today to express my respect for all of you, for your customs and your knowledge, and your way of holding meetings, though they do take forever!

Maasai chuckle among themselves, she smiles and continues.

I am quite excited about the discussion that is happening here. It reflects much of what we have been finding in our research but is rarely talked about. Unfortunately, we often see the sort of generalized statements made by Peter. *Looking over in his direction, she gives him an apologetic smile.* I do not mean to insult you Peter; you are merely repeating what you have learned, which is the standard narrative about the impacts of livestock on savanna landscapes. But, after researching the history and ecology of savannas across the continent, I can honestly say that it is just not true. Or rather that it is much too simplistic. Let me explain.

There have been two competing narratives. One says pastoralists destroy the landscape by overgrazing and keeping more animals than the range can withstand or, to use the common term, as you did, beyond the *carrying capacity*. And then another narrative, coming from nonequilibrium ecology says that arid and semiarid rangelands, such as this one here [*she sweeps her arms around her to refer to the surrounding landscape*], are not so much impacted by grazing as they are by rainfall.[35] Of course, it is often somewhere in the middle, as Turner has showed us for West Africa [Turner 1998], and as the elder over here [*she points to Meshuki L, who chuckles*] just explained.

Furthermore, some argue that grazing—by **both** livestock **and** wildlife— can improve the range, for instance the work of Gufu Oba and his colleagues [Oba, Stenseth, and Lusigi 2000]. Ecologists working in the Serengeti have shown that wildlife grazing can improve the pasture through the production of "grazing lawns" (McNaughton 1979, 1984). And we have found similar effects with livestock grazing around Maasai homesteads. So we can say "that savannas in east Africa were, in a sense, 'preadapted' to the herders and their stock when they arrived from the north several millennia ago and started grazing and burning" (Reid 2012, 127). *She pauses and looks around to smiles from Maasai. She continues in a serious tone,* "There is no reason to suppose, however, that these savannas are adapted to more recent forms of disturbance, such as heavy and continuous grazing by livestock" (such as a herd of 3,000! [*she looks again back at Meshuki L, who laughs harder this time*]), "replacement of many species of wild herbivores by a few species of domesticated animals, frequent burning, plowing for crop cultivation, permanent settlements, wells [dams], and . . . [*she pauses here and looks around, then says with a serious smile*] the removal of pastoral people from protected areas for wildlife" (Reid 2012, 127). So, what I am saying is that if you stop moving with your livestock, then the effects could be damaging to the range. So, it **is** important to talk about what will happen with the creation of the dam **and** restrictions on Maasai grazing inside the Manyara Ranch. For we did find that when the boundaries between protected areas are soft, meaning mobility and use of fire can occur across them, then pastures are healthier. It's complex, and in addition to more research, we need more pastoral herders like you all here [*she says with a sweeping gesture and a broad smile*] to contribute to the conversation, "to bring much-needed nuance and sophisticated local understanding of savannas to the discussion" (Reid 2012, 161). *She turns around on her feet, smiles around the meeting, and sits back down.*

Dr. Raphael Mwalyosi: *A professor from the Institute for Resource Assessment (IRA), at the University of Dar es Salaam, he has a great deal of experience in the Lake Manyara area (Mwalyosi 1981, 1990, 1991, 1992).*[36] *He speaks in a confident and professional tone.* It is true that the effects of grazing on the range are complicated. I have done a lot of research here, in the Lake Manyara area, and have found that both wildlife and livestock can impact vegetation composition as well as soil structure and that livestock are not always to blame for changes. For instance, we found that the most likely cause of the decline in *Themeda trianda* and *Hyparrhenia* species, grasses favored by wildlife is "overgrazing by game animals and restriction of burning" by pastoralists (Mwalyosi 1992). We also found that in this area "most of the bare ground comprises rocky surfaces which were not man-made" (Mwalyosi 1992, 586). *He looks around at the Maasai elders and nods.* Perhaps this is what you call *olpura*? *He smiles, then continues.* Additionally, the gully erosion as related to cattle tracking to and from grazing and water sources was minimal. All in all, we could say that the soil conditions here are fairly stable, and that primary production and range condition are good (Mwalyosi 1992, 583, table 2). In fact, I recommend the introduction of controlled burning to encourage the recolonization of *Themeda triandra* and *Hyparrhenia* species, which are favored by wildebeest and zebra [McNaughton 1979, 1985; Talbot and Talbot 1963] and can be stimulated by fire [Van de Vijver, Poot, and Prins 1999]. Others have argued that moderate to heavy grazing can help to stimulate *Themeda trianda* [McNaughton 1979; Coughenour 1991]. *He looks around to see the reactions of others and catches Dr. Reid smiling. He then adds,* So perhaps Dr. Reid is correct, that herders do not always destroy the range but can sometimes improve on it.

Makaa LAK:[37] This is true, what the professor says. We, Maasai, we have always used burning and grazing to manage the pastures; and this is especially important for certain grasses. For instance, "if there are two places with *olkereyan* [*Sporobolus pyramidalis*] and *oloyeti engusero* [*Sporobolus rangei pilger*] grasses, and one was grazed and the other not touched, the place that was grazed by cattle will be better than the place left ungrazed, which will become *pori.*" It is the same with fire. A place that has been burned will be better than a place left unburned. So for instance with *alalili* (our reserve pastures for calves and sick cows), we burn it every two years so that good, healthy grass grows back.

Landis P: *Starts to speak while sitting and everyone stops to listen.* What the elder said is true, and it is very important. If you don't burn, the grass will die this year and then others will grow on top of it. The grass near *Simbi* [*he is interrupted by exclamations from the crowd, "oosho," "o yie kake," all showing their disapproval and dismay at the state of the Simbi pasture*], it is *pori,* it is no longer any good for cattle or even for wildlife.[38]

Lonana:[39] *An educated Maasai elder (of the Makaa age-set), he is involved with pastoral civil society building and nongovernmental organization (NGO) work. Recently he was asked by TLCT to act as a liaison between communities and the Manyara Ranch. He is not originally from this area but now has cattle in Esilalei.*[40] *He has been exposed to multiple sides of the story regarding grazing in the Manyara Ranch. He is extremely well respected by all (Maasai and non-Maasai), so as he stands to speak, there is a hush as people quiet down to listen carefully.* This has been a very interesting conversation and brings up many useful points. Let's bring it back to the Manyara Ranch. I am new to a lot of this, so I brought an ecology professor down from Nairobi to look at the ranch and tell me what he saw. Well, he said that the ranch, in its current state, is no good for wildlife or livestock grazing.

While burning is important, grazing is even better than burning for pasture maintenance. When grass is eaten, it grows back. I know that with the Mara Count in Kenya that Dr. Reid has been part of [*he looks over at Dr. Reid with a smile, and she smiles back*], they found that grass was the *greenest* in areas that had either been burned or grazed prior to the arrival of rain [Reid et al. 2003, 46]. And there is no doubt that the need for grazing exists in the villages! In addition to the problem of tall rank grass, "there is the problem of *endundulu*."[41] This shrub is very bad. I don't even think it is eaten by animals, except what they can get on the edge of the thicket, and then they just continue to spread it [through seed dispersal]! Manyara Ranch is the breeding center for it, spreading it out to the villages. The manager thinks it is due to overgrazing and fire but that is unfounded.[42] The ecology professor told me that it needs to be dug up. *As he returns to where he was seated, Maasai look at each other in disbelief. He is always so calm, controlled, and cautious in his criticisms, but he made it clear that he was unhappy with decisions being made on Manyara Ranch.*

Makaa Lak:[43] *A confident and respected elder far removed from politics, he is not afraid to speak after Lonana.* It is true, long ago, there was not as much *endundulu* in the villages as there is now. It does not "like" fire. If you burn, *endundulu* will go away, most of it will burn off. Of course, some of it will grow again, but only a little bit, so fire will keep it in check.

Seuri K:[44] *A respected elder who was born here, he speaks calmly.* It is true. *Endundulu* has increased a lot since we were young, but cattle grazing didn't do this. If it is a place that trees like, it just grows. And fire? *Oosho!* [this elder who said it likes fire is wrong], that is not possible. It will burn if there is a fire, but it won't die. But if you burn it every year, it won't increase, it will stay the same. I guess I can say that cattle did contribute to the problem though, because after heavy grazing you can't burn again. What will you burn if the cattle have finished the grass? And those trees, if there is no grass underneath it, fire can't kill those trees [it won't get hot enough], so they continue to grow.

There is lots of commotion, with Maasai talking to themselves about endundulu. The ilmurran complain loudly of its uselessness, hands flailing in the air: "If only fire could get rid of it!" Then elders speaking up, calmly cautioning them to be specific. Yes, endundulu o sirikon (endundulu *of the donkey) is a nuisance and is not as "afraid of fire." But there is* endundulu narok (*black* endundulu, *the one of people), which is a very important medicine and actually is "afraid of fire."*

Chairman O: *The chairman of Oltukai and of the* enkiguena *stands up slowly, looking around and waiting for just the right moment to stop the commotion, when an* ilmurran *rather than an elder is speaking. He calls the meeting back to order through a series of whistles and then begins talking in a tone that reveals his underlying nervousness.* OK everyone, I think we have all agreed to the dam? *Nods around the circle, proclamations of yes, we agree.* And that livestock should not always be blamed for overgrazing; so we should be allowed into the Manyara Ranch! Actually, I think we still need to talk about that and so I wanted to formally introduce the second agenda, which we have already talked a lot about, regarding how wildlife and livestock coexist. Do they compete? Help each other? Avoid each other? Stay together? Let's talk about this.

Game Scout 2: *He is young (Landis age-set) and is the only Manyara Ranch game scout not from one of these two villages. He was one of the few selected to study at Pasiansi Wildlife Training Institute in Mwanza. He is shy but speaks clearly.* It is true that there is a lot of grass in the ranch. I don't think that is the reason the management doesn't want too many village cattle inside. They are not just coming into the ranch for grass, but also for water. If they all come in for water freely, they will eat all the grass near the water, and it will become an open plain. Also, if people dig [wells] in the *korongo*, when it rains the soil is easily carried away and the animals can fall into the wells. Even if they are dug big enough so that the elephants can use them, the elephants will cover them up after using them. That is certain. The elephants always cover the water after drinking. Another thing, when cattle come into the ranch, they bother the wildlife. The problem is with the herd boys, who chase away wildlife with their dogs.[45]

Olmurrani Lekei: *Only a warrior, he is not afraid to speak against what the young Landis has just said. He saunters into the center of the circle and, leaning on his walking stick, speaks with just a touch of arrogance.* Maybe what the game scout says is true **sometimes**, but we share our wells with wildlife. I was just out there digging wells in the dry Mto wa Mbu dam inside Manyara Ranch. We take our goats there for water. "And wildlife come to use the water as well, even elephants. Elephants come and use the wells we dig. They can even come in the afternoon when we are still there. If they come, we just move out of the way and let them drink first, and then we return to give water to our animals. There is no problem. They don't ruin the well. They don't step in the well. They stand outside and drink from it. They try to cover it up though, like the game scout said, but this is not a big problem because every time we come, we have to fix the wells anyway before they can be used by our animals. So, we don't have any problems sharing our water with wildlife.[46] But Manyara Ranch management does not want us there. I guess they think we are interfering with wildlife. I don't know." But the other day the manager caught us there. *He looks over at the manager with a combination of shy respect and anger before continuing.* "He said we weren't supposed to be there. He threatened to cover our wells up . . . but the *mzee* [elder of the *enkang'*] begged permission, and now we are allowed to be there. We have no place else to go. There is no water anywhere."[47]

Elder:[48] "Wildlife and livestock can stay together, drink the same water and eat the same pastures, as long as the wildlife have already come to know people. Or if they don't see people, the wildlife will stay together with livestock because they don't bother each other; they are not afraid of each other. They [wildlife] are afraid of people. They have become afraid of people because they are chased away by herd boys every day. So they have come to know that if they see cattle, the herd boy is not far behind, and he will come to bother them, he will push them away. What else are the herd boys to do, out in the pasture all day? It is a game for them; they don't know any better. Like the game scout said, the herd boys usually have dogs. But a dog cannot chase away zebra without people, so zebra are not afraid of dogs if they are not with people. But at the same time, if a herd boy is out without a dog, the wildlife will likely be less frightened." And if we tell the herd boys not to chase the wildlife, if for instance we were benefiting from having wildlife around, *basi* [that's it], they would stop![49]

Landis K: *Sitting with MG and Landis M, they were talking about all the wildlife they see during their work, and Landis K was encouraged to stand and speak. He is usually shy around elders and not one to speak at meetings. Since he will be talking about the transect data, he feels confident but still speaks quietly, leaning on his walking stick.* It is true that wildlife can be afraid of people, and maybe that is why during our transect work we sometimes found more animals in the Manyara Ranch than in the village. But some of the animals, like zebra, got to know us and were no longer afraid when we were walking the transect, whether it was in the ranch or the village. Sometimes they wouldn't even move; they would just look at us and then keep grazing. Wildebeest though, they are different. They are always scared. If we approach them by car, they run as far away as they can. When we were on foot, sometimes they would just run nearby and then stop. But the funny thing is that while wildlife might be afraid of herders during the day, they come to our homes at night for protection against the real danger—*olowaru* (predators, usually lion). Now it is the dry season, so all the animals are back in the park. But as soon as it rains, *Oosho*. . . . There are so many wildebeest by my *enkang'* out in *Engusero* that it's dangerous to go out at night because of all the lions![50]

MG: *Looking through her papers and comparing tables with M, she slowly stands to speak with the papers in hand.* What Landis K says is true, at least in 2003, the highest recorded total wildlife density was over 370 animals per km² for the Bwawambili transect, which goes into the Manyara Ranch from Esilalei, during *orkisirata* (the early rains) in December [see figure 18].[51] The second-highest recorded density that year was over 350 animals per km², recorded during the same period, also inside Manyara Ranch, on the Simbi transect [see figure 19].[52] These numbers are truly striking. The numbers mostly reflect large herds of wildebeest and zebra, as well as 64 impala, and 100 gazelle, all fairly evenly spread out [see map 6]. The numbers on the Simbi transect are even higher, including approximately 1,822 wildebeest and 1,256 zebra on the ranch side of the transect, as well as approximately 106 gazelle on the village side. At the same time, the cattle densities on these transects were zero inside the ranch.[53] Even if we look at recordings of dung and footprints (marks) on the transect line from the past few days we still see very low densities of cattle for (T6) Bwawambili in December 2003, with most of them outside of the ranch, along with high counts for wildlife marks, although there were other times when cattle marks were also high in both of these transects (June and August 2003; see figure 21).

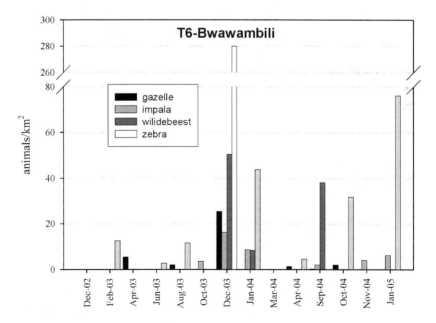

Figure 18 Wildlife density (by species) for T6-*Bwawambili* (wooded savanna, MR)

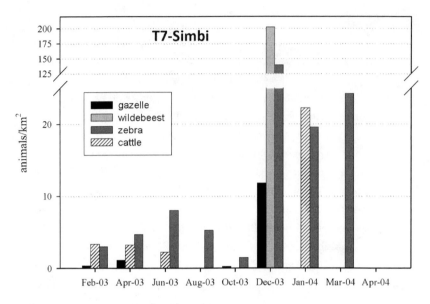

Figure 19 Wildlife density for T7-*Simbi* (grass savanna, MR)

There has been some mention here and at previous meetings that many parts of the ranch, such as Simbi, are overgrown and no longer suitable for wildlife or livestock; so you might be wondering why all these wildlife and livestock were there. First of all, the cattle marks need to be read with caution, as this area is crossed often to get to the Mswakini dam southeast of the MR. Also, it is now 2005; even in 2003, when we conducted these transects, the grass was very overgrown, with dry rank grass mixed in with fresh green sprouts and full of ticks. Most of the animals we saw were in the portion of the transect either just over the boundary from the village where the grass had been grazed by cattle or toward the end of the transect, where the grass thinned out again by the (breached and dry) Simbi dam. Unfortunately, we don't have much data to talk about the trends in Simbi because that transect was discontinued after April 2004. The area had become thick bush, or *pori*, and walking transects were no longer safe for fear of lions.

In this sense, I guess we can talk about this part of the ranch becoming good for some wildlife, like lions, which are better conserved in protected areas with limited access by people. *Grumbles from Maasai throughout the crowd; some of the* ilmurran *present touch their spears, which are standing in the ground next to where they sit.* And that gets at what Landis K was talking about: that many

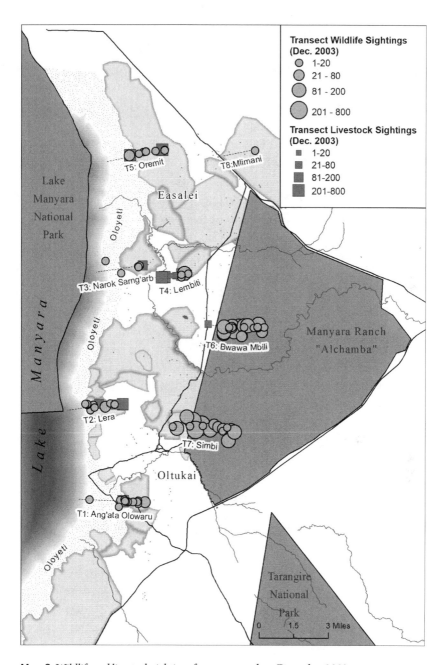

Map 6 Wildlife and livestock sightings from transect data, December 2003

of the wildlife leave Manyara Ranch at night to escape the lions and come by
Maasai homesteads for protection (see also Reid et al. 2003). This can cause
problems as well though. Some people argue that it brings lions to their home,
where they can prey on livestock. The rising numbers of lions on Manyara
Ranch have led to an increase in predation of Maasai cattle inside and outside
of the ranch (Goldman, Roque de Pinho, and Perry 2013).[54] In such cases, it
is difficult for the *ilmurran* to be held back from organizing a lion hunt (*olamaiyo*), but in all the cases where the predation occurred inside one of these
two villages (Oltukai and Esilalei), *ilmurran* were prevented from going on
olamaiyo by the village government and the MR management. This suggests
"coexistence" is possible. However, the lack of follow-up and compensation by
Manyara Ranch only increased antagonistic relations with villagers over time.
Noises of agreement mixed with anger come from Maasai around the circle. Some
conservation scientists have suggested that Maasai traditional hunting of lions
shows that their presence is *not* compatible with wildlife conservation (Prins
1992). These hunts, however, are regulated by the elders and are not arbitrary
(Goldman, Roque de Pinho, and Perry 2013). Some Maasai have explained
to me that hunting lions helps "coexistence" by teaching lions to stay away
from cattle and *ilmurran*. It reinforces relations of respect/fear. Additionally,
it has been shown that when Maasai are on the side of conservation, wildlife
numbers increase because they can be a vigilant antipoaching force (Western
1997; cf. Homewood and Rodgers 1991). It will be interesting to see if the
wildlife numbers in the village rise with the antipoaching efforts that will come
with Corbett's hiring of the newly trained game scouts.[55] Anyway, there are of
course other animals that also do better in places without people, such as eland
and rhino (Reid et al. 2003). We often saw large herds of eland (up to twenty-
four) on the *Simbi* transect (February and June 2003; April 2004; usually by
the end of the transect). We even saw an elephant on this transect once (February 2003). *She looks back at Landis M and Landis K for their reaction; they seem
happy, but Landis M is anxious to say something. MG is ready to sit down, and many
men are vying for the next chance to speak. Landis M requests to speak specifically on
what MG has just said, regarding the transect data. He promises to be brief.*

Note on competition: It is difficult if not impossible to "prove" competition.
One needs to illustrate that resources are shared, that resources are "limited,"
that there is joint "exploitation" of these resources or interference in accessing them, and that there are negative effects on the species involved (Prins

> 2000). Prins and his students have tried to do this, despite their data sug-
> gesting resource partitioning was actually happening, which implies the use of
> resources at different times and places. We tried to see if wildlife and livestock
> used the same space, and if not was it because of interference?

Landis M: I just wanted to speak briefly on the high densities of wildlife in Manyara Ranch that MG referred to. They were very high, probably even higher
than she reported, as we were unable to count them all. And it is true that on
those same transects, as MG said, there were almost no cattle present. But we
need to be careful to not draw conclusions from this. First, wildlife (particularly
zebra and wildebeest) follow rainfall, and from what I recall, in late 2003 Manyara Ranch received better rain in *orkisirata* than other areas. This is common;
it is one of the reasons the ranch has always been an important grazing area
for us during *orkisirata*. However, now we are not allowed into the ranch with
our cattle without permission and then only during the dry season, **not** during
orkisirata. *He looks firmly over at the manager as he says this.* And it is normal that
during this time (October/November–December) there are many wildebeest
and zebra and they can even outnumber cattle, especially in Manyara Ranch,
but also in *Engusero* and *Lera*, where they graze together with cattle. There are
also lots of gazelle in all these places during this time, and they mix together
with the goats. This can be problematic though because there is a disease that
the goats can get from gazelles. At least it can be treated, not like the disease
that cattle can get from wildebeest. When the wildebeest give birth, in February or March, we need to keep cattle far away from them because of a disease
(malignant catarrhal fever, MCF) that is spread through the calves to cattle. It
is deadly and there is no cure. *He looks over at the chairman, who is picking other
people to speak next. He decides to end here and sits down.*

> *Note on predators:* In discussing wildlife-livestock compatibility, it is important
> to discuss predators. Predators can prey on livestock, wild herbivores can bring
> predators into communities, and predators introduce a difficult component
> to human-wildlife relations, which is necessary to pay attention to in order to
> maintain good "pro-conservation" relations (Woodroffe, Thirgood, and Rab-
> inowitz 2005; cf. Naughton-Treves, Grossberg, and Treves 2003).

Seuri OL: *An old elder, stands to speak. He is highly respected and liked by all for his
amiable and gentle character* [mpole]. *He was born here and is also respected for*

his in-depth knowledge of the area. He speaks calmly and slowly. It is true, what MG has said. There are many lions in the ranch now and they want to "to keep wildlife like buffalo, hyena, lion, elephant, and even rhino. These are all very dangerous animals. Will they live with people?" I had three donkeys killed by a lion from Manyara Ranch, and "the ranch says that I am unable to do anything. My cattle die, and they do not kill that lion.[56] [What can I say] when they prohibit us from entering the ranch and wildlife from the ranch leave and eat our cattle? We [Maasai] know the character of lions. If a lion eats cattle, it will keep eating cattle until you kill it. It will run to eat cattle until you kill it or you move. But this is not my problem alone. I cannot go and complain alone, because my donkeys could also die from the dry season. I cannot say anything. Today it is me; tomorrow it will be someone else. . . . This is everyone's problem."[57]

Landis Taeto: *Young but self-assured, he speaks confidently with a bit of defiance.* "Of course there are a lot of animals in Manyara Ranch. We agreed to let AWF manage it as a conservation area. But lions don't have boundaries. So if the lions are being 'kept' [*kufuga*] inside the ranch, fine. But if they come out and eat our cattle, is AWF ready to pay? They are not allowing *ilmurran* to kill lions, so are they ready to pay for cattle eaten by lions if we can't kill the lion?"[58]

Korianga LEK:[59] *Educated and the son of a wealthy herd owner, he is not shy and speaks loudly and clearly.* It is bad enough that we are not allowed to kill lions, but "when we hear that livestock are not allowed into conservation areas we get angry. Why not? Cattle are not also animals? What is wrong?" *He pauses and looks over at the* wataalamu *(experts) present representing conservation, the MR manager and Corbett. He continues.* "We say let livestock in [to the ranch] and we all will graze together. We can mix livestock and wildlife. We Maasai, we have no problems with wildlife being here. And now we also see that there are benefits to having wildlife for both villages, through wildlife tourism." *With this final statement he nods in the direction of Corbett, and there are many sounds of agreement around the crowd.*

Meshuki OK: *An old man born in this area, his respect has waned in recent years because of his heavy drinking. Yet when he is sober, like today, he can speak clearly, and people listen.* What the young man says is very true. "You can't divide cattle and wildlife. God [*Engai*] produced grass for the purpose of pasture for all of them. And all those that eat grass, eat that pasture. So it is not possible to separate them out. The only animals that don't eat grass are predators [*Olowaru*]." And, as has been discussed already, they can cause problems for cattle. "All other animals eat grass and God put forth grass so that they can all eat together."[60]

M. Voeten:[61] *A researcher from the Netherlands, she is a student of Dr. Prins. She conducted her PhD research in the area, looking at wildlife and livestock-grazing patterns and resource partitioning.* It is true that there is often a great deal of resource overlap between cattle and wildlife, particularly with wildebeest and zebra, which are the most dominant wildlife in this ecosystem. I conducted research in Lake Manyara and Tarangire National Parks, and in the Mto wa Mbu Game Controlled Area, of which I believe most of these two villages are a part. We found that there was a great deal of both habitat and dietary overlap between cattle and wildebeest and between cattle and zebra. That means that they like to graze in the same habitat (short grass plains) and eat the same plant species (e.g., *Sporobolous* and *Chloris* species). But . . . [*she pauses and looks around at the crowd a bit nervously*] . . . we believe that this means that there is a high **likelihood** of competition between wildlife and livestock, if not always present. Let me explain. A high degree of diet and habitat overlap between wildebeest, zebra, and cattle occurs in the wet season grazing areas in the Mto wa Mbu Game Controlled Area. Now, since the amount of high-quality pasture at this time is not limited, competition is not likely (Voeten and Prins 1999). In the wet season, "wildebeest, zebra and cattle use their food resource differently, thus accomplishing resource partitioning" [Voeten and Prins 1999, 292; cf. Bell 1971].[62] We found that wildebeest consistently selected for short grass swards, and zebra selected feeding sites with taller grass. Cattle, which are ruminants like wildebeest, and similar in body size, surprised us by feeding on taller grass. And in the dry season, when resources are scarce, many of the wildlife move back into the parks, so "we postulate that wildebeest and zebra, by moving to Lake Manyara NP, are able to **avoid** competition" [Voeten 1999, 125]. However, there is resource overlap between cattle and zebra in the early wet season and between cattle and wildebeest in the early dry season [Voeten and Prins 1999, 292]. These are both times which **could** result in resource limitations, as grasses are at the very beginning and very end of the growing stage. We therefore suggest that competition is possible at these times, **if** resources are limited. So, *she looks around nervously,* to return to the comments made by Mr. Peter, we must look at stocking rates. "Prins analysed stocking rates and energy requirements of livestock and wildlife and concluded that livestock competes with wildlife" [Prins 1992, 293].

Meshuki L:[63] It is true that "there can be competition between the animals during the first rains [*orkisirata*], when the grass is just starting to sprout and the water is just starting to collect." But they are not always in the same place at the same time, because like the scientist explained, they have their ways of separating out. For instance, "wildebeest graze in the morning, zebra too, and then they sleep in the afternoon and eat in the early evening and into the night. Zebra eat a lot, but they don't get full, but they don't finish the grass like wildebeest can! They also prefer different parts of the grass. For instance, zebra like all the grass, but they especially like the top of the [taller] grass. They like it here on top." *He motions with his hand to the top part of the long grass on the top of the* korongo *wall.* "Wildebeest like the short grass. Cattle like it all, but they especially like the shorter grass. They can all graze together because zebra can help to shorten the grass and make it available for the others. But then wildebeest can really finish the grass." Now wildebeest, if there is any competition, they are the ones to benefit. When they come out to the village pastures and give birth, no cattle can use that area until all the calf placentas are gone because of MCF![64] That can be a couple of months (e.g., February to April).

Landis OK: *Only a Landis junior elder, he is the son of a very respected and knowledgeable elder, and he holds a fairly high position in the village government. He is respected for both his "book smarts" and the knowledge "of home," which he receives from his father. He speaks knowledgeably but in a modest tone.* From what we see, wildebeest and zebra usually graze together, and they both eat a lot, finishing the grass because they eat in the night and in the day. They don't sleep. Cattle only eat during the day. Wildlife eat more because they eat day and night. When cattle are sleeping at home, wildlife are eating and drinking water. And when in the morning the cattle go to eat, the wildlife are still eating. When cattle go in the afternoon to drink water, the wildlife are still drinking. *He chuckles at this. Maasai around the crowd make noises of agreement, repeating bits of what he has said out loud.* And when the water in dams gets low, the wildlife keep drinking it and dirtying it up, even after cattle are no longer able to drink there. And even when we run out of water, sometimes they will stay in the village for the grass, especially in Oloyeti. For instance, "wildebeest can come here to eat grass, at night they will go to the park and drink water and then in the morning they will come back here."[65]

Makaa SK:[66] *A very wealthy man, he does not often speak at meetings, but when he does, he gets a lot of respect, mostly out of fear more than anything else. He speaks in a slightly arrogant tone.* It is true what the young elder has said; wildlife eat a lot because they eat day and night, especially zebra (just like donkeys, they are never full!). "Oosho! Ee pae!" *and other exclamations of agreement and dismay at the eating ability of donkeys and zebra, from the men and women.* Even wildebeest will eat at night. They can sleep starting at 9 a.m. until 4 p.m. (during the period when the sun is very hot) and then start eating again. If there are a lot of them, they can finish the grass so that cattle have none to eat. This often happens in *Ang'ata Olowarak*.

Landis M:[67] *Excitedly he starts to speak while he is getting up so as to not lose his chance.* I agree with what is being said. Even though there can sometimes be competition, it is also like Meshuki L explained, the different animals can help each other out in the pasture. For instance, elephants can break trees and make a big path where others (zebra, wildebeest) can go through to eat and see predators more easily. Zebra can see lions and run before wildebeest, so they help wildebeest to know that there is a lion nearby. Gazelles cannot enter places of tall grass, nor can wildebeest. But zebra can eat the grass until it is short, and then it can be eaten by gazelles. Wildlife can also open up an area until it becomes accessible to cattle. Wildlife, because they are out there [in the pasture] all the time, they usually eat first, and in so doing, open up the bush for cattle. Elephants come first [opening up the thick bush], then zebra, and then wildebeest, and then it is good for cattle. Other times, cattle can pass through a place that is *pori* because they are led by people. Like near the *korongo*, back in *Engusero*, or near dams, cattle go first and break open the bush, and then wildlife can enter. So yes, wildlife and livestock can help each other out. And they often graze in the same places, as long as there is water available, like the elder mentioned earlier.

This is not always visible though from the transect work that we did, that MG will discuss. This is because we started the transects early in the morning, except for the transect at *Lembiti*, which we always did in the afternoon, as an extension from the *Narok Sarng'arb* transect.[68] We did the transects in the morning so that we would observe wildlife, which go looking for shade in the afternoon sun. Yet cattle are rarely out that early in the morning. So, the transect data is a much better marker of where wildlife are than cattle. The exception is *Lembiti*, which was conducted in the afternoon and where we often counted a lot of cattle [see figure 20]. This is particularly the case when people in Esilalei were watering their cattle at *Embarimbali*, which is right at the end of the *Lembiti* transect and an important source of water in the dry season and in the early rains. On other transects, especially *Ang'ata Olowaru, Lera, Oremit, Simbi*, and *Bwawambili*, we would often see cattle as we were walking back from the transect. When we did see cattle on the transects, they were often very close to wildlife, particularly zebra and gazelles. If the herd boy wasn't paying attention, we would even see zebra mixed in with the cattle [see figure 9].

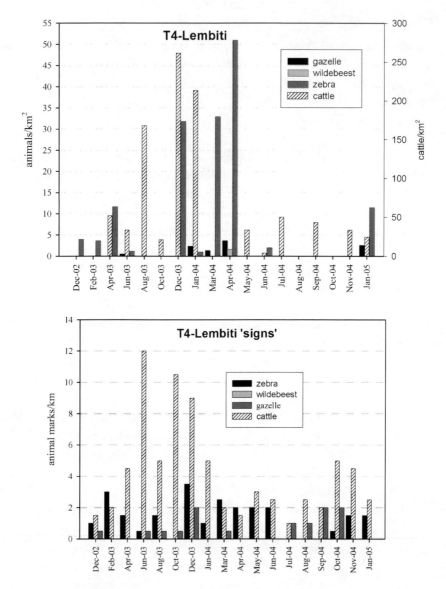

Figure 20 Wildlife and livestock in T4-*Lembiti* (mixed wooded/grass savanna) (a) density and (b) marks

MG: *The chairman looks at her, giving her the opportunity to follow up on what Landis M has said. She stands again to speak, holding on to the papers with the graphs and tables.* One of the ways that we tried to get an idea of pasture use more broadly was by recording marks (signs) of animal presence on the transect lines within the past couple of days. Looking at graphs of marks in comparison to graphs of sightings of the same transect, the distributions of wildlife and livestock seem more similar [see figures 21, 22, 5a, and 5b]. Looking at wildlife across the entire area, we can see some of the separation of wildlife and livestock in the dry season that was discussed by Voeten. Most wildlife leave the village in the middle of the dry season (June–October). Cattle numbers also decline at this time, although not as much. There is variation by transect though, with higher wildlife numbers during this time found in T6-*Bwawambili* [see figure 18] because of remaining water in the dams inside the MR, which are off-limits to village cattle, and T8-*Mlimani* [see figure 6], because of remaining water at *Oloturo*, and/or moving through the area on their way to water sources elsewhere.[69] *Lera* is also an important area during the dry season for both wildlife and livestock, but cattle use is not reflected in the graphs very well for the reasons mentioned by Landis M [but see figures 5a and 5b]. *Lera* is also one of the first places that cattle will go to during *orkisirata*, and this does appear in the graphs. So if we look at marks, we can see that wildlife and livestock are positively correlated [$r = 0.22990$ at a significance level of 0.01]. This is mostly related to gazelle [$r = 0.21850$ at the 0.05 significance level (see figure 14)]. Perhaps this is because gazelle, unlike wildebeest and zebra, are in the area for most of the year, with gazelle marks found across all months on some transects. *Sounds from Maasai around the circle of* "Oosho! ee pae! [of course!] They are always here."

So what does all this say for wildlife-livestock coexistence? It is complex. The transect data shows both spatial segregation and spatial overlap by transect [see maps 5 and 6], with more overlap with marks, which we didn't map. Variations in use can be related to regulations to access, poaching, and water. However, overlap or segregation in use does not tell us much about compatibility or competition. People have already been speaking a lot about that. Maybe there is more to say about this?

The meeting chairman takes this opportunity to speak and thereby try to steer the meeting.

MK O: We have talked a lot about the different areas that wildlife and livestock use for pasture and water. And a lot of different views have been expressed regarding the relationship between wildlife and livestock. Does anyone have anything

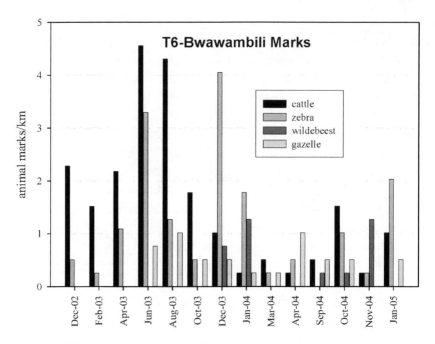

Figure 21 Wildlife and livestock marks (dung, prints)/km for T6-*Bwawambili* (wooded savanna, MR)

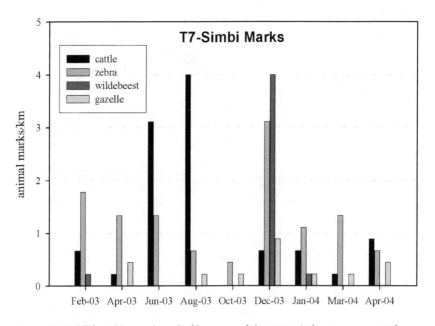

Figure 22 Wildlife and livestock marks (dung, prints) for T7-*Simbi* (grass savanna, MR)

else to say? We have not heard much from the women. *Before a woman has a chance to speak, an older man has stood and begun to talk.*

Seuri Elder: Wildlife and livestock can help each other. If wildlife are together with cattle in the pastures, they get help against lions (especially if there is an *ilmurran* herding and he has a spear!). The same at night, the wildlife come near our homes [*inkang'itie'*] to get protection from predators (*arripito*—they protect each other). Wildebeest help cattle because they know where rain is. It can rain at night without people seeing and then in the morning you see animals moving in a certain direction and so you follow them to bring the cattle there. It also works the other direction, because wildlife see cattle going to a certain place every day. Wildlife cannot know where good grass is, so they follow cattle. Wildlife have no herders, so they follow cattle. But not in the dry season, because cattle drink water from the wells [and wildlife need to be in places where there is water available]. Wildlife like places where there are people, because people are their protectors. Because lions are afraid of people, and lions are the enemies of these animals (herbivores) and they are also the enemy of livestock. So those animals, if it was not for people hunting them or chasing them away, they would stay near people and livestock. But people don't like to let this happen because the animals attract lions, which are also the enemy of livestock.

Koko Y:[70] *An old woman who was born here and knows the area very well, she is encouraged to speak by the other women. A widow and the village midwife, she is highly respected by men and women, though often laughed at for speaking in a sometimes incoherent way (in Maa and Swahili!).* Wildlife and livestock eat in one place, except when the wildebeest give birth; cattle are taken to a different place. Otherwise they are in the same place. They just pass by each other—cattle here, wildlife there, but one place. They don't necessarily compete, but cattle will drink more water than wildebeest because wildebeest are scared that they will be chased away by the herd boys, and they can go longer without water because they are used to dry country. On the other hand, after cattle stop using a water source (like a dam) because the water level is low and it has become too dirty, the wildlife will keep drinking the water until it is all gone. *Murmurs from the women about wildlife going for water. She continues.* They can also help each other with grazing. Like my brother here just said. It is usually the wildlife that open up bushed [*pori*] places, but in other places, like near the *korongo*, animals can't open it up except for cattle because they are led by people; then the wildebeest come in. But also, like the other elder mentioned, wildlife can help us find the rain. If you know that it has rained and then you see wildebeest running to a certain location, you think "Why?" Maybe grass has already grown there, and so you send warriors to look and then go back with the cattle.

Koko B: *She is even older than the previous woman. She is her older sister and has also lived here her whole life. She speaks loudly.* Wildebeest come near to the *enkang'* for grass. They can run away, and then the small calves (cattle) will follow them. If the elders know that the wildebeest are passing, or if they begin to pass near the *enkang'*, they will tell the youth to push the calves to the other side so that they won't be lost into the herd of wildebeest. If they go, that is it! They are lost. They will enter the middle of the wildebeest herd and not be able to leave, will just be pushed along with them. To try to go after them is fruitless, as you won't be able to catch them. *She uses her arms to show that you get so far, and then the wildebeest pass here (a bit in front) and then you reach here, but the wildebeest are there—they will always remain a bit in front.* When I was a child, we would get beaten if cattle were lost to the wildebeest. Because they can end up far, far away and then they are lost for good and they will die.[71] *Laughter among the women and then chatter among people around the circle sharing similar stories.*

Landis LW:[72] *A young Landis, he is not usually around, off in the cities looking for work. He grew up here, herding cattle. He is political and brash, speaking nonchalantly.* We are just talking in circles. Of course wildlife are near our homes, in the pasture, they are near Maasai. "If you see animals, Maasai are not far. If you see cattle, animals (wildlife) are not far. They are both things of the wild (*pori*)." Tourists know that. Tourists come to Tanzania to see two things—wildlife and Maasai. We, Maasai, just need to learn how to start profiting from it now!

Landis M: *A Maasai, he is not from this area, but is well known as he is a veterinarian from Simanjiro, which is within the TME. He has been attending meetings as a part of a larger project looking at different socioeconomic dynamics in several Maasai-wildlife systems in Tanzania and Kenya. He is working for ILRI, as a representative of the TME ecosystem and knows the issues being discussed very well. He kindly requests permission from the chairman to speak.* I am very happy to hear all the things being discussed today. It is important to discuss these issues openly and with each other. *He nods in the direction of Dr. Reid and Manyara Ranch/AWF personnel and then back toward the Maasai circled around him.* Too often, we are having parallel conversations and are not speaking to each other. There has been more recognition lately by the conservation community of the compatibility of Maasai pastoralism with wildlife conservation and the need to support it. Yet sometimes the partnerships that are created remain very focused on wildlife, as often reflected in the titles of the projects such as the Simanjiro wildlife forum. If it is really about wildlife **and** livestock, why not call it the Simanjiro pastoralist forum? There has been some improvement though. For instance, the Tanzanian wildlife forum is now called the Tanzanian Natural Resource Forum (TNRF), and the steering committee is full of Maasai! This is because we cannot look at wildlife in isolation anymore. However, nor can we look at pastoralism in isolation. The different contributions today have talked about different kinds of wildlife-livestock relations, as well as the ways in which things are changing. There are farms today and there is less grazing land available, and the boundaries with the parks have become "hard," with farming and guards at the boarders. Wildlife tourism is also becoming an important source of income for Maasai, if they are involved [Kristjanson et al. 2002; Thompson and Homewood 2002]. But to separate out a place that is for wildlife only, as Corbett has suggested for his camp, is not feasible. In Simanjiro we are even suggesting a vaccination against the MCF virus. Long ago it worked well to separate out wildebeest and cattle, but today there is no space available for this to continue to happen. And as we have heard today, wildlife and livestock can coexist. The grazing succession that the researcher Voeten has discussed and which others referred to includes livestock as well. We have heard that today, and we have heard it from people in Kenya for a long time now. David Western explained that in the Amboseli swamps Maasai enter after elephant and buffalo have "improved the structure for cattle," who in turn "improve the vegetation (through grazing) for smaller stock (shoats)" [Western 1982, 195]. He has also shown how livestock and elephants impact the environment in different ways, in ways that work together, something we Maasai have known for a long time. In Western's words, elephants and livestock transform the habitat in ways "inimical to their own survival but beneficial to each other, they create an unstable interplay," that Maasai note when we say, "cows grow trees, elephants grow grasslands" [Western 1997, 229].

In fact, studies in Kenya have shown that integrated livestock-wildlife systems are more productive than either livestock or wildlife systems alone [Western 1989]. My colleagues in Kenya, like Dr. Reid who has already spoken, assert that conservation policies that exclude low to moderate levels of traditional pastoral use such as grazing and burning, may actually impoverish the very lands they were designed to protect [Reid et al. 2003, 129; see also Western and Gichohi 1993]. Yet again, the study in Maasai Mara did find that there are certain species "that are best conserved in places with no people and no livestock (rhino, eland, most carnivores)" [Reid et al. 2003]. This corresponds with what MG was discussing earlier in terms of the lions and eland in the Manyara Ranch. But MG also touched on the importance of good relations. Maasai can handle predators, and can even hold back the *ilmurran* from killing lions, **if** they see the reason for doing so [Goldman, de Pinho, and Perry 2013]. This has been clearly displayed in Amboseli over the years [Western 1997]. At first Maasai *ilmurran* speared entire prides of lions in protest of their removal from the park without benefits and lack of compensation to lion predation. However, when the park became "theirs" for a short while, the elders kept the *ilmurran* from killing lions, and even poaching declined dramatically. So Maasai-wildlife compatibility is not just about wildlife-livestock coexistence, but people and wildlife coexistence.

Coexistence, therefore, is dependent on good management. The study in Maasai Mara by my colleagues at ILRI found that as the number of *inkang'itie* increases or the distribution changes, there will likely be consequences for wildlife. They talked about "a density of bomas ideal for promoting abundant species-rich wildlife; any increase or reduction in the number of bomas may decrease the number of wildlife" [Reid et al. 2004, 129–30; see also Reid 2012]. But this kind of research has not been forthcoming in Tanzania. That is why this meeting today is so important. Coexistence of Maasai and wildlife **is possible**, but it is not a guarantee. It is important to bring in the kind of tourism venture that Corbett is starting, and along with it development for livestock—like the dam, but also dips and better veterinary care. And to have the elders keep the herd boys from bothering wildlife! However, it is also important to manage the land **as a whole** for wildlife and livestock. What good will the Manyara Ranch be if all the wildlife come to the village to graze? If the entire area is managed as one, then all the animals will be better off—wildlife and livestock. Well, I have spoken enough. Thank you again for letting me be a part of this meeting today.[73]

Chairman O: *He stands proudly, grinning, taking responsibility for the success of the meeting. He speaks confidently.* So can we all agree that the dam should be built together with the campsite? We will need to monitor change and continue our discussions with MR regarding grazing inside the ranch if wildlife numbers increase in village lands. The transect work that we have decided to continue to conduct will help us to detect changes in wildlife numbers after the dam is constructed. That is one of the reasons we have agreed to the transects. We have our knowledge of where the wildlife are at different times, and changes in their numbers. But sometimes our words are not taken as seriously as those of the *wataalamu*. These transect data will help us to speak together. At the same time, we need to make sure that wildlife provide benefits for us. "We can now start to see wildlife like our cousins . . . we can start to drink their milk."[74] Are we all in agreement?

Conclusion

My goal in this chapter was not to propose a definitive conclusion on wildlife-livestock coexistence versus competition, or the ways in which herders impact the range with their livestock. My intent was rather to suggest that the situation is complex and multiple, related to many factors often excluded from traditional social and ecological scientific methods, such as land-use histories, changing grazing practices, rainfall histories, soil type, Indigenous knowledge, livestock management, conservation management, and the politics of land grabs and knowledge production. Many of these factors do not even come into the picture without talking to the very people who use the landscape in question and providing the space for them to talk about wildlife and livestock on their terms.

My intent was also to look at boundaries in a critical way—where and how they are drawn, with what impacts on the ground, and how we structure research questions. For Maasai, animals are animals, though wildlife are often positioned differently for political as well as cultural and ecological reasons. Yet the boundary between domestic and wild is not a firm one, it can shift in time and space. What would it mean for social and ecological methods if we made this ontological shift and started our research and planning conversations by just talking about "animals?" And what would it mean to approach the boundaries that now exist in a more nuanced way—not taking them for granted but seeing them as ongoing processes of becoming, between Maasai, animals of all kinds, conservation policies, and land-use change? And finally, my goal was to show that moving beyond standard methods to maintain nuance, complexity, and multiplicity is the only way to move beyond simplified models of wildlife-livestock interactions and conservation versus development debates. This is not an innocent exercise. The policy ramifications have immediate and long-term impacts for people and wildlife, as discussed a bit more in the next chapter, which takes us once more out of the *enkiguena* to historically situate the boundary-making processes of conservation in this space, in contrast to Maasai orderings of space, people, and what we have come to call "nature." We then return to current policy discussions in the final *enkiguena* agenda in chapter 5 on conservation corridors.

| Interlude II |

The Lost Calf

THERE WAS A Maasai man who had a large herd of cattle, around seven hundred in total.[1] One day a young calf was at home waiting for the mama cow
to come back from grazing to milk. Meanwhile, a herd of wildebeest came
by making their noises (sound of grunts of wildebeest on the move). The small calf,
waiting for its mother to come home was confused and followed the wildebeest. He
followed the wildebeest herd for three days over a huge distance. He was, however,
still a young calf, and soon became tired and hungry, with no mother to milk and too
young to eat grass. He lay down to sleep, and the wildebeest didn't care; they just left
him there and moved on.

A herder was out with his cattle and came across the lost calf. He picked him up
and brought him home and nursed him back to health, allowing him to milk off one
of his own cows. The calf grew to be a great bull and helped the herder to increase his
herd by mounting many of the females and producing many new calves.

Then one day the original herder was traveling and stopped at this *enkang'* to spend
the night. In the evening he stood with the herder and watched the cattle come in from
the day of grazing. As the lost bull passed him, he noticed that he seemed familiar, as
did many other much younger members of the herd, the offspring of the original lost
bull. "I say," proclaimed the man, "this bull seems so familiar to me, like he is one of
our bulls. Where did you get him from?" "Oh this bull goes way back in our family,"
lied the herder, "back to my grandfather. They know where he originally came from,

but I don't. He is just ours from long ago." "OK," said the visitor reluctantly, and they went on with their evening.

This bull, however, made a very particular sound when it was mating. Every time he mounted a female, he cried out with a strange, low grunting sound. When the visitor heard this sound, he was stunned. "I know that sound," he said to himself. "That sound is of my cattle." All night long he could not sleep and was woken in a surprised state every time he heard the bull mating. The next morning, he approached the herder again, asking about the origins of this bull. "I ask you to be honest," he told the herder. "Where did this bull come from?" Surprised at his visitor's persistence, and getting angry, the herder again told his visitor that this bull was from way back in their family and that his grandfathers know about his seeds [origin], not him. But the visitor was not convinced. He explained about the sounds that the bull made while mating and that he knew that those seeds were somehow his. He remembered then and explained to the herder that long ago a young calf was lost, and that he believed that this was in fact that calf. The herder refused to listen and denied everything. So the visitor went to talk to the elders, and a meeting was held. A meeting, another meeting, a meeting, on and on. Finally, the *olaigwenani* said that he wanted to end a meeting and postpone it for another day; he asked everyone except his fellow *ilaigwenak* to leave. He then instructed the *ilaigwenak*. "The medicine for these two men," he explained, "is as follows. We will send them off tomorrow during the meeting to different locations," he explained. He then assigned different elders to hide out in the two different places where the two feuding men were to be sent. He instructed the elders that they needed to remain hidden from the men and had them agree to his plan. It was certain that the men would talk out loud when they were alone, and the truth would be discovered.

The final meeting was held. The *olaigwenani* announced that they were ready to make their decision but that they needed to talk among themselves first. He asked the two arguing members to leave, for one to go over to that tree and the other over to that tree. He explained that they were likely to argue if they were together, and so this was why he was separating them. The herder who denied finding the bull sat under his tree and spoke his thoughts out load. "This man is clever, where did he come from? He must have gone to a really powerful *oloiboni* to find his bull. Why can't he just die tonight, and tomorrow we bury him? If they favor him, he will not just take that bull, but he will take so many of my cows, all the ones fathered by him, oh I say, this man!"

Meanwhile the initial herder sat under his tree and talked to himself. "That cow is mine, and I am certain of it. When he was born there was a problem in the birth, and we had to burn with fire the end of the umbilical cord. I bet that scar is still there; if they would let me look, I could prove that that bull is mine."

The meeting was reconvened. The *olaigwenani* asked his fellow elders for assistance: What did they think should be done? He called first on the elder who was hidden out by the tree where the herder who found the calf was. The elder explained what he heard. "Do you have anything to say to that?" the *olaigwenani* asked the man. "No," he said. The *olaigwenani* then asked the elder who had been hidden out by the other man's tree what he thought, and he repeated what he had heard. "OK," said the *olaigwenani*, "it looks like this calf belongs to you, but we need to check first if it is true that there is a scar still on the bull. If not, then you will not be able to take the bull." The man enthusiastically agreed, and they checked the bull and found the scar. The man took his bull back, along with two hundred cattle, all of which had been birthed with the seeds of this bull. Had the man who found the original calf not lied and deceived him, he would only have taken the bull and one or two milking cows. However, because the man refused to tell him the truth even when he had discovered it on his own, he took all that he saw as rightfully his as being the seeds of his cow.

This story was told to me to illustrate how well Maasai know their cattle. But it also tells us something about Maasai ontologies of nature and society, or how "wild" and "domestic" are conceptualized. Cattle are domestic not because they are controlled and managed, as in the Western sense, but because they have an intimate relationship with people. The man *knew* his calf personally and was emotionally affected by the sight and sound of "one of his own." Yet at the same time, when he wasn't watching, his calf took off with wildlife, which he had mistaken for his own.

Chapter 4

Bounding Nature and
Reorganizing Maasailand

Today even the wind has changed. The country has changed. . . . Everybody asks why did you come to this place? Long ago, we moved like the wildebeest. [But today,] people have gone to Maromboi and been taken by the police; it has become a park.[1]

There were a lot of pastures long ago, but they are no longer used because people were shrewd/cunning [Swahili: *ujanja*] in the way that they took [the land]. Like in the dry season we would use the area of Mto wa Mbu, a place with springs, but now? It has been taken by farms. And Manyara Ranch was taken [by conservation].[2]

BOUNDARIES OF VARIOUS KINDS have been enacted, challenged, negotiated, and crossed, by individuals, groups, and phenomena that helped to create the categories we find today—including "Maasailand," "conservation areas," and administrative villages, districts, and regions. While some of these boundaries were introduced in chapter 2, here I very briefly outline the historic and contested ways they have been enacted, challenged, and appropriated—between groups of people and between people and what has been defined as "nature." This review is brief, as these stories have been well covered in the literature.[3]

Reorganizing and Dividing Maasailand

The particular spatial demarcations—historic and contemporary—referred to as "Maasailand" must be seen in light of a series of historic and ongoing processes that include: attempts by various Maa-speaking groups to gain access to and control over resources after a set of devastating ecological disasters in the late nineteenth century;[4] colonial attempts to contain Maasai as a people while alienating much of their land for farms and conservation; state attempts to control land and promote development;

and ongoing attempts by individuals and organizations to claim rights to and influence over an area coveted by conservation agencies and farmers. I begin my review with colonialism.

In 1905, in what is now the United Republic of Tanzania, the German colonial regime (in control from 1884 to 1919) moved Maasai to a reserve south of the Arusha-Moshi Road (Fosbrooke 1948, 10–11), allocating the remaining territory to white settlers. Similar, if more drastic, events occurred in Kenya in the 1900s where Maasai were moved at gunpoint into two reserves, freeing up valuable grazing resources for white settlers, many of whom remain today in the Laikipia plains (Hughes 2006). The reserves were designed by the colonial regimes to create and maintain categories of control—Maasai as a people, and Maasailand as a place (Hodgson 2001).

In 1919, after World War I, when Britain took over Tanganyika as a protectorate under the League of Nations, they found that Maasai were not restricted by the reserve boundary but had spread throughout the protectorate. In line with their policies of indirect rule, the British confined people into distinct categories—"tribes"—"then placed these tribes within demarcated, controllable spaces" (Hodgson 2001, 49), each with its own set of "customary leaders." Despite British recognition of Maasai having a decentralized leadership structure, they created the Masai Native Authority (also called the Masai Council, or *Olkiama* in Maa), comprised of elder men from different areas, headed by the "Laibon" (*oloiboni kitok*), a spiritual leader for an entire section [*olosho*], whom colonial administrations misinterpreted as a "chief" (Spencer and Waller 2017). Boundaries of the "Maasai Reserve" were strictly enforced, with Maasai found outside fined ten heifers (Ndagala 1992). In 1926, the Maasai Reserve was renamed Maasai District. Although the reserve was 63,000 km², it did not provide adequate water and pasture resources, and could not contain Maasai mobility—which continued to follow *olosho* and *enkutoto* delineations, as well as long-distance networks within and external to Maasai society.

With independence in 1961, tribal identities that formed the basis of colonial rule and sociospatial organization were discouraged, and Tanzanians were persuaded to adopt a national identity. Tribal reserves were abolished, and Maasai District opened for settlement. As a result, many agricultural groups, also displaced by the British, began to seek land in Maasai areas. The Maa-speaking Waarusha in particular, previously excluded from Maasailand by British tribal distinctions, were now able to call on kinship, clan, and age-set relations within Maasai communities to access land (Spear 1997). Independent Tanzania adopted the British legal framework regarding land, which worked against pastoralist land rights, knowledge systems, and management regimes. Formerly held in "trusteeship" by the colonial governor, land was now held by the Tanzanian president. Customary land rights associated with common-property management of rangelands, were formally recognized as "rights of occupancy," but systematically disregarded by the federal government (Shivji 1998a), particularly when left vacant (seen as "unused") for much of the year, as was often the case with pastoralists.

The governing ideology of the newly independent Tanzanian state was defined by the first president, Julius Nyerere, as *Ujamaa*, a Swahili word that roughly translates as "familyhood" or community. Despite its romantic appeal to traditional African societies, *Ujamaa* policies reinforced the value of modern science and development techniques (Nyerere 1968). In Maasailand this meant the promotion of modern range management and the reorganization of space into smaller and smaller managerial units, beginning with the 1964 Range Management and Development Act, which demarcated Maasai District into twenty-two Ranching Associations (Ndagala 1992, 71).[5]

In 1974, Ranching Associations gave way to villages with the passage of the National Villages and Ujamaa Villages Act, which stated that all Tanzanians were to live in "proper" *Ujamaa* villages (Jacobs 1980, 8). Through this process, known as villagization, rural communities were resettled into proper villages with a village center, where social services could be provided and residential units clustered. Villagization became known in Maasailand as "operation *imparnati*," meaning permanent residence (Ndagala 1992, 29). Villagization eventually increased land alienation and introduced new boundaries, modes of organization, and leadership through elected and appointed government positions. Valuable grazing areas peripheral to village centers were targeted for subsistence agriculture by outsiders. Land was also alienated for large-scale parastatal farms and ranching operations, including the Manyara Ranch (Igoe 2000).

By the mid-1980s, Tanzania officially abandoned the *Ujamaa* governance system and embarked on economic and political liberalization. This began a new period in Tanzanian history, with a focus on a "liberalized" economy (i.e., deregulated markets, increased foreign investment), while "democratized" politics ushered in multiparty elections and the rapid proliferation of NGOs. The private appropriation of Maasai land for farms accelerated, and large government parastatals (including the Manyara Ranch) were dismantled. Tracts of land were leased to private companies for export cash crop production, and agricultural development projects were initiated through donor funds. Well-connected government officials parceled up government ranches into smallholdings, and land seen as unused was proposed for the resettlement of landless peasants in overcrowded areas (Igoe and Brockington 1999). Ironically, the promotion of village land titling, which started with villagization and only accelerated during economic liberalization, provided the mechanism for continued land loss during this period, as land left unregistered and not in "use" could be confiscated by the government. Land titles also provided the means for corrupt government officials to lease village land to outsiders.

> **Note on the land law:** In the 1990s widespread concern over unjust land appro-
> priations led to a national review of land laws (Shivji 1998b) and eventually to
> land reform (Wiley 2003), culminating in two major land bills in 1999: the Land
> Act and the Village Land Act. While "ownership" of all land remained with the
> president, individuals, villages, and companies could now obtain legal rights of
> occupancy and use, in theory supporting customary tenure (United Repub-
> lic of Tanzania [URT] 1999a). Formal processes were put in place for village
> governments and land committees to secure property titles for village land,
> allocate land to village members (and outsiders), and resolve land disputes
> (United Republic of Tanzania [URT] 1999b). In order to distribute land titles,
> village governments need to *formalize boundaries*, build a land office, create
> land-use plans, and demonstrate "use" of all village lands.[6] Lands not in active
> "use" can still be appropriated by the state and reallocated for other uses or
> people. The new land laws do not help to support customary management
> and continue to reinforce the power of the state, but the land title remains the
> primary means through which rights and security are sought.

Maasai villages and activists alike have promoted individual and village land titles to protect their land. In some places, fear of land appropriation by outsiders has led to the division of village lands into individual plots. Activists have promoted land titles as a means of securing land rights—either for collective-village control or at the household level for women (Goldman, Davis, and Little 2016). This parceling up of land into manageable, legible categories has reordered social relations while continuing to chip away at Maasailand. Until 1974, "Maasailand" was entirely con-stituted by Maasai District, the largest administrative district in Tanzania (Ndagala 1992), entirely within Arusha Region. It has since been subdivided into five districts: Longido, Monduli, Ngorongoro, Simanjiro, and Kiteto, which now stretch over two regions (Arusha and Manyara).

Within villages, zone-based land-use planning has been promoted (by state agen-cies, conservation and development NGOs), which in pastoral areas has meant divid-ing village lands into wet season grazing, dry season grazing, and "village center" zones (Oikos 2002a; Hodgson and Schroeder 2002). Zone-based planning can be problematic for Maasai, who historically organized grazing at the level of *enkutoto*, which encompassed many villages and was estimated in the 1960s to cover, on average, 500–800 km² (Jacobs 1965, 174). Additionally, *inkutot* boundaries overlapped to assure territorial "spillover" during emergency times. With the village as a discrete unit, this flexibility has been lost, particularly as zone-based planning is required for a village to receive a land title and to then engage with outside investors, who often seek wildlife-only zones.[7] Villages with land titles can lease land to outside investors for conservation purposes (i.e., exclusive safari zones, camp/hotel sites; see Gardner 2016) or they can be coerced into creating the "Authorized Association" needed for the creation of a wildlife management area (WMA), that might include several villages (Benjaminsen et al. 2013; Igoe and Croucher 2007). Outside entities can obtain a land title for conservation purposes on land otherwise claimed by villages (but untitled)—as occurred with the Manyara Ranch. Legal codes (both land and conservation laws) have only facilitated these processes, which continue to divide and fracture Maasailand while drawing hard boundaries around what is considered nature and society.

Bounding Nature?

People sit in Arusha and Dar and partition up our land? This is a reminder of the Berlin meeting, dividing up Africa. This is not correct. They need to come to the village and make decisions together with the village under the direction of the village government land-use planning [committee].

—MAASAI JUNIOR ELDER, AUGUST 7, 2008

Historically, Maasai did not draw strict boundaries around wild and domestic, nature and society, but maintained intimate links with "the environment" through everyday practices and ritual events. According to Hodgson's historical analysis, "Nature and its elements were understood as manifestations of *Eng'ai* [God] or expressions of Her will, and therefore central to Maasai religious beliefs and practices" (Hodgson 2005, 25).[8] These links were particularly clear in the spiritual qualities associated with grass, used as a sign of peace, welcome, and blessing. Trees and shrubs were also associated with *Eng'ai*, referred to as *olcani* (sg.) which is also the Maasai word for medicine, or *ilkeek* for plural, also the word for firewood. The bark, leaves, and roots of trees continue to be used by Maasai today to treat multiple ailments, give strength, get rid of afterbirth, purge, serve as a toothbrush, clean calabashes, and make rope. The ficus tree (Maa: *oreteti*), is particularly associated with *Eng'ai*, and often the site of spiritual delegations of women.

Many of these associations continue today, with places in the landscape often named for the dominant or most important tree, and "wilderness" or wild spaces seen as relative, malleable, changing in time and space, and never entirely separate from humans and their everyday activities. *Entim* and *osero* are probably the closest approximations for the English words "wilderness" and "bush" and the Swahili word *pori*. *Entim* refers to bushed-forested areas and *osero* to overgrown areas of grass/ bush. While *entim* and *osero* are not always desired places, for people or cattle, they are entered, utilized, and in the process transformed and reshaped by the mediating factors of Maasai, livestock, rainfall, and fire. Women enter *entim* and *osero* in search of grass (for the roofs of their houses), water, *olcani*, and firewood, and in the process thin out and reduce "the bush" whether *entim* or *esero*. The distinction of a place as *entim* changes with time. Wooded or scrub savannas, recognized as *osero* or *entim*, can be heavily grazed or browsed, and by the end of the dry season nearly bare and thus no longer "wild" bush. After the big rains such areas can become *entim* or *osero* again. This shift into and out of states of *entim/osero* suggests that the boundary is flexible and porous. Human interventions—fire and grazing—prevent a grazing area from becoming *osero*, while restrictions on human activities (e.g., tree felling and farming) are used to maintain forested areas as *entim*, which can continue to supply firewood, *olcani*, food, and shade for livestock and wildlife, and help bring the rain.

Even the boundary between areas that Maasai mark as home space is far from discrete. The *enkang'* is usually enclosed with a thorn fence (*esita*), which is left open during the day and closed off at night by a large thorn branch, called *oltim*. Arhem (1985, 79, note 8) defines *oltim* as "the protector," in that it closes off the *enkang'* from the unknown wild nature of the night. Yet the literal translation of *oltim* is quite differ-ent. *Oltim* is the male version of the female word *entim*. In Maa, feminine words often connote the unknowable. In this case, *entim* is the forest/bush/wilds (of unknown size and contents), "that is out there, far from the *enkang'*." *Oltim* is a large thorn branch that is known; it is "like a piece of *entim*, it is just right here, close to the *enk-ang'*."[9] It is the women's job to place the *oltim* branch on both the cattle kraal and the *enkang'* fence (*esita*), and while it is meant to create a barrier between the *enkang'* and the unknown outside, it does not always work.[10] Predators get through the *oltim* and the *esita* and kill livestock. Yet the immediate area just surrounding the homestead is not considered *entim* or *osero*; it is called *auluo* (cf. Arhem 1985), an *in-between space*, "neither home nor *pori*, but in between."[11] Such in-between spaces are important for ritual events and connote a gradual and shifting boundary between what is considered "home" and "the bush."

In a similar way, Maasai will even characterize their cattle and themselves as occupying a middle ground between wild and domestic. This is illustrated with *orpul* rituals, where Maasai *ilmurran* go into *entim* for several weeks to regain their strength and health for the coming dry season. As such, they go into "the wild" to prepare for their "domestic" duties, particularly herding livestock long distances. At *orpul*, *ilmurran* eat copious amounts of meat and drink soups made with *olcani*—that give them strength and keep them healthy but can also make them "go wild" like lions. Maasai will often say that wildlife are of the bush, but so are they.

> Anything that is out here in the bush [*entim*] is *ing'uesi* (sg. *eng'ues*)—buffalo, elephant, monster (*olkukun*). There used to be Maasai *ilmurran* that would go to the bush to eat meat [*orpul*] and then would not want to go back home again, so they would stay in the bush, steal cattle from Maasai and become monsters. They would eat wildlife, have no clothes, and live in the mountains, long ago.[12]

This shifting boundary between "wild" and "domestic" is also seen in the ways in which Maasai categorize animals. When talking about how animals were grouped, I was told that animals were all considered one group, and then further breakdowns were made. Sometimes the first breakdown was into domestic and wild animals, but other times cattle were kept together with wildlife, placed within the appropriate groupings. The first breakdown was usually into *ing'uesi* and *ilcang'it*—harmful and harmless animals (see appendix).[13] In one group interview I was told that sometimes cattle fit both categories "because even a cow, when it gives birth, is very dangerous and therefore like (*ing'uesi*). God [just] came to give these animals to people to care for."

There is a Maasai story that is often told about the origin of wildlife:

> Long ago wild animals used to be women's cattle. Then, one morning before the cattle were taken out to graze, a cow was slaughtered. Soon the cattle started moving away to graze by themselves and wandered off. One woman told one of the children to go and drive the cattle back before they went too far. When the child's mother heard this, she said: "My child is not going until he has eaten the kidney." It followed that whenever a child was asked to go, his mother forbade him to go until he had had a bite of the meat. This went on until all the cattle, sheep, and goats wandered away into the bush and got lost. When all the children had eaten the meat, they tried to bring the cattle

back, but they found that they had all gone wild. And so that is how it came about that women lost their cattle.[14]

This story is often cited to show the gendered nature of cattle ownership and the reasons women do not have control over cattle today (Kipury 1983, 32; Hodgson 2001). Yet it also tells us much more. It shows that in the beginning wildlife and cattle *were one*, and the places of wildlife and the places of cattle were the same. Wildlife were seen as part of *Enkai's* creation, just like people and livestock (Hodgson 2005; Roque de Pinho 2009), with some herbivores called the "cattle of God" (*inkishu eEnkai*) and the "goats of God" (*enkinej eEnkai*) (Mol 1981). As "manifestations of *Enkai*," wildlife were not historically hunted, except for the ritual hunting of lions by *ilmurran*. Yet even then, lion hunting was seen as part of regulating *relations* between wildlife and people, teaching the lions to respect/fear *ilmurran* and keeping them from preying on cattle (Goldman, de Pinho, and Perry 2013). Stories still circulate about particular lions protecting women and children from other predators or less polite lions (Goldman, Roque de Pinho, and Perry 2010; Roque de Pinho 2009). Maasai often voiced their frustration to me about outside attempts to separate out the places of wildlife from the places of cattle and people. But these boundaries have worked to create new categories for many, who now often refer to wildlife as the livestock of "the state" or of the "Manyara Ranch" and are more inclined to kill lions in political protest, particularly when they cross these boundaries and prey on their livestock (Goldman, de Pinho, and Perry 2013).

ENCLOSING EDEN

Just as the German (1884–1919) and then the British (1919–61) colonial powers sought to contain and control Maasai in reserves, so they sought to contain nature—by bounding it in space—at first for controlled exploitation through hunting and later for conservation and tourism. Such containments relied on boundary-drawing practices to create spatial and ideological configurations of inclusion and exclusion. Practices that the independent Tanzanian state continued apace, all the while supported financially, structurally, and ideologically by international conservation organizations based in the United States and Europe (Bonner 1993). These boundary enactment practices have always been, and continue to be, contested and challenged by Maasai residents and activists, as well as by wildlife and ecological processes. In this section, I provide a broad sketch of these historic and ongoing boundary enactments that seek to separate nature from people, particularly in the study area.

During the colonial era, wildlife legislation acted to protect game animals and ensure hunting as a "socially exclusive pleasure pursuit" by a privileged few: white hunters granted licenses (Beinhart 1987, 16). By the 1930s, however, the tide was changing globally. Overhunting of at-risk species (e.g., rhinoceros), combined with a growing preservationist trend in the United States and Europe, led to pressure from outside the colonies to preserve nature in national parks. The emerging view, stemming from U.S. conservation policy, aimed at preventing all hunting and human habitation inside designated areas to preserve "wild" nature. Such goals were solidified at the London Convention for the Protection of Flora and Fauna of Africa, held in 1933. All European powers sent representatives to sign the agreement, which obligated them to investigate the possibilities of establishing national parks, free of human occupation, in their respective colonies. In 1940 Serengeti became the first national park in British Colonial Africa, with Maasai initially allowed in, but eventually expelled from it, to protect "pristine nature" (Shetler 2007; Neumann 1995b).

Large tracts of land have steadily been taken out of Maasai use for the creation of conservation areas ever since. With independence, after losing access to Serengeti and Lake Manyara National Parks,[15] Maasai faced eviction in Tarangire National Park (1970), Mkomazi Game Reserve (1988/89), and increased restrictions and threats of eviction in Ngorongoro (see table 7).[16] Maasai just outside of Serengeti, in Loliondo Division, continue to be subjected to ongoing attempts to restrict their access to land, which they have official village titles to, for international elite tourism and hunting (Gardner 2016b). As early as 1989, a Maasai member of parliament, Moringe ole Parkipuny, outlined attempts to capture more of Maasai land on the periphery of protected areas—including this proposed "corridor" in Loliondo, the expansion of LMNP, and a new conservation area in Simanjiro to "cushion" TNP (Parkipuny 1989, 11).

While there was no official expansion of LMNP, forest reserves were established along the park, and Lake Burunge WMA was created on village lands to the southeast; Randilen WMA was created on the northeastern side of Tarangire

Table 7 Protected areas in Maasailand

Park/Reserve	Date of creation; evictions	Area/km²
Serengeti NP	1951; people evicted in 1958	14,763
Ngorongoro Conservation Area	1959; Maasai evicted from crater in 1974	8,292
Lake Manyara NP	1960	325
Tarangire NP	1957; people evicted in 1970	2,600
Mkomazi GR	1951; people evicted in 1988/89	3,726

National Park; a new conservation area was proposed (and resisted) in Simanjiro; and Manyara Ranch became a new conservation area in 2001. Although hailed as "community-based," these latest conservation interventions have all involved a combination of evictions and land-use restrictions.[17] In doing so they enact the same stories used to remove Maasai from Serengeti in colonial times, stories that separate nature from society and portray Africans as misusing the environment (through overgrazing, farming, hunting, burning) (Brockington 2002; Adams and McShane 1992). The history of the creation of Manyara Ranch is particularly important for the study area.

According to local elders, there used to be Maasai homesteads inside the ranch, which was part of what became Esilalei Village. They were located near the current headquarters but were abandoned in the 1930s because of an increase in tsetse flies. Shortly thereafter, an *mzungu* man named Farab came to request the land from the elders. He was a herder and requested an area to graze his cattle. Since Maasai were not regularly grazing there, the elders agreed to let him "have" that land; they were not aware that by doing so they were giving up the land for good. For Maasai, land was a not a discrete object separate from its use. The following words from an elder born in the area, sum up this dispossession process:

> Farab came to request the land. There were only two *in-kang'itie* then. We were going to this *pori* [bush/wild] area only for *orpul* [meat feasts], because of the tsetse flies.... So we told them OK, take this area and reduce the tsetse flies. We didn't write anything or get any money. [And then] people started to increase.... We started to need this area more, but we saw that we can't go in there because they put a border up.

The border never stopped Maasai from accessing important resources inside the ranch. According to elders, throughout the various ownerships (to George Dam in 1965, then the National Ranching Company [NARCO] in 1974), they maintained rights to access certain locations for water, *orpul*, and prayer. And although it was often forbidden, Maasai *never* stopped grazing inside the ranch, often taking livestock in at night at the risk of being fined and beaten. As one elder responded to the question of how long he had been grazing in Manyara Ranch:

> Since a long time ago. Since we were *ilmurran*. We were bothered by the *wazungu*, and by the government, [we were] thrown in jail, had our cattle confiscated, but we would beg to be forgiven and we'd return. They don't permit us even now, but we steal [pasture].

Maasai in Oltukai and Esilalei insist that they wanted to use the Manyara Ranch for dry season grazing *and* wildlife conservation and were willing to work with AWF to manage it as such. But they were not trusted. They were deceived and told they were "given" the ranch by their member of parliament, when it was signed over to a new body formed by himself and AWF, the Tanzanian Land Conservation Trust (TLCT). TLCT was comprised of wildlife experts (from Tanzania and abroad), with villagers included as "trustees," not as managers, as discussed in chapter 2.

Boundary demarcations ideologically separate nature from society, while also reconfiguring the material landscape. Legal codes facilitate this process, with separate laws in Tanzania regulating wildlife ownership and use. All wildlife in the country, like land, is owned by the state. The Tanzanian National Parks Association (TANAPA) controls all wildlife inside national parks, while the Wildlife Division (WD) of the Ministry of Wildlife and Tourism controls all wildlife outside of parks—including inside game reserves (GRs) and game controlled areas (GCAs), where hunting is allowed on a permit-only basis. Today GCAs are surrounded by ambiguity and confusion—as their boundaries overlap with demarcated village and private lands. Hunting within GCAs is allocated by the WD to private hunting companies. All of the *Emanyara enkutoto* falls inside the Mto wa Mbu GCA.

National parks, game reserves, and forest reserves cover more than 27 percent of Tanzania's territory, yet remain insufficient to protect wildlife, which do not stay inside park boundaries. Consequently, conservation agencies and the Tanzanian state are continually finding new ways to demarcate land for wildlife conservation—through the drawing of new boundaries for buffer zones, corridors, and wildlife management areas (WMAs). Many of these new units of conservation were spelled out in the wildlife policy (1998), which claimed to be the beginning of a new "community-based" era in Tanzanian conservation. The policy claimed to provide rural Tanzanians the means to control wildlife on their lands, through WMAs (Ministry of Natural Resources and Tourism 1998). WMAs were the subject of extensive debate by NGOs and community members, and the new law (2009) was critiqued for maintaining much of the centralized control present in the initial 1974 wildlife legislation (Benjaminsen et al. 2013; Goldman 2003). Both the policy and the act continue state promotion of scientific supremacy and antipastoralist sentiment regarding land and wildlife management (Ministry of Natural Resources and Tourism 1998). Maasai were critical of the policy and continue to fight some aspects of the new law, including WMA implementation and conservation corridors. Not interested in hunting rights, they see the new law as the continued enshrinement of rights in wildlife and land in the hands of the state, and WMAs and wildlife corridors as dividing up Maasailand. For this reason, and with the threat of land alienation ever looming, Maasai often resist signing on to new conservation projects. Not only do such projects threaten to impose new boundaries with associated access restrictions across their lands, they also bring with them a certain set of ontological politics. For conservation interventions promote Western assumptions that separate people from nature in ways that Maasai do not. As seen in the following example regarding conservation interventions in Simanjiro district, in the TME.

Over the past several decades conservation agencies have attempted to protect the Simanjiro Plains, which provide important wet season grazing for migrating wildlife from TNP and are used by Maasai and their livestock across several villages. In reaction to the threat of new conservation boundaries, some village leaders persuaded villagers to settle or farm in the plains—to prevent them from "becoming conservation" (Cooke 2007; Goldman 2009). In Terrat Village, Maasai had already divided much of their village land into private parcels and needed to keep their portion of the plains open for livestock grazing. They succeeded at negotiating with a tour company and conservation agency to create the Terrat Easement, to protect important pasture in the Simanjiro Plains for wildlife and livestock (Davis and Goldman 2017). The easement applies Maasai land management techniques, with a board of customary leaders coordinating grazing. Its widespread success suggests the possibilities of doing conservation otherwise—in ways that do not alienate Maasai, their livestock, and their forms of management. But this is not always so simple and includes revisiting the ways in which boundaries have been drawn, and crossed, over time and space. This is best illustrated in the following conversation with a village leader in Emboreet, a village in Simanjiro where conservation agencies and researchers have been pushing to protect the Simanjiro Plains for wildlife, especially wildebeest.

The village chairman explained how it was more complex than just "saving the plains" for wildlife.

"Emboreet has a different geography," he explained. "In Terrat, they have a very small area of the plains left—it's the only area in the whole village still open, so they need to keep it that way for livestock and wildlife.

"In Emboreet, our place of wildlife is in the *pori*, against the boundary of the national park. People tell us to stop farming in the plains and to farm in the *pori*—but if we cut down the *pori* to farm, how will the wildebeest get out to the plains? And we will stop the rain. Now we go there because it gets rain. And all Maasai come there to follow the rains.

"Terrat has a *chemchem* [natural spring], and so people followed that to put in farms. There is no water in the plains. For us, we had one *chemchem* and one dam. The *chemchem* was turned into a borehole during the colonial era. And it's in the plains.

So this is where people came to live. Where the school was built. . . ." He pauses and chuckles. We then take a slight diversion so that he can explain to me why it is that the plains became the village center. "Well. . . . The story that the elders tell is this. The British came here and asked the elders where they could build a mission. The elders thought and talked amongst themselves and decided to have them settle in the area covered by black cotton soil [*engusero*, which becomes completely impassable when it rains], so as to isolate them. They said, 'OK, they want to come, let them come and stay until they need to be pulled out by tractors! And if they are here to attack us they cannot escape on any side. They will be isolated on an island that they build in the middle.' That has now become the center of our village!"

"And you can't now ask people to move their residence and leave the plains. We want to keep the area open so there's still space for wildlife to move, to graze on around twenty acres around the edges and keep the middle open, but it's hard for me to do. To kick those out that are already there. We'll have to send them to the *pori* to do this. And the government tells us to farm the *pori*. So if we cut down and farm the *pori* the whole village will be plains?"[18] He ends his story with a questioning tone, unable to make sense of the plan that is being proposed.

Conclusion: Ongoing Border Crossings

Long ago, there was a place that was like a hole and inside there were bees and honey. But if you touched the bees or ate the honey, you would die. The bees didn't hurt people, but if you took their honey you'd die. When the English came, they discovered this place and the delicious honey, and they tried to take the honey back to their country. They put the honey in the airplane, and they ate it during their trip. By the time they reached home [England] they had finished all the honey. They then died at home [in England]. Maasai told the English not to do this but they said that they had special expertise. But even they failed, and the bees followed them. Maasai don't touch this place anymore. It is the place of God.

This story, told to me when in the field, can be read in different ways. I use it here to introduce a Maasai reading of colonial interventions in nature—against the knowledge, desires, and even cautions of Maasai. Maasai have regularly challenged and crossed the boundaries delineated by the colonial and then Tanzanian state on the ground—first the Maasai Reserve, then Maasai District, and now many villages inside different districts and regions, as well as national parks, game reserves, and WMAs.

Yet they have also, over time, drawn on and utilized some of these boundaries, such as when demanding recognition of customary leadership at district levels, using village land titles to create arrangements with wildlife tourism companies, and to access land for grazing and farming. In doing so, they are simultaneously using and challenging categories that define what it means to be Maasai and how nature is to be managed. Maasai civil society organizations have been active in this process, helping Maasai leaders at national, district, and village levels to assert their rights and speak out against a history of land alienation for conservation. Through these processes, and on their own, Maasai have challenged their image as "pure pastoralists" by claiming rights to farm, while simultaneously claiming their ability to preserve wildlife historically by virtue of being pastoralists. This means they sometimes farm to claim land and resist conservation, and sometimes collaborate with conservationists to protect pasture from farming.

Boundaries reconfigure the world in certain ways. They are not natural, nor purely discursive, nor are they permanent or solid. Boundaries are enacted through knowledge-making practices—regarding who "Maasai" are, where "nature" is. They are epistemological and ontological practices—enacting particular ways of knowing and being in the world. Boundaries not only reflect knowledges but produce new realities—places where nature is, separated from society. This separation has biophysical as well as social impacts that enact new realities on the ground, such as wildlife conservation corridors, discussed in the final *enkiguena* chapter.

| Chapter 5 |

Enkiguena Agenda III

Wildlife Pathways and Conservation Corridors

DIFFERENT USES OF THE WORD "corridor" overlap and coexist in conservation discourse, particularly in Northern Tanzania where the word has become so ubiquitous that it has entered the vocabulary of many non-English-speaking Maasai and other rural Tanzanians living there.[1] Despite the great deal of uncertainty surrounding what a corridor actually is, it has become the accepted term to discuss wildlife movements (as in migratory pathways), the places in between national parks (as in the Kwa Kuchinja Corridor), and a very specific wildlife conservation intervention.[2]

The prominence of corridors means that there were many meetings and discussions about corridors when I was in the field. I interviewed Maasai on the topic, including their thoughts on the appropriateness of designating conservation corridors in the villages of Oltukai and Esilalei. And I presented research findings to a group of village representatives (elders, *ilmurran*, women), MR and AWF staff, and outside members of the Maasai advocacy community. My presentation was only the beginning of a several-hour-long meeting, designed to initiate dialogue, where many Maasai voiced their concerns, and I present many of their statements here, as they occurred at the meeting, along with interview findings. I also draw on a meeting regarding a project proposed by AWF, called KEEP (Kwa Kuchinja Environmental Easements Project), to designate a wildlife corridor in the village of Oltukai (and several surrounding villages). I situate the *enkiguena* in Oltukai Village, which has been targeted by AWF to join the KEEP project. Landis T, introduced in the last meeting, is now village chairman for Oltukai. He has experience as a game scout in MR but is also quite critical of "conservation" and more interested in community well-being then the last village chairman. The views of people from Esilalei on the corridor concept are weaved throughout—from interviews to participation in meetings, cited appropriately.

THE SETTING

Today's *enkiguena* is being held under the large baobab (*olmesera*) tree that is often used for village meetings in Oltukai (see figures 10a and 10b). The large tree towers over the slightly raised area of the village center (*Enkung'u Oltuka*) and is close to many *inkang'itie*. Sloping downhill from the *olmesera*, the *oltuka* trees thin out into an open grassland scattered with Maasai *inkang'itie*, and then again to open grazing areas all the way down to Lake Manyara. The lake is visible, from the raised ground of the *olmesera*, as it glimmers in the sunlight just below the looming rift valley wall on its far western edge. Sloping south of the *olmesera* is the Oltukai *korongo* [seasonal river], marked by dense vegetation, twisting and turning its way to the lake. This view, afforded at the slightly raised spot where the *olmesera* stands, makes it an ideal meeting spot. More importantly, the massive size of the tree provides adequate shade (when it is in bloom) for a sizeable group of people, and the large roots of the *olmesera*, clumped at its base and spreading out in all directions, provide places for people (men in particular) to sit. Clusters of people sit around the base of the tree, finding little nooks in the large roots that make for seats in the shade. As these roots form chair-like crevices and supports, they are the most coveted seats. But for this reason, this area also tends to be crowded. Others circle out in front of the tree, preferably sitting on a rock. There are groupings of people sitting together, close to each other, many leaning on each other, some behind others, forming a large circle panning out on the slightly raised eastern side of the tree. Enough space is left in the middle for someone to stand and speak, and to walk about as they do so, addressing all the sides of the circle. This is not a closed circle though—there are many open spaces between clusters of people. Spaces with no rocks to sit on. Spaces in the sun. Or just spaces too far from another person. For no one would want to sit alone—this will be a long meeting, and so one must be near others to whisper to, to share snuff with, and to just lean on. Women sit together in a shady, grassy spot on the southern edge (near to the closest *enkang'*, where they all meet first until they are a large enough group to make their way to the meeting).[3] Visitors and important elders are provided with seats, which are carried over to the site from the nearby houses (see figure 10b).

Just adjacent to the *olmesera* stands a partly constructed village office. When complete, the office will provide an alternate meeting location—inside, or on the large mezzanine that is being built to face the *olmesera*—to provide shelter from rain or from the sun, if the *olmesera* is not in bloom and thus providing only limited shade in the late afternoon sun. Most of the non-Maasai visitors (i.e., those from AWF or the Manyara Ranch) have come by car, which can be driven right up to the meeting place and parked in the slightly shady area just west of the tree, or a distance away to the north. Drivers lounge in the cars while the meeting begins.

> **Note on governance:** There has been a change in village government since the last two agenda items were discussed. You might be wondering why this would really matter since an *enkiguena* is supposed to be an open forum dictated by Maasai tradition rather than government rules. In the general way in which I have been utilizing the *enkiguena* as a methodological tool, this is true. However, this third agenda item directly addresses conservation politics, and the new government is more aware of the issues and wary of the dangers conservation present. Their predecessors were both naïve to the politics of conservation and interested in using it for their personal gain. The new government is also more open to the contributions of women at meetings and in village decision-making than the former government was, and receptive to the views of outsiders, while confident in their own knowledge and decision-making capabilities. Moreover, the new village government is acutely aware of the failures and politics associated with their predecessors, which made them adopt a more open approach to governance. The data presented below was collected during both the old and the new village governance. Interview responses regarding the appropriateness (or not) of conservation corridors and data regarding movement pathways come mostly from the period of the old village government (2002–4). During this time, there were some who stood out for speaking their views, even if (or sometimes particularly if) they conflicted with what the village government was saying. Many of these people became part of the new village government. Excerpts or statements from meetings regarding corridor design, particularly in relation to the new KEEP project, come mostly from the period of the new government at that time (2005). The meeting is enacted as if it occurred under the newer village government leadership.

The blessing: *An elder from Oltukai, from the* Ilmeshuki *age-set, stands to bless the meeting. He stands hunched over and leaning on his tall walking stick, his eyes foggy with age and blindness, and speaks in a low, loud voice, which expresses the confidence and respect lacking in his physical stance. Like many of the elders in this* *village, he is poor and most often drunk. Unlike many, however, he can remain sober for days at a time, and so he still accords the respect of a knowledgeable elder. Many others have drunk away not only their capital (cattle) but also their knowledge and respect. He is sober today and present at this important meeting, for which he has volunteered to bless, but he will later sneak across the river to buy some of the illegal brew sold by the neighboring Waarusha.[4] He blesses all of us at the meeting; he blesses our cattle, and our children. He thanks Engai (God), for the rain we have received and blesses the country (enkop) to continue to receive rain, keeping the cattle healthy. Throughout the blessing, participants respond appropriately with "Nai." He sits back down among his peers, on a large rock positioned just so in the shade, and the meeting begins.*

Chairman T: *The chairman of today's* enkiguena *is the village government chairman of Oltukai, because the issues being discussed have raised many important questions regarding land-use planning in the village. In order to make decisions, they have called this meeting to bring together their neighbors, friends, and family from Esilalei, visitors from local conservation agencies, and knowledgeable researchers/scientists (*wataalamu*). He opens the meeting by thanking them all for coming and then explaining the agenda:* Today we have two agenda items to discuss. One concerns corridors in general, and the other concerns the KEEP project.

He speaks in Maa but says the word "corridor" and the acronym KEEP as a word in sharply accented English, and this is repeated by the person translating everything (except "corridor") into Swahili. The word is repeated by many of the Maasai sitting around him (young and old; men and women). They say the word to themselves and to their neighbors, in either a questioning tone, "corridor?" unsure of its meaning, or in an affirming tone, "corridor," as in "Yes, that's right, I know about that!"

He looks around at all the confusion and continues. I know that some of you are not quite aware of what I mean by "corridor," but many others of you are tired of talking about corridors. We do have some *wataalamu* (experts) here to tell us more about it, but briefly let me explain. You all know that wildlife move across the village between the parks and Manyara Ranch? *There are murmurs around the crowd of agreement.* And there are places that certain animals like to pass through, like at Kwa Kuchinja, or by the *enkang'* of Sulel. *As this is translated, the conservationists look back and forth at each other as if they have just been privy to some privileged information; they jot down notes on their pads. The chairman continues.* The *wataalamu* call these "corridors." They say our village is inside the Kwa Kuchinja corridor. And the conservation people, well, they want to protect these places, like down by the lake, they want to carve out conservation corridors in village lands to protect the movements of wildlife. *Maasai in the crowd listen closely, some raise their heads or eyes in agreement, as the visiting* wataalum *look around anxious to see how people are reacting, to catch the tone of the meeting.* Today, we are here to discuss all of this. We are here to discuss corridors. What are they? Where are they? And is it appropriate, should we agree, to carve out corridors, or set aside land for corridors in the village, should we agree to the KEEP project?[5] But let's wait to discuss KEEP till the end, as it is not as relevant to our Esilalei guests, and this will allow them an early start home if they wish to leave. I have now said enough; please, if you have something to say on this matter, *karibu* (welcome), the *enkiguena* is now open. *He starts to sit down but looks over at the guests, the* wataalamu *sitting together on a row of chairs in the shade, and addresses them.* Perhaps our guests would like to speak first? I am not sure if you agree with how I explained a corridor; you are the experts and this is your word, maybe you have something to say?

Professor Raphael B. Mwalyosi *volunteers; he is a professor at the Institute for Resource Assessment (IRA) at the University of Dar es Salaam, with a great deal of experience in the area. He has conducted research inside the LMNP and on the need to set aside corridors throughout the area (Mwalyosi 1991, 1990, 1981).[6] The IRA has historically done most of the resource-related consulting for the Tanzanian State. He stands up and, with a casual confidence, addresses the crowd. As a well-educated, respectful Tanzanian, he follows the Tanzanian protocol of using polite (formal) Swahili and thanking his audience before he speaks.* Thank you for having us here today and for giving me this opportunity to speak to you all. I have done a lot of research in this area and have much that I could talk to you about. First, I would like to do as the village chairman requested and explain to you all what a corridor is. But I first want to address what a protected area is. "The concept of game reserves presupposes that 'island' reserves contain all essential life-sustaining ingredients for the animals and should therefore thrive" (Mwalyosi 1991, 172). This, at least, is what conservation biologists have discussed (Wilcox 1980, cited in Mwalyosi 1991, 172). But we also know that many times national parks do not provide all the necessary ingredients for wildlife survival, in which case the concept of a sustainable "island" reserve becomes invalid, and wildlife migrations occur (Mwalyosi 1991, 172; cf. Fryxell and Sinclair 1988). And this, of course, is very much the case here, in this area called the Tarangire-Manyara-Simanjiro Ecosystem. The name itself implies that animals move not just beyond the park boundaries to access resources but also back and forth between the two parks and into Simanjiro. As such, we can talk about a "corridor" connecting the two parks, the Kwa Kuchinja corridor, of which this village is a part.

He pauses and looks around to check that there is agreement with what he has just said. Many raise their eyebrows and make sounds of agreement. He continues. Now, wildlife used to move freely outside of the parks, but that is changing with accelerated population growth and increased agricultural development, especially in the areas immediately surrounding LMNP, like Mtowambu (Mwalyosi 1991, 173–76). I am sure there are some elders who remember when there were far fewer people in this area.

Elder 1: *Ee pae* [of course]! There were only three *inkang'itie* [homesteads] in this village when I was born!

Elder 2: There used to be so many wildlife long ago, even rhinos were here.[7]

The elders are cut off by the professor, who continues.

Professor Raphael B. Mwalyosi: Yes, there has been rapid population growth in this area, at a rate of 3.4 percent, which is higher than even the national average of 2.6 percent (Mwalyosi 1991, 174), mostly from in-migration and mostly into the towns of Mtowambu, Minjingu, and Makuyuni, where there has also been rapid conversion of land to agriculture.[8] In this situation, it is likely that wildlife will lose access to areas beyond the park boundaries and that the national parks will become isolated "islands." But, as you know, "Lake Manyara NP is very small (110 km² of parkland) and is therefore not viable as an 'island' park" (Mwalyosi 1991, 175). In addition to regular movements outside of the park for grazing and water, the wildlife in LMNP need an escape route from the park in case the lake floods and inundates the lake shore grasslands (Mwalyosi 1981). And if the animals inside the park don't have a link with other populations (or groups) in other places (like in TNP), then when a disease strikes the park, like the rinderpest epidemic for buffalo in 1959 or the anthrax outbreak among impala in 1977 and 1983, then the animals might go extinct. So. . . . *He pauses and looks around, making sure that everyone is paying close attention before he continues. He adjusts his stance to assure confidence in what he is about to say.* "In anticipation of increased land-use pressure around Lake Manyara NP, a game corridor connecting it to Tarangire NP is important particularly to migratory species as a route for local dispersal. The corridor would maintain connectivity between the two Parks, and thus enhance survival of wildlife" (Mwalyosi 1991, 176). "Within the corridor, only fuelwood collection and livestock grazing would be allowed. Since the game animals involved migrate between

National Parks, the corridor would be managed by Tanzania National Parks [TANAPA]" (Mwalyosi 1991, 180). Now, I have done the calculations. . . . Looking at how much the animals (wildebeest and zebra) need to eat in a day. And assuming they will move through the corridor in twenty-four hours, the corridor will only need to be 1 km wide to provide enough forage for them to get from LMNP to TNP and back again.

> *Note:* Mwalyosi draws heavily from conservation biology and island biogeography theory. He does not outline these theories or discuss their relevance to LMNP in any detail, but the link is far from subtle. He discusses "island" parks and states that LMNP could not survive as one, citing examples of why this is the case. He argues that corridors are needed, not so much to protect preexisting movements, but to prevent localized extinctions, citing the island biogeography literature (Diamond 1975; Margules, Higg, and Rafe 1982). Yet in deciding on the placement of the corridor, he draws from data on wildlife use patterns (Mwalyosi 1991, 176, and table 1, 178). But these, it turns out, are just for guidance, for he is really interested in designing an animal highway of sorts. For in determining the appropriate width the corridor should be, he takes data on the estimated population numbers for wildebeest (10,000) and zebra (800) and multiplies it by two (assuming a "return trip"), to come up with 20,000 "wildebeest days" and 1,600 "zebra days." He uses this to determine how much fodder would be needed within the corridor area ("about 67840 kg per migration season"). This estimate comes from an assumed maintenance requirement of 3.12 kg of dry grass per animal per day for wildebeest and 3.5 for zebra (Mwalyosi 1991, 179). All this suggests that 1 km would be wide enough to enable safe passage across the landscape. The corridor is proposed above the lake line, to ensure passage during floods. This means that in nonflood years, available grazing in the corridor would be much greater, extending down toward the lake. This is an important buffer, especially since he does not seem to consider temporal and spatial variability in rainfall patterns and grass productivity characteristic of semiarid savanna areas. Nor does he acknowledge that the actions—movement, grazing, resting—of the animals themselves will impact the vegetation and soil composition within the corridor (Turner 1998). The corridor is proposed to protect the area from human-induced transformation. Once that happens, will it persist indefinitely in the same state? This is unlikely (Coughenour 1991; Walker and Scholes 1993; Westoby, Walker, and Noy-Meir 1989).[9]

> Mwalyosi's use of island biogeography theory is strategic, and perhaps more appropriate for the small LMNP than for discussions regarding the larger ecosystem and TNP. And he argues his point well, with many examples. Yet he fails to maintain the dual argument for corridors that he begins with and that carries the import of the concept throughout the TME. That is, that the animals already move outside of the parks and need to have those routes protected. His mathematical calculations for corridor design do not reflect this reality. This is perhaps the reason that despite its obvious relevance, this paper has had little impact on conservation activities in the area, in direct contrast to the Borner article (1985), which focuses on maintaining preexisting (but threatened) pathways.

There was much commotion after Mwalyosi spoke; the chairman selects Landis P, a knowledgeable, respectful, and politically aware junior elder.

Landis P:[10] *Walks, smiling, into the center of the gathering, pointing his olkuma outward as a sign of the respect he knows he deserves despite his young age, and in a confident but friendly tone, speaks.* Thanks to the professor for explaining things. I for one, agree with some of what he said, but disagree with much as well. It is true that the animals come out of the park, which is not news to any of us. *Sounds of agreement and support come from Maasai men and women.* "Wildlife are here more so than they are in the parks! Especially in May there are a lot of wildlife, more than cattle," all along this side of the lake. But "it is not a corridor. They are just there." *Again sounds of agreement from the crowd,* ee pae *[of course].* "They don't stay all year of course, and after the seventh month (July) they have already moved to Manyara and Tarangire, they spread out. They can even stay here if there is no water, even wildebeest, they can go to Mtowambu for water and come back, they have pathways everywhere."

It is true that people near Mtowambu cause problems for the animals though, this I will agree with, especially the "Mbulu [a neighboring tribe]. [They] capture [the wildebeest] by rope, when there are a lot." And I will also agree that when the lake floods the animals can have problems. But they don't come here then, because if the lake floods it floods here too. This happened during El Niño and the wildebeest didn't come. Water filled up the whole area, so they had no place to go by the lake, which is where the wildebeest usually go.

You are speaking of a corridor that comes above the lakeshore, through where our homes and farms are? To this we cannot agree. We have already fought it. "We know that TANAPA wants this land, and that if we hadn't come here and settled, it would have been selected to be [inside] the national park. TANAPA says that this area *will* be inside the park. In 1995 they tried to get this area to be inside a corridor from Manyara to Tarangire. And a corridor doesn't allow for homes and farms. From *Lembeti* and *Olmukutan*, from my *enkang'* [in *Oleketalokeon*] to the lake, even up to *Embarimbali*, would be inside the park [see map 3]. When TANAPA asked us to move we refused to leave because this is an important grazing area. Water from the *korongo* spills over into the pasture and there are good places for farming. People have already built homes in this area, it has already become a subvillage, we can't just leave it now and have it go back to being 'bush' [*pori*]. We farm here too. Not much, but we get something. The soil is good for farming; even if it rains only a little, you get a crop, not like in other places in Esilalei village. If we moved into Esilalei proper it would be too full. Even today, we hear talk [about moving for a corridor], but not much." We hear from the Manyara Ranch that "they want to decrease the farms [here]. We don't want to stop farming. It has benefits. We get corn for our children and beans to sell to buy cattle."

If we stop farming, "this whole area will come under the control of conservation," and then we won't be allowed to farm at all. If we don't farm, then they will change everything, and then someone that does farm will get thrown in jail. We don't want to have it be like that. They have tried to make it all a conservation area. "The ward secretary of Manyara came in 1995, 1997, and 1998 and said that this area will be a corridor. He was here for five days. In Naitolia [Village] there are two places. There are two corridors, one from Saburi that passes through the mountains going to Mbulubulu, Serena, Ngorongoro.[11] But we refused, and we continue to argue over the corridor. But it doesn't bother people; we can still live here."[12] *There is much commotion, many sounds of agreement, and chatter among Maasai and exchanges (in looks and words) of concern among the conservationists. Many Maasai clamor to speak; the chairman chooses a guest, an elder from the neighboring village of Losirwa.*

Melita:[13] What the young elder has said is all true, but it goes back even earlier than that. Since 1992 there were plans to make a corridor. A corridor from LMNP passing the *msitu ya mbogo* (the forest of buffalo; *Olmukutan*) in Esilalei, passing through Makuyuni Maasaini Chini (a subvillage of Esilalei, where Landis P lives) into Manyara Ranch. *An elder from Oltukai, a popular, jovial man, stands to speak.*

Makaa S:[14] *With a serious look, holding on to an* olkuma *that looks a lot more like a weapon then a meeting stick, his presence quickly fills the open space. He is a new* olaigwenani *for the Ilmamasita clan, a close relative of the new village chairman,* *and very loud and outspoken.* This talk of a corridor by the lake, it is true. And TANAPA **is** there. They come with their cars sometimes from Lake Manyara and drive around, monitoring the area. I live down near the lake and I see them. Just the other day, I had to help my neighbor out because his young boy [*olay-ioni*] was caught killing a zebra down there. Now, granted he should not have killed a zebra, and who knows why he did; he's *mweng'ati*,[15] not Maasai. *He makes a joke about the foul smell of zebra meat that many tribes eat but Maasai refuse, which brings bursts of laughter from Maasai.* He was caught by Maasai from Oltukai, a couple of those guys from the village that completed game scout training at LMNP, and they brought him to the park. When the TANAPA guys at LMNP got a hold of him he was fined. The fine was reduced because he is just a kid, good thing since I had to pay it! *Again laughter from the crowd.* And they said we should know better, because we know that this is a **corridor**. And this is true, the area by the lake, *Oloyeti*, as far as I know, is an agreed upon corridor, meaning that we don't build or farm down there. But, what does that really mean? If it is only in *Oloyeti*, then we can't farm or build there anyway! (It gets waterlogged and flooded in the rains.) If they say we can't graze cattle there then that's when the problems will begin! *And with that strong statement, he walks away with a serious face.*

The many faces of the conservation "state": In Tanzania, the governing body in charge of wildlife depends on where the wildlife are located. TANAPA only has power inside national parks, while the Wildlife Division governs wildlife outside of parks—including inside GCAs, where the study villages are located. While the Wildlife Policy of 1998 introduced WMAs as "community" run conservation areas for villages inside GCAs, they mandated the involvement of NGOs (like AWF or Honeyguide) in management and at times forced villages to participate along lines dictated by the state (Benjaminsen et al. 2013).[16] The Wildlife Conservation Act of 2009 increased the power of the Wildlife Division to intervene in the management of village lands for wildlife protection, such as through the creation of corridors (United Republic of Tanzania [URT] 2009). The act was not yet passed when the below conversations occurred but was being debated, and various state agencies were already working closely with NGOs for corridor delineation and protection. These factors, combined with the shared use of vehicles and similar "game" attire worn by scouts, across state agencies and NGOs (AWF, TLCT, and now Honeyguide Foundation), makes it difficult for local people to ascertain the difference between them. It

> is therefore unclear, nor does it really matter to villagers, which state division (or NGO) is patrolling and enforcing the rules. The confusion works to create a shared sense of fear of "the state" and local NGOs, which are often seen as working together.

TANAPA 1:[17] *The chief warden for Tarangire National Park stands to speak, with a big friendly grin on his face; he addresses the crowd in Maa, before switching to Swahili.* I thought I should contribute, since we are talking about TANAPA (laughter from the crowd). First, what the elder has said is true; there is a general agreement among us all to maintain the strip of grazing by the lake as a corridor. We all know that wildlife use that area to move between the parks, and to graze during much of the year, as the young elder explained. However, this is just an informal agreement. There is currently no formal legal mechanism in Tanzania to protect wildlife corridors.[18] Moreover, TANAPA has no legal jurisdiction over wildlife outside of the National Parks. So, referring to the professor's proposition made at the beginning of this meeting, despite his good intentions, his proposal would be difficult to implement. Now, there is a new wildlife law coming into effect, but it is not yet law, and it does nothing to change the TANAPA mandate.[19] That being said, if it was up to me, I would say that there is no reason for restricting livestock grazing in a designated corridor. Livestock grazing is perfectly compatible with wildlife protection.

With that last statement there are sounds of agreement and side discussions among Maasai, many of whom are eager to speak, but the local conservation manager stands before anyone else has a chance, and the chairman nods for him to go ahead, while his hand stretches out to quite the others.

Local conservation manager:[20] *A British expatriate, he speaks in formal but heavily mispronounced Swahili, before switching to English.* Thank you TANAPA 1 for clarifying things a bit, but I need to clarify them a bit further [*he lets out a hearty, good-natured laugh*]. The new wildlife law is now in parliament and likely to pass, and it has a provision to set land aside as a wildlife corridor. So, while it is true that TANAPA does not have any jurisdiction outside of the national parks, there is now a legal mechanism to protect corridors—and this can be done directly by the wildlife division, or more appropriately, by the villagers themselves. That is what the KEEP project is all about, helping the villagers to set aside land for the purpose of a corridor, before the government comes and does it for them! But we can talk more about KEEP later; I just wanted to clarify this important point.

TANAPA 1:[21] *Without standing, he speaks.* Even without the new law, the government has been pushing corridors as a form of land use and trying to use land-use planning as a legal mechanism to put corridors in place. If we produce a land-use plan in a participatory fashion directly with the communities, then they are the ones who decide to make a corridor and the by-laws governing its use. The district oversees implementation.

TANAPA 2:[22] *A Tanzanian ecologist by training, he is not from the area and can barely hide the annoyance and arrogance in his voice. He leans on his vehicle and chews on a piece of grass as he speaks.* Wildlife migration routes are very important. Blocking them is problematic for wildlife; they must be protected. And like my colleague has said, this can be done through land-use planning, and the best way to work out proper land-use plans is with appropriate data about wildlife. Bring this [to the villagers] and help them make their decisions. We explain the benefits that will come if land is left for grazing for wildlife and livestock. If villagers decide [to make it a corridor] in their land-use maps, it will be followed. The Kwa Kuchinja corridor is here and there is a beacon from LAMP (Land Management Program); it is about 6.5 km wide.[23] Wildlife are used to the corridor; they pass there one day and then again and they remember it. The beacons are along the lake. There is also a dispersal area along the lake, and the MR will look after it all.[24] *With this he looks over at the MR manager, who seems both happy and a bit startled by what he has heard.*

Land surveyor:[25] *Someone from the district land office stands to speak. He has been working with AWF on several corridor projects and is involved in the KEEP project. He speaks matter-of-factly.* It is true that while there is no law for corridors on the wildlife side, there is on the land side. And with land demarcation, a corridor is legally binding as a place left open for wildlife to pass. In Selela there is a corridor; we measured it on the ground, put it on maps, and it passed through Dar es Salaam [at the ministry of land]. Now people can't do anything inside, but livestock can enter. And we are doing it in West Kilimanjaro, but people there want to take it to court, to fight the corridor because farms will not be allowed inside. They don't farm much now but they will want to, and they are worried that their kids will have no place to farm. But the country is big; they can go elsewhere. In Tanzania, a few people cannot stop many. We still have a lot of wilderness [*pori*], which is not used. But you can't force animals to pass in a certain place. You can find out where they most often pass and protect it; this is a better than doing nothing. We survey the area, and then it gets sent to the ministry of lands and it becomes final. We did this in Esilalei, but it has only been planned. Once the plan is agreed upon by the ministry, it comes back to us at the district and then we demarcate the area. Once it is a formal corridor, villagers do not have the right to put anything there—houses or farms.

Mwenyekiti E:[26] *The village chairman of Esilalei stands to speak, motioning to the others (who were waiting and had started to stand) to sit and let him speak first; the meeting chairman nods in agreement. He is an elder (Makaa), and an olaigwenani for the Ilmamasita, he thus speaks with an overwhelming sense of authority.* What these people from TANAPA are saying is true. Even we, the government of Esilalei, put a corridor on our land-use map, which we did with the district land officer. But we did not realize this was final. "You see, putting a corridor on the map, was just what we see, it is not a plan. It is appropriate [*inafaa*] because it is an area that is important for cattle and wildlife and so will not be farmed. It is not good to fill all the pathways; it will not be agreeable [to wildlife]. Even if you refuse to protect an area, [wildlife] will pass, even if it is a farm. If you protect an area, the wildlife will know, and they will pass there."

Landis Taeto:[27] *A resident of Esilalei, he is now the appointed executive secretary of Oltukai Village and taking minutes for the meeting.*[28] *He is Ilaiser, his father is an olaikwenani, and he is always trying to show he is better than the Ilmamasita-led government. He is considered one of the smartest men in the area, though not always trusted. He is very outspoken at meetings, though not very diplomatic or a particularly good speaker. He is not concerned with the reaction his words might provoke. He starts speaking before standing to ensure his chance to speak.* What the *mwenyekiti* says is true. The animals have their places to go, and they will go there regardless. We learned this in Mwanza. People who live near Serengeti National Park complain that wildlife come to their farms. We did an experiment to see if the animals were targeting the farm, or if the farm had just been placed in a location that the animals had historically used. So certain areas were not farmed that year, and the animals came anyway. We found out that this was the area they have always gone to. So maybe it wasn't such a good idea to put the farms there.

Landis K:[29] *A very young, educated Landis, he is not very comfortable speaking in front of elders. He walks quickly into the center and in a soft, casual tone speaks.* Maybe the farm in Landis Taeto's story was put in the wrong place, but the way I see it, it doesn't matter where the farm is; the animals will come to it, especially elephants! The elephants have created new corridors coming out of Manyara Ranch to our farms to eat maize, and then they go back into the ranch! Have you seen our farms this year (in Endepesi)? All eaten by elephants, and I can show you the pathways they have made back and forth (from our farms to the ranch). *Murmurs of agreement and quick stories back and forth, especially among people who live in Endepesi and in the neighboring part of Oltukai, where elephant raids of farms are common.*[30]

Elephant R1:[31] *The "elephant researcher" or* bwana tembo, *as he is called in Swahili, greets the gathering in Swahili but then speaks in English, which is translated.* "Elephants are like people, they pass down knowledge from generations." And so yes, they have places where they normally go to, and they will return to these places every year, if they can; if they can't, it can cause serious problems. The elephant populations in TNP suffered high mortality among the elder population because of poaching, and this resulted in the loss of knowledge among the whole group. So, during the drought of 1992–94 only those elephant groups with members that still had knowledge of where to go during a drought (the last bad one being in 1958) survived. The rest just stayed inside the park and died. In order to keep areas available for elephants, and other animals, villages should set aside an area for wildlife. You can make more money from wildlife than from farming. I am not suggesting giving up legal rights to the land, just changing its use (from farming to wildlife conservation) in certain places. The money will trickle down. But we don't have much time left. We only have three to five years left to try to save the ecosystem. *Murmurs of discontent pass between Maasai.*

Elephant R2:[32] *Called* Mama Tembo *in Swahili, she is the GIS specialist of the team. Soft spoken but confident, she stands, and the crowd quiets to listen.* I would just like to say that we have seen specific corridors used by elephants. When we track their movements closely, the corridors show up as specific routes, through which the elephants can move quite fast—up to four times as fast as normal, for instance, when they move from TNP to a dispersal area in the Lolkisale Game Controlled Area (GCA, northeast of TNP; Foley 2002, 34). We don't have this kind of detailed data yet for this area, but we know that the elephants do use the MR as well as the villages to move through, together with wildebeest and zebra, and that elephants at least can often move through these routes quickly.[33] It is important to map out the corridors as they are currently being used by the animals and then find ways to keep them open, like Elephant R1 said. The one that I mapped going to the Lolkisale GCA was 3.5 km wide.

Landis Papai:[34] There are places in the village where the animals stay, like down by the lake, and we call this area *Ang'ata o n'geusi* (open plains of wildlife). It is used by all—cattle, lions, and wildebeest. They sleep at *Oroboti*, the place where the lake has receded and there is no water or grass; they like to sleep there. . . . They don't like to sleep in the grass. [But, is there a path (Maa: *engoitoi*)?] There is no path, they just graze. The wildlife do not have a *pario* [Swahili: path], they do not have a corridor, they pass everywhere, they do not have an *engoitoi*. They even pass through the middle of the village, even by my *enkang'*. It is true that when they move they create a pathway near the lake, but these change all the time, every year, every day even! Only elephants have special routes that they use (like *Mama Tembo* explained), because they don't separate. They are the only animal that has a big track . . . because they travel together. They pass through Kwa Kuchinja,[35] near *Elwane Orok* [the black dam], entering *Alchamba* (MR) from Tarangire. But here in the village, they don't have any corridors. This is what I say/think of course,[36] but if anyone thinks differently, let them speak and say so.

Maasidaan:[37] Maybe what Landis Papai means is that there is no secure, planned corridor for the animals, or that their movements change within a general area, but there are corridors here in the village [Oltukai], or rather, regular paths that the animals use to move around. There are three main ones that are used on a regular basis. One is along the lake, as we have been talking about. The animals move along the lake between LMNP and TNP and they just stay down by the lake, like Landis Papai and others have said. There is another path that the animals use to get back and forth from this area by the lake and Manyara Ranch, because sometimes they will stay by the lake but go to the ranch for water. They move in between the *enkang'* of Sulel and the *enkang'* of Olbioto. And then there is another path that cuts up from *Lera* by the *enkang'* of Malaso, across the *korongo* and then up through *Endepesi* into Manyara Ranch. These are pathways that the animals regularly move through, when they move across village lands.

Landis M:[38] It is true that the animals stay in the village to graze, and also that they have their pathways that move through the village (*he pauses, and looks back at the elephant researchers and adds*) or corridors, which go all the way from LMNP to Tarangire. If the wildebeest decide to move,[39] they come from LMNP, loop out into Losirwa [the village north of Esilalei], through *Oleketalokeon* in Esilalei and into Manyara Ranch and then Tarangire. Another path is along the lake, like the elder explained, and this one cuts out straight across [the road] into the park [TNP] [*he motions with his arm in that direction*]. Others go across the village [*he points with his arm in the direction of the ranch*] and into the ranch. It is common for animals to pass *through* the *enkang'* of Sulel as well as in the area between his *enkang'* and that of Olbioto, going in and out of the ranch. *He pauses, looks around, and notices that he has the attention of the crowd, that there is no one else* *vying for the chance to speak or people upset with what he is saying, and he continues in a more argumentative tone.* You see, the animals are **not afraid** of the *inkang'itie*. They move right near and right through an *enkang'*. The corridor that was mentioned by the elder that goes by the *enkang'* of Malaso, sometimes it loops near my *enkang'* as well. And then there are animals that come out to the *inkang'itie* at night for protection from predators. If you spend a night at my *enkang'*, you will see wildebeest and zebra late at night as well as early in the morning. They don't just move through . . . they stick around to graze and sleep.[40]

> ***Observing gazelles around Maasai settlements:*** While I was in the car one day with Landis M, he stopped me to look at gazelles running around in between a couple of Maasai settlements [*inkang'itie*]. "See how they are running near the *inkang'itie*," he pointed out. "They are completely in the area of *inkang'itie*," he said, "they are looking for a place to cross. This is why Maasai are able to live with wildlife." When I asked why this was the case, he explained, "Do you see how close they are to the homes? Look, they are practically entering an *enkang'*. If this area was Waswahili, *oosho!* They would have killed and eaten them. Maasai don't mind, they let them be. Maybe small boys will chase them, but they will just come right back, they will just return." This was a common sentiment expressed by Maasai in the area. The confusion over whether there are corridors or not is related to this understanding that wildlife, livestock, homesteads, and Maasai are all together. When corridors are thought to be permanent passageways free of Maasai settlements, this is hard for many to register.

There is much talk among the Maasai about wildlife near Maasai homes, until the chairman quiets them.

Chairman T: Does anyone else have anything to add about where the wildlife pass? *Noo yeyio* [*call to the women*], don't you have anything to say about this?

Mama P:[41] *The wife of one of the oldest elders in the village, she does not live with him, but lives with her son who is the old village chairman. These factors combined with her strong personality give her the freedom to speak; she does so loudly and confidently (if a bit abrasively); she speaks from where she sits with the other women.* All of Oltukai is a wildlife corridor because it is between Manyara and Tarangire National Parks. It is a place of animals, the whole village. Some stay, some pass through. Elephants, buffalo, wildebeest, giraffe, and zebra, some just pass through and some stay.

Mama J:[42] *She is a young woman, married in to the community from a neighboring tribe. With a primary school education, she has the confidence to speak. She does so in a shy and quiet manner, but in perfect Swahili.* There are animals that come out to the village for the farms, like Landis K said, but not just elephants, even zebra. They come from over there [*she motions with her hand*], from TNP to our farms. Sometimes they stay after that, sometimes they go back.

Mama PL:[43] *An elder woman, several of her sons have leadership positions, and she too is considered a leader among the women, known to be tough and not afraid to speak her opinion.* It is true that there are wildlife everywhere and that they don't leave certain places, like *Oremit*. But they also have their pathways, like the men have been saying. There is one that runs just below the cultural boma in Esilalei; wildlife run through it all the time. When the rain comes, a lot come through! Especially wildebeest and zebra.

Makaa Lameck:[44] The animals do not have definite pathways—today here, tomorrow there, the next day over there. [But what my mother has said is true], animals, particularly wildebeest, like to pass by the cultural boma. Wildebeest come from Selela and LMNP during *orkisirata* [the early rains] and *koromare* [the end of the rainy season], passing by *Olotoro*, going to Manyara Ranch. They cross the road and then cross below the cultural boma.

Ilpayiani:[45] I think that what this man has said is true. The pathway by *Olotoro* and the cultural boma is there. And animals can come down from Selela, into *Engososi*, across the road, and then below the cultural boma and into Manyara Ranch. But in Esilalei there are several other corridors too. There is one that comes up from the lake, through *Orumukutan*, across *Lembeti* and into the ranch. And of course, there is the corridor that runs the length of the lake, that has already been mentioned. But animals also move back and forth from the lake to *Engososi*, without going to the parks (or to MR). Another corridor crosses *Enkeju Olayioni*, near the milling machine. Another is in the mountains, near the *Oloiboni's enkang'*. This one crosses over the mountains, into the area where his farms are (at the base of the hills), across the road and into Manyara Ranch. *As he is speaking, there are exclamations of agreement from the crowd, mostly those from Esilalei, but also from many people from Oltukai, men and women, who know the area well.*

MG: *Stands up to speak, stepping into the center softly, looking around at all those gathered.* When we are doing our wildlife transects in *Lembiti* we often see a lot of animals crossing through, but also grazing in the area which they say is a corridor (or passageway?) for wildebeest, zebra, giraffe. The Landis working with me noted wildlife crossings by the milling machine, when they were out doing their vegetation work, or just walking in the area. We also see animals crossing, or just coming for water, at *Oloturro*, when we are doing the transect in the mountains. At first we didn't have a transect there, but I was told that it was an important corridor and so we added one. And when we ascend the mountain we can also see animals crossing down below, by the cultural boma, as people have spoken about. *She looks over at the men she is working with and they raise their eyebrows in agreement. She continues.* The corridor mentioned by the *enk-ang'* of Sulel is used by wildebeest on a regular basis, and oddly enough during about the same time every day—usually in the late afternoon, early evening. I have seen it myself, and I receive reports by people walking by the *enkang'* on their way home and from Sulel himself, who will stop by my house and fill me in on the latest wildebeest crossings.

Landis Enkinyi:[46] *A young, confident man, stands up and with a broad smile speaks. He is very young but very wealthy and generous, and so well respected and liked. Yet he has not honed his speaking abilities and has a hard time keeping the attention of the crowd.* There is a path that comes from the park (he points in the direction of TNP); the animals come from there, they rest in the *korongo*, pass near our *enkang'* like the elder has said (in the mountains) and they go up into the mountains—elephants, zebra, buffalo, in the rainy season.

Game Scout L:[47] *A young man dressed in the green army suit worn by game scouts stands up in a slightly shy manner. He looks over at the elephant researchers and then back at his fellow game scouts before addressing the gathering.* I am not from here; my home is in Selela, but working in the Manyara Ranch and for the elephant researchers, I can speak with confidence about the corridors that run through this area. The elephants, for instance, move from Manyara Ranch into the Losi-mingori Mountains, like the last two men mentioned, and into Selela, even up to Ngorogoro. And then they come back to Selela and then enter LMNP. We learned from Elephant R1 to look for the footprints and dung and if you see the footprints of the animal, you will see the animal. So we stayed in the Losimingori Mountains, put up a camp to watch the elephants, their children, birthing, and so forth. But it was too cold. They can't birth there; they go back down and separate out. Like wildebeest, the elephants move to give birth. But I also knew these things before I started working for the elephant researcher, but I just didn't think it was something important. I just knew from being here and looking and seeing that elephants pass, from being a herder or traveling to different places and seeing animals. But now that I am working for the MR,

I follow the animals every day and see where they go, and then we call those places they pass a corridor. *He looks over at the two elephant researchers who grin back at him.*

Local conservation manager:[48] *He stands up smiling, looking first at his game scouts; he then addresses the gathering.* The game scouts have been working with Elephant R1 and R2 to monitor the elephant corridors that cut through the ranch and village lands. But we still need more work to monitor the corridors of the other animals. The game scouts are doing a great job and working with the elephant researchers on this. This is an important part of our mandate, for the ranch was bought by TLCT to protect part of the Kwa Kuchinja corridor. Marcus Borner told us back in 1985 that the original corridors [pathways] were disappearing and we needed to protect them to prevent the parks from getting isolated (Borner 1985). Like the original documents for the Manyara Ranch say, "long-term conservation goals for the two national parks require linking these core protected areas with corridors of undeveloped land across which wildlife can move, and the acquisition of Manyara Ranch serves as an initial major step in this direction"[49] But the ranch is only one part of the corridor; the rest runs through village lands, and this is why we need to better understand where they are and start talking about protecting them. That is what the KEEP project is all about.

Olmurrani Micheal:[50] *A young olmurrani stands up; as he walks into the middle of the gathering, there is a jingling sound made from all the beads he is wearing (from bracelets and necklaces, to his belt, and the beaded piece in his long-braided hair). Standing with the confidence of an olmurrani, leaning on his walking stick, he speaks.* I don't know anything about this KEEP thing, but I do know that you can't set aside a separate place for only wildlife to go. When it rains, cattle and wildlife are one; they all go to where there is water and grass, where it has rained. It wouldn't work. Animals go where it has rained to look for grass.

> **Note:** *Ilmurran* are often hesitant to participate in a general *enkiguena* where elders are doing most of the talking. Yet they are the ones out herding the cattle, traveling long distances with them, or just exploring the bush with their age-mates—all the while observing wildlife. After one has stood and spoken, another has the courage to do so.

Olmurrani Laiser:[51] *Looking back at his fellow ilmurran, all sitting together at the base of the olmesera, he speaks to the gathering.* I don't see the reason to build/

protect an area in addition to where the wildlife already pass. Because, as we have always seen it, they pass through the village and just stay in village land. They pass near the lake and they pass near the *inkang'itie* [homesteads]. Even if you do carve out a corridor, the wildebeest will still come near the *in-kang'itie* [at night] to escape lions.

IIMeshuki N: *A frail elder man stands up slowly and enters the center to speak.* My son has spoken wisely. I too cannot agree with building new corridors when there are already the usual corridors. There is no reason to set aside a new area [*kutenga*] because the animals will just pass as they do, and we don't chase them away.

Makaa Leke:[52] *A young elder, one of the wealthiest people in the area and thus someone who commands immediate respect, stands, and there is a sudden hush as the chatter comes to a halt.* "It is good to place a corridor for wildlife but wildlife and cattle and *inkang'itie* are one. Therefore, I would advise that we protect the corridor for the purpose of wildlife and then we mix [with them] as usual."

Landis Lamba:[53] It would be good to carve out a wildlife corridor from Manyara Ranch going to the mountains, toward *Engososi* [in Losirwa], passing through *Oloturo*. *Another man, of the Makaa age-set, chimes in from the crowd.* "Yes, we could carve out a corridor from the ranch going into the mountains."

> **Note**: This has already been done, with the agreement between AWF and JKT to protect former army land in the mountains as a part of the corridor.[54] There has been a retired army training base there for a long time, and the elder whose *enkang'* is there had initially received permission from the army. It remained uncertain whether he will maintain rights of occupancy after the area had come under conservation status. People at AWF suggested he will. For not only would it have been difficult and politically dangerous to relocate the many families that are now a part of this *enkang'* of the richest man in the area, his son became a local politician, and the *enkang'* could draw tourists into any new conservation corridor area that is designed. However, if the corridor would pass all the way down to *Oloturo*, which is a dam near the Esilalei School, it would involve negotiations with many other families within Esilalei, that are less powerful. It is still possible that Maasai *in-kang'itie* will be displaced, with many lying outside official village boundaries. As of 2017, the *Oloiboni enkang'* was still there and, as predicted, had become a big tourist attraction with a private campsite just up the hill.

Makaa Rangi:[55] *An outspoken young elder stands and speaks with a sour, angry look on his face.* I don't know about *Oldonyio*, in Esilalei, but here in Oltukai, "we won't agree to put forth a corridor because the [village] area is very small. Wildlife should pass anywhere and everywhere, like they currently do."

Landis R:[56] *Another Landis stands to speak now, young and small in stature, but with the speaking abilities of an elder and the presence of someone who matters, he speaks quickly.* Wildlife should pass every place, like they do right now because if we say they should pass here [*he motions with his hands across the village, like a corridor*], they will just pass as they like to themselves, and we are not bothered, we do not have a problem with it.

Many elders yell back from the crowd: This is true, the animals should just pass as they do now. They pass everywhere; how can they be put in a corridor?[57]

Seuri Ole Tete:[58] *A respected elder from Esilalei, stands to speak.* "I don't agree with moving *in-kang'itie* to put in a corridor. [The animals] should pass like they do now. I don't see any other option."

Seuri L:[59] *Another elder from Esilalei, highly respected for his age and good-natured character stands to speak; he is soft-spoken and modest, but speaks firmly.* Of course, *inkang'itie* should not be moved. The animals (zebra and wildebeest) that fill the Manyara Ranch, they drink water there and then visit [*tembea*] the villages, walking in between our homes. The wildlife have their corridors. If they come from anywhere, even from Serengeti, they rest at Selela, [and then] they pass through this corridor until Tarangire, but they pass in between the *in-kang'itie*. And if you know the place they pass, you don't place your farm inside. Even me, I have my farm near the corridor, but not inside it. But *in-kang'itie* the corridors go right by them.

Elder L:[60] It could be good to carve out a corridor for wildlife if it was possible, but I don't think that it is possible because they pass every place. I don't know if it would work, if the wildlife would agree to pass in only one place, one line, without passing homes, farms, and eating here and there.

Makaa Jona:[61] I say that we cannot (and should not) carve out a corridor, because they [wildlife] would not know where to pass. Wildebeest in particular don't like to pass through *pori* areas, so if it is *pori*, it won't work.

Landis Lema:[62] *A slightly controversially man, he is the* olaigwenani *for the Ilaiser, respected for his knowledge but not trusted. He speaks with an air of authority.* I say that it would be good to carve out a corridor for wildlife—starting from the settlements in *Engusero*, Olutkai into Esilalei. The *inkang'itie* in *Engusero* would all move to be here in Oltukai.

There is a lot of commotion in angry and anxious voices from residents of Engusero, "Oi
yie yie! He can't be serious," *they mutter out loud.*

MG: *Whispering with one her assistants, she is pushed by him to stand and share what
she is saying with the crowd. She speaks with confidence in Swahili.* Research in
Kenya suggests that wildlife prefer areas with a moderate density of Maasai settlements, *inkang'itie* in Maa [*she says in a decent Maa accent and Maasai
smile*], and livestock. The study by (Reid et al. 2003) found that such areas had
higher wildlife densities than areas with no settlements, or areas with very high
density of *inkang'itie*.

Landis Taeto:[63] I would like to support what the elders are saying. "The corridor
should just stay as it is. You can't move people. If you do, wildlife won't know
where to pass, they follow people, and they follow cattle." And like MG said, an
enkang' can attract wildlife.[64] "Of course people shouldn't be too many and the
farms shouldn't be too big in the areas where they pass, but wildlife should be
allowed to pass as they do now. And wildlife should be able to mix with cattle
as they do now. I say that we should not be talking about a corridor, but rather
a grazing area, *malisho* [Swahili, *shoo* in Maa], for wildlife **and** livestock." Where
are the wildlife now? All that is left [outside of the parks] are in Maasai areas.

> **Note:** This is a common sentiment held not only by Maasai, but by conserva-
> tion workers in the area, that the remaining wildlife in the country are in Maa-
> sai areas. Even someone at the game office in Monduli stated in an interview
> about corridors that "in Maasai land, there are a lot of wildlife. . . . They are not
> inside the parks. Pastoralism and wildlife are no problem, they can be planned
> together."[65]

Gideon:[66] *He has been sitting in his car paying attention to the meeting but, as the driver
for the MR, not participating. He is Maasai and spends his days in the villages and
the ranch and is therefore quite knowledgeable about the topic at hand. He speaks
in a casual, confident tone.* [Landis Taeto is right], here, in Oltukai and Manyara
Ranch, the wildlife are not moving, they are staying. But in Esilalei, they are
moving, [like people have already explained], from between the cultural boma
and the school (*Oloturo*), they are moving to and from the ranch and into the
mountains. Here, a corridor, which from my understanding should be about
3–6 km wide, would permit the free flow of animals like wildebeest, zebra, and
elephant—which are not eating along the way when they are moving. And
farms? Farms are not the enemy of wildlife, but the animals cause problems for

people farming [*loud exclamation of agreement from Maasai in the crowd*—Ee pae! *(of course!)*]. It is like a leopard and goats. You cannot let a leopard in the middle of goats and not have it eat them [*exclamations of* Oosho! Oi yie yie!, *and laughter from Maasai*]. But if we can find a way to protect farms then it would solve the problem.

TANAPA 3:[67] Yes, corridors are important for keeping open areas, which are important for wildlife and have not yet been ruined. But you can't say that a corridor should be 3–6 km wide. This wouldn't work because wildlife do not have boundaries. We need to look at the whole area. And different animals have different patterns. Like elephants have their paths. They can leave it for three years and then use it again. Buffalo, wildebeest, even zebra. They come from one place and move to another. Not always back and forth from the parks.

Lonana:[68] *A Maasai elder who is a guest, an educated man who is acting as a liaison of sorts for the Maasai community and TLCT, and who is extremely respected by all, stands to speak; there is a hush as people quiet to listen carefully.* What everyone has been saying is true. In fact, there is no word in Maa for corridor. We can talk about *orogous* or *embolos*, which translates as neck or waist, but also means pathway, as in a narrow path through the woods, but corridor, we have no word like that. And I think that is part of the confusion that is coming across in the different statements being made here today. There needs to be some clarification on what this word means and if a corridor, as being proposed by AWF or another organization, would allow livestock to mix with wildlife. *Enthusiastic sounds of agreement come from Maasai.*

Professor Gamassa:[69] *Gamassa was president of Mweka College of African Wildlife Management, which has a research station within the Kwa Kuchinja corridor (southwest of Oltukai Village in Babati District). Despite his stature, he speaks in a modest, soft-spoken, and friendly tone. If I may? he asks, since there was the assumption that AWF would speak next. Those at AWF, the* wataalamu, *and the chairman all motion for him to go ahead.* I feel I can contribute here. In general, "a wildlife corridor can be defined as a springboard passage route used by wild animals to move, during a certain season of the year, from one place to another according to migratory behaviour." For the purposes of planning, a corridor "needs to be defined in spatial and temporal settings according to a series of criteria," including, like Professor Mwalyosi explained, a minimum area such as the length and width needed by the migratory animals [Gamassa 1989, 8]. And of course, it matters which species we are talking about—today there has been discussion of wildebeest, zebra and elephants, the dominant species for this area—and whether they use the area at night, during the day, at dusk, and so on. And then we need to know the season and the specific use of the corridors by the different animals—are they in transit to their dispersal, congregation, or breeding destinations, or are they using the corridor for more than movement, such as for breeding and calving, resting and feeding? The management authority for the corridor [*he looks around to AWF, the district representatives, and Maasai*] needs to be aware of all these issues in designing and implementing a conservation corridor. "In terms of wildlife management, corridors are as important as national parks and game reserves and need protection. They need to be identified, demarcated and protected by law but restrictions on their use need not be as severe as in national parks. Livestock grazing can be practiced, even crop cultivation in selected areas if crop types can be planted and mature before animals start moving in the area" [Gamassa 1989, 9].

TANAPA 4:[70] I would just like to add that Kwa Kuchinja is very important as a wildlife corridor. It links TNP and LMNP. LMNP is very small, too small to be viable [as in an "island park"], it needs to have this link. There are a lot of ecological dependencies between TNP and LMNP; if [the corridor] is blocked, the impact will be very big on LMNP. It won't be so big on TNP because the animals have space and they can move to Simanjiro. But for LMNP, the Kwa Kuchinja corridor is very important. Everyone—TANAPA, Wildlife Division, communities, NGOs—need to work together to protect it. We know you, the communities [*he looks at the Maasai sitting around him*], depend on this area for your livelihood. [We need to look at] how to support you and to protect wildlife at the same time. NGOs also need to play a role to keep the area protected. The big problem is coordination. It is still weak between the different stakeholders and institutions [but AWF is working on this, and we are working with them].[71] *He looks over at the local director for AWF and then sits down.*

Dr. K:[72] *Another highly respected guest, he is Tanzanian and the director of AWF in Arusha, he is well liked and respected by Maasai. He stands up and speaks where he is standing, smiling.* "A corridor dictates a form of land use. It ensures access to land so that wildlife can go through village land. It is not something new; it is rather to make sure, to accommodate sustainability, to allow wildlife to get from point A to point B."

Landis Taeto:[73] *Stands again quickly and speaks in direct response to the last speaker.* Then we need to change the name of the Kwa Kuchinja corridor! Where is the end? You are coming here to this village talking about corridors, but this corridor goes all the way to Selela, Engeruka, and maybe even further! We should just call it *malisho* [grazing areas]. And the project should be to improve the places where the animals stay, not to set aside [*kutenga*] a corridor. Or maybe you could call the project "Helping those people who stay with wildlife and mix with them." We need to be talking about improving this relationship and this land, and not about carving out or protecting a corridor! *He sits to loud sounds of agreement and enthusiasm from Maasai.*

Local conservation area manager:[74] *Standing, he speaks with a serious face.* I completely agree with what Landis Taeto has said, and I am happy to hear this. And I would like to say that KEEP is just that kind of opportunity; if it means changing the name from corridor, that's fine with me. Maybe we could talk about KEEP now?

> **Note:** There is a great deal of malleability with the word "corridor." Maasai have used the word to discuss "pathways." But these pathways don't always go between national parks; they also move around the village. Pathways, and wildlife, they argue, move between and among settlements, and next to farms. It follows that rather than talking about carving out "corridors" we should leave the animals to pass as they always have, but what happens when things change and little room is left for animals to pass? Landis Taeto suggests we should change the language altogether and talk about protecting grazing areas not corridors. The conservation manager agrees with this, because that is what they are, after all, proposing—to protect grazing areas. But they are doing so in a manner that still assumes the need to protect a route from "point A to point B" rather than an open area of mixed land use. However, if it is understood that the villages of Oltukai and Esilalei are inside a corridor (Kwa Kuchinja) then the ultimate goal would be to treat the whole village as a corridor—as Mama P suggested it is, and as the conservation literature argues. Yet, as Landis Taeto has pointed out, this corridor doesn't start or end with these villages, or even with the national parks. How then, he asks, can we really be talking about a corridor?
>
> If there was a shift in *language and focus* to grazing areas, there would be more room to negotiate with Maasai on their own terms. For instance, the statement above suggesting *inkang'itie* be moved out of *Engusero* expresses a common concern among villagers that this part of the village, which used to be open grazing area for livestock as well as wildlife, is filling up with *in-kang'itie* and farms. A focused dialogue on the need to protect *Engusero* as a grazing area would, of course, meet resistance from those residing there. Yet it would make sense to many (even those residing there) and encourage land-use plan-

ning at the village level to preserve pasture (for livestock and wildlife). A recent conservation intervention in Terat, Simanjiro, has done just that (Davis and Goldman 2017).

Chairman T: The manager is right; we should move on to a discussion of KEEP now, unless anyone has anything else that needs to be said regarding corridors in general? *He pauses, and there are murmurs among the crowd suggesting that no, there is nothing left to say.* OK, then can we all agree that perhaps there are many corridors in this area, in terms of pathways that animals use, but that planned corridors as in new conservation areas wouldn't work? Can we agree that perhaps we should be talking about *malisho* [grazing areas]? *To this there is a lot of noise, with people speaking out loud that yes, this makes sense, yes they agree.* OK, then, we have agreed. We have finished agenda one. Now, let's move to agenda two, which is about the KEEP project. Let us hear what people have to say about KEEP.

Landis M:[75] *He moves into the center with ease and confidence. He looks around, and back at members of Manyara Ranch and AWF, for whom he is working. He speaks in a confident but gentle tone.* I have been spending time looking for a place to live in Esilalei because we (myself and the village chairman) have been told we are getting kicked off of our land, getting relocated by those people from KEEP. *At this statement, there is a shocked, frustrated look on the face of the manager of MR, who is also the manager of the KEEP project. He starts to interrupt but lets the elder finish.* They said that we are inside the wildlife corridor. They said that we are inside the *ramani* [Swahili: map/border], which is being redrawn. When I asked them why, they said because we are in a wildlife corridor. Since when? I asked. For twenty years it has been a corridor, they said. But where will we go when our ancestors are all from here? Where will we move when under every tree in the whole country, there are people? If the corridor was here twenty years ago, where was the government? We did not agree to any corridor, and we will not agree because they have no rights [to this land] like we do. We ourselves [*he gestures to himself and to the village chairman, whose enkang' is adjacent to his*], we have been here for more than thirty years, and our grandfathers were here more than one hundred years ago. They cannot move us.

The chairman looks over at the MR manager who is eager to speak; he stands.

Local conservation manager:[76] I am very surprised to hear what Landis M has just said. I am coordinating KEEP, which is a *project* by the way, not a people and not an organization! And it is not even a project without agreement from the village. Anyway, I am the coordinator of the project, and I know nothing about what was just said—the moving of settlements. The project has not even really begun; we have just been in the research stage the past year to see if the project is feasible. So what Landis M just spoke about should not have occurred. As we all know, any discussion of land and of wildlife is political, with a lot of misinformation thrown around provoking fears. I would like to know who it was that visited Landis M's boma claiming to be from KEEP. *His words reflect a mixture of concern for what he heard but also frustration and mistrust that it was all true.*

Landis M:[77] *He answers without standing, since his words are brief and in response to a question.* "The people were from AWF and from the district, in an AWF car; there were a lot of people." And you know, *he pauses and looks around,* "there was never a village meeting held about KEEP," so this was the first I had heard of it. "But they told us we are inside the corridor."

> **Note on KEEP and lack of transparency:** The KEEP project was introduced in late 2003 by AWF, who was working together with district and village level government officials and insisted they were still in "planning stages" and that nothing could be done without the consent of villagers. I was told they would involve me (since I had been working in the village for nearly two years and looking at wildlife movements), but they needed to keep outside involvement minimal at first and to work closely with villagers. They started with meetings in the AWF office in Arusha, with village government leaders and selected "traditional leaders."[78] At these meetings they discussed the goals of KEEP and received general consent from village representatives. I would find out about the meetings from village government members who were attending. On a visit to district offices in Monduli, I was told by the regional surveyor and others that they were waiting for an AWF car to go out to the villages to start measuring boundaries for the KEEP project. During this time, I began to ask villagers in Oltukai if they had heard of the KEEP project, and most replied that they had not.

Chairman O:[79] *The former chairman for Oltukai, a young elder now of the Landis age-set and Ilmamasita clan, he was only an* olmurrani *when he was first elected. A primary school educated and kind man, he was naïve about politics and was quickly dominated by members of the village government of the age-set above him, and of the Ilaiser clan who were more powerful and knowledgeable, but more concerned* *for their own welfare than that of the village as a whole.*[80] *He stands to speak, in a slightly arrogant, but somehow humbled, manner.* We did hold meetings about KEEP, but not everyone came to them, and so now they say we didn't have them but we did. KEEP wanted to place a corridor up from the lake into the Manyara Ranch, but we said no. *He says this proudly, looking around the crowd.* We told them this was not possible because there were *inkang'itie* and *shambas* there, which could not be moved. They wanted us to still be able to participate in the project, so that is when someone suggested adding one hundred meters to Manyara Ranch by expanding the boundary into the village. I could not tell you who that was, I believe someone from the district. If you expand Manyara Ranch boundary west one hundred meters, it enters the space where Landis M and the current chairman's *enkang'* is are. So maybe that explains the visit that Landis M mentioned.

Local conservation manager:[81] *Clearly flustered and confused, stands up immediately to speak.* I must say that I really do not understand what I am hearing. I believe you both of course [*he directs these words at Landis M and Chairman O*] but will need to investigate who is behind this one-hundred-meter idea, because it is complete nonsense. The KEEP project is about protecting corridors, or grazing areas [*he adds as if an afterthought*] and adding one hundred meters to the ranch does nothing of the sort. So please, take my word on this, as the manager of the ranch and as coordinator of this project [*he laughs as he says this out loud; he should be an authority on this issue!*]—there is **no** one-hundred-meter extension of the ranch boundary and **no** movement of homesteads. There is **no** KEEP project, yet . . . not until you all agree to it first. *He shakes his head and sits to the sound of laughter from Maasai, playful friendly laughter that says we understand your frustration and appreciate your honesty.*

Chairman T:[82] *In a confident but respectful tone, he addresses the crowd, looking between the conservation manager and Oltukai villagers.* The former government may have agreed to the KEEP project, but they did so without our consent. If there was a meeting in which an agreement to participate in KEEP was made, there is no formal record of it. If there are such records available, we would like to see them, as we currently have no information on this KEEP project. *Sounds of agreement come from Maasai, except members of the old government, who whisper among themselves.*

MG:[83] *Stands to speak, turning as she does to make sure all those at the gathering can see and hear her.* From what I am aware of, the KEEP project is to be completely participatory, which means that you—villagers of Oltukai—are to be involved in all decision making every step of the way. It is your decision if *inkang'itie* need to be moved out of a corridor or not. You are the ones that know where the animals pass and if an *enkang'* gets in the way or not. For we all know that often animals come to *inkang'itie* at night. But farms can get in the way of wild-life and will likely need to be moved from any corridor. But livestock? It is all up to you, and you should not let anything be decided that you do not agree with. Does anyone here know what KEEP means? *Various responses from Maasai, such as* eh-eh *(no)*, mikiyielo *(we don't know)*, ooh! Maiyeilo *(oh, I don't know!).* *MG looks around to take in the voices and expressions and continues.* KEEP stands for Kwa Kuchinja Environmental Easements Project. The notion of an environmental easement comes from America, where people live on land which is important for conservation and they lease out the rights to the land or agree to only use the land for certain purposes and not to sell it in exchange for a financial reward. Here, it is as if you were to decide that rather than farming this year you will lease out the land to wildlife. That is, the land will be kept open for use by wildlife, and you will receive money like when you lease your land to people. The money would come from the KEEP project. But after a while, you might discover that leaving the land open for wildlife is more profitable than farming, even if the direct leasing payment stops, because the wildlife numbers increase, which will increase tourist numbers and bring financial benefits into the village. The payments at this point, from KEEP, could stop, and the process of "leasing" the land to the wildlife will become self-sustaining. Does this make sense? *Sounds of agreement come from Maasai men and women, with excitement to finally understand what the project is about.*

Landis R:[84] *A young Landis of the Ilaiser clan, he is close friends with the old village chairman and implicated in the past village government corruption. He speaks in a confident if slightly angry and frustrated tone.* Thank you, MG, for explaining the meaning behind this KEEP project to us. We can understand this leasing concept; it makes sense.[85] There are many of us who are getting tired of farming. For three straight years now we have gotten nothing, or if we get a crop, it is eaten by wildlife. So we would be open to discussing such a plan.[86] However, I need to say that I do not think we should sign on to KEEP for several reasons. First, we have all these problems with Manyara Ranch right now. Why would we start another project with the same organization while there remain other problems unresolved? This KEEP project has started off poorly; there has been miscommunication and just lack of communication. One person says one thing and then someone else says something different. There are things done in the name of the project (like creating a one-hundred-meter extension of the ranch boundary), which the leaders of the project say they know nothing about! Why should we agree to such a project? If we were to agree to a project and then down the road problems were to occur, that is OK, that happens. But to agree to a project that is starting off with such problems? That does not make any sense to me.

Makaa MN:[87] *A well-respected elder speaks in a casual but confident tone.* We have been here protecting wildlife for so long. Maasai live with wildlife. Wildlife are here because we protected them, and now they want to come in and tell us how to protect them? *Reactions from the crowd in agreement* (Ee pae!) *and raising new questions.*

Conservation manager:[88] It is true that Maasai have been good at conserving the environment and wildlife, but things have changed, and they will continue to change. "Some of you remember what it was like long ago—there were less people, and lots of wildlife." *Maasai respond in the affirmative, "Yes, this is true," with many elders expanding on the issue, but the manager continues.* "You also know that the government of Tanzania gets a lot of money from wildlife. Twelve percent of the national economy comes from wildlife. They would like to increase the money they get from tourism to over 20 percent in the next ten years. This means we need more tourists. Why are tourists coming here?"

Maasai elders: To see wildlife.

The manager continues: Tanzania is unique because we have a lot of wildlife in open areas. . . . There are no fences, and the wildlife continue to graze in open areas outside of national parks, and tourists like this. But over the past thirty years there has been a dramatic decline in animal numbers. There are regular censuses that are conducted, which show major decline in numbers of certain animals like wildebeest and zebra. And some animals have disappeared altogether, like the rhino. If you disagree with this, say so.

Maasai interject with agreement: "Yes, there used to be many rhino here, but now they are gone. And wildebeest numbers have declined. But zebra numbers have gone up in village lands." But this last comment about the zebra was said softly and is not picked up on by the manager or his translator.

"Imagine yourself as a top government official and you need money for development, you need to increase tourism to get money, but the tourists come to see wildlife and the wildlife numbers are decreasing. . . ." If you understand that *one of the reasons* is because their pathways are being closed off, you can decide to put in corridors from TNP to LMNP. The government tends to do things like that, which it sees as being in the interest of the people of the country, but which are not usually in the interest of the communities involved. There is a chance that [the government] will just put in corridors, and there is now new wildlife legislation that allows them to do this. But people working in conservation for a long time, we know that this is not likely to work. The history of taking land to conserve wildlife has paid no interest to the people and has caused a lot of problems. We are concerned that if the government comes to put in corridors, they will get a lot of resistance from people living there. This is where the seeds of the KEEP project were sown. It is better to benefit the local communities so that everyone benefits, not just the government and the wildlife. "So how can we do this? Not by acting like the government and just saying that this is where the corridor is! That's why I was surprised to hear that this has happened." *He shakes his head in annoyance. Then looks up and, clearing his throat, he puts on a smile and continues.* Talking to all of you, I realize that maybe "corridor" is not the right word. You have said that wildlife pass through the whole village. So please don't think that we just want to carve out pathways across village lands. But it is important that we realize that there are key areas to protect for wildlife so that they can continue their "passage through" village lands.

> **Note:** There is still a focus here on *passing through* village lands rather than *coming to village lands*. The problem is not just with the word "corridor" but the description of what is happening, with the verbs used—passing, moving through, moving from A to B. However, the manager, in response to the rejection of KEEP, is forced to reshape the description of the project—from corridors to land-use planning. However, the project remains couched in terms of "protecting the corridor."

Makaa Ntoipo:[89] *An elder of the same age group as the last, but younger, stands to speak. He is more politically aware and politically active. He speaks with conviction.* This is dangerous—all this talk of corridors. This is just another way to steal our land. We need to be careful. We should not agree to the KEEP project.

Chairman T:[90] I would like to summarize things. It seems like we should not agree to KEEP. People have provided many reasons why. They have said that there is no reason to demarcate a corridor when wildlife cover the whole village. And while we have talked about various existing wildlife paths, they all include other villages, especially Esilalei. Why talk about a corridor here when Minjingu, Mswakini, Esilalei, and Losirwa are not discussing a corridor? *Murmurs* *of agreement among Maasai.* The project proposes to move *inkang'itie* and to change the lives of people. This we cannot accept. And finally, We are already conserving the environment and wildlife. Do we agree? *Loud murmurs of agreement come from Maasai, with clear grunts of frustration from the conservation community. The meeting comes to an end.*

"But There Was No Space to Speak"

T'S EARLY 2002. Members of the steering committee for the Manyara Ranch stood around the village school grounds, waiting for the car to arrive to transport them to the ranch for their monthly planning meeting. Unsure when the car would arrive, they waited patiently, talking among themselves—excitedly, nervously—about what to expect at the meeting, and what to say. I had my own car and agreed to carry some people over early in a bit more comfort than the overcrowded MR Land Rover. The two oldest elders and an outgoing younger one convinced the others that it was their right to ride in my car, squeezed their way in, and we were off. As we drove on the barely visible dirt road that cut across the short grass plains into the ranch, the elders spoke excitedly. They had waited a long time for this meeting, and they had much to say. They explained to me in detail why they needed to speak up and what they were planning to say. Their excitement was contagious. I too grew impatient for the meeting to start and was anxious to see how these elders would negotiate their speaking space with the ranch manager.

As the meeting continued into the early evening and none of the elders spoke their minds as they had said they would, my enthusiasm began to wane, turning into a mixture of curiosity and concern. Why were these elders not raising any of the contentious issues they had discussed so excitedly in the car? When the manager asked for their opinions, he was met by silence. Moreover, not only did they not participate in the meeting in more than a very minimal way, they agreed (in their silence) to a proposal put forth by the manager that I knew they disagreed with; a plan to monitor use of MR pastures by villagers through a cattle headcount system. They agreed without argument. Why? What prevented them from participating as they had planned? What had gone wrong? After the meeting, the manager also seemed discouraged, and asked me in a confused and concerned tone, "Why did they not participate? I gave them every opportunity to do so." Unable to answer him, his question fueled my own curiosity.

Driving back from the meeting, I questioned the most vocal and respected elder of the group: "Why did you not speak up at the meeting as you had planned? Why did you not share all those thoughts you shared with me on the drive over?" His response was quick and direct, said as if I should have known the answer, "But there was no opportunity to participate. There was no space to speak." His answer caught me by surprise. As I had observed, there was "space" to speak. The manager had asked several times for them to share their views, yet each time he was met with silence. He himself was distressed and concerned about their lack of participation. Now I found myself asking the very question he had asked me: Why did they not participate?

After regularly attending Maasai meetings of all kinds for two years, I started to look a bit closer at *how* the steering committee meetings were being held. The meetings were always held outside, where old school benches were placed in a semicircle facing a main table where the manager and his liaison officer sat. In Maasai custom, the meetings were always blessed by the *oloiboni* (who was also the oldest man present). The ranch manager, an elder white man, would lead the meeting. He usually had an agenda with multiple items to discuss, which he would introduce at the beginning of the meeting along with a lengthy discussion of his opinion of the best solution or course of action for each. Then, he would inevitably say something like, "I have much more to say, but I would like to give you all a chance to speak. I want to hear what you think," which was nearly always met with silence. For Maasai, the manager openly said he was not done speaking; it would be disrespectful, unthinkable, for a Maasai to begin speaking until the manager (who was an elder) was done. He was someone whom they respected and saw as an authority, which was confounded by his placement at the front of the meeting space. Since he had proposed a possible conclusion along with the presentation of the agenda, he had foreclosed further discussion. The agenda item, for Maasai present, had already been decided.[1] There was literally and figuratively no space for them to speak.

| Chapter 6 |

Mountains Do Not Meet
but People Do

A Postscript to the Enkiguena

Accounts of a "real" world do not . . . depend on a logic of "discovery," but on a power-charged social relation of "conversation." The world neither speaks itself nor disappears in favour of a master decoder. The codes of the world are not still, waiting only to be read. . . . The world encountered in knowledge projects is an active entity.

—HARAWAY 1991, 198

Metumo ildoinye, kakai tumo iltunganak
—MAASAI PROVERB, "MOUNTAINS DON'T MEET BUT PEOPLE DO"

MAASAI ELDERS are renowned for their eloquence with the spoken word and for their use of proverbs regularly in everyday speech (Saitoti 1980). The title of this chapter comes from the above proverb, which is used on different occasions in slightly different ways. It is commonly spoken when people are parting ways, not sure when they will meet next, or in response to meeting someone new and finding their multiple connections to your life. I suggest it may also allude to the centrality of meetings and dialogue in Maasai society—the bringing together of people, knowledge, and ideas. For according to Maasai, *memut elukunya nabo eng'eno* (one head does not encompass all knowledge) and *ore enkang' nemeiguena, nemeshe-tayiu* (the homestead which is not discussed is not built) (Massek and Sidai 1974, 41). It is through dialogue, in meetings (*inkiguenat* pl., *enkiguena* sg.) that disputes are settled, ideas exchanged, and decisions made. And there are *always* meetings in Maasailand.[1]

It is often said, with some degree of admiration and romantic embellishment, that Maasai make decisions through consensus at these meetings. But what is a consensus? Does it represent a Maasai singular viewpoint? How does it enact and/or displace multiplicity? I hope that my use of the *enkiguena* in the prior chapters as a narrative device and methodological tool of diffraction may have shed some light on these questions. My intent was to decolonize the process of debating conservation plans in two ways. First, by disrupting existing power dynamics that privilege Western ways of knowing, being, and narrating nature-society relations, and instead privilege a Maasai framework. And second, to create ontological openings where diffraction rather than reflection is the goal, and where *multiplicity is exposed and hangs together* in the enactment of a consensus.

I am not proposing the *enkiguena* as a romanticized trope of Maasai indigeneity or an idyllic model for democratic decision-making. All knowledge production and decision-making practices are shaped by and enact power dynamics. And this is true with the *enkiguena* as well. Yet, I suggest (and have hopefully shown) that the structure and guiding principles of the *enkiguena*, based in oral practice, provides a more active space to enact multiplicity, rather than representing singularity (as we are often promised with scientific truths). It also creates a space for power to be exposed, manipulated, contested, and deflected. In this chapter, I will outline how this works through a series of principles that frame the *enkiguena*. I will also touch on the way a consensus is enacted. I close the chapter with a discussion of the ever-present and changing power dynamics within Maasai society and how they are mediated by/through/with the *enkiguena* as method.

The Art of Speech

Over time, as I observed meetings of all kinds across Maasailand, it became clear that in addition to *what* was being said, *how* things were said mattered. This is common in African oral literature, where the art of speech, or how people do "things with words," matters significantly (Finnegan 2007, 27; Mbembe 2015, 2001). The importance of the spoken word in Maasai society is illustrated by the fact that in Maa, the verb for "to think" and "to speak" are the same, *a-jo*. The importance of speaking is closely linked to the importance of "listening" or "hearing," as expressed in the two following proverbs: *Mengor olekutuk inkulukuok*, "He who talks misses no target," and *epolos engiok enaimen*, "The ear penetrates darkness [an eye cannot]" (Even in darkness, the ear hears) (Saitoti 1980). In this section, I explain a particular "art of speaking," or way of "doing things with words" performed by Maasai on an everyday basis. I then proceed to discuss the importance of the *enkiguena* as a place where the art of speech is formalized with a set of guiding principles that can form the basis for building decolonial conservation dialogues.

I: *AINOS ILOMON* (EATING THE NEWS)

For Maasai, to share the news with someone, to sit and catch up with an old friend, or to find out more about a visitor, is to eat the news (*ainos ilomon*).[2] News is "eaten" because it is not just passed back and forth but presented by one person and taken in, digested, ruminated on by another. While much time is devoted to eating the news with an out-of-town visitor, it is a ritual that is also performed daily with one's neighbors, age-mates, relatives, and friends.

To eat the news is a ritual, with a structure and rhythm. The process is initiated when one person asks one of a series of possible questions regarding the other's condition/state of being, such as "You are well?" "You are not sick?" or "You are rested?" This signals the other to begin talking, and so they do. They answer the question always in the positive, regardless of their state of being: "Yes we are well," "No, I am not sick," "We are well rested." They then repeat this notion in multiple ways: "We are well," "We are at peace," "We are all healthy," "There is nothing wrong," and so on (*kirasidaan, kiserian, kirabioto, miti entokin tohrono*). After this, they begin to discuss the real state of affairs: "The children all have malaria, the cattle are all sick, the dry season has hit hard," explaining, of course, that all is *not* well. Nonetheless, and regardless of how bad a person's condition might be, they continue to repeat, as a chorus of sorts, the various ways in which they are well.[3] The more talented an orator the speaker is the longer, more musical and rhythmic the news is told.

The entire time the speaker is talking, the other participant in the dialogue just listens. This is not a back-and-forth conversation. The one listening is not to speak, except to acknowledge they are listening by responding accordingly with the affirmative sounds of *ooó* or *eeé* or with a quick word: *tedo?* (you say so?), or *esipa* (it is true). Failure to do so suggests that one is not listening. If the listener does not respond in this way, they are often reminded to—*tedo ooó* (say *ooó*) or *tedo eeé* (say *eeé*)—by the speaker.[4] When the speaker is finished sharing their news, they make it clear by calling out a long tone, raised at the end. Then, and only then, does the listener know the speaker is finished and that it is now their turn to speak. And so, the speaker and the listener switch roles. There is no need to ask the opening question again. The listener has been cued that it is now their turn to speak, to share their news, and so they do.

This formal sort of news exchange can occur between men, women, elders, and *ilmurran*, all with the right to their own time to speak, in line with complex social relations and power dynamics mediated by age, clan, and gender. Historically this was the main way in which news and knowledge traveled across Maasailand, particularly before cellphones. And it continues today, facilitated by cellphones, when a visitor comes to visit, at markets, and at the beginning of meetings. According to a junior elder from Sukuro Village, Simanjiro:

> When someone would travel from here to far away, they'd stop at each location along the way and eat the news. So from Sukuro to Loborsoit, he brings the news from Loborsoit. When he gets to Emboreet he brings the news from Sukuro and Loborsoit. When he gets to Lobersirrit, he brings the news from Loborsoit, Sukuro, and Emboreet, and so on. In one day, news from five different villages is passed.

This holds true today, and can be seen at an *enkiguena*, where the meeting begins with people from different locations standing to share the news of their area. In this way, the entire meeting is informed about livestock or human illness outbreaks and recoveries, if it has rained somewhere, how much, how the pastures are, and so on.

II: THE *ENKIGUENA*

The rhythmic pattern of speech, mutual respect, and shared time for speaking and listening that occurs when Maasai "eat the news" is performed in a more formal way at the *enkiguena*. The literal translation of *enkiguena* is discussion, meeting, consultation, debate, and counsel (as in legal dispute) (Mol 1996). In the literature, an *enkiguena* is sometimes referred to as the counsel, assembly, or meeting of the "elders" (Rugumayo 1997), where the eloquent oratory skills of elders are contrasted with the impatient, virulent character of the *ilmurran*. Yet *ilmurran* also take part in meetings, where they plan events and settle disputes while learning the art of speech, the importance of unity, and the value of dialogue. Historically, these practices were cultivated in the *emanyata*—separate *ilmurran* villages that no longer exist in Tanzania. Yet even without the *emanyata*, *ilmurran* maintain a tight social circle and have regular meetings coordinated by their *ilaigwenak*, where decisions are made by consensus. An *enkiguena* can also be called by a family, an *enkang'*, local clan members, women, or an *olaigwenani* (age-set or clan-based). There are village government meetings (government council), village assembly meetings (all adult residents), and NGO-initiated meetings, all which are referred to as *enkiguena* and often run as such, with minutes kept for government records.[5]

The subjects dealt with at an *enkiguena* range from development issues, such as road maintenance or dam construction, to petty theft, age-set transgressions, age-set ceremonial planning, clan needs, wedding preparations, questions of inheritance, warfare, murder, election fraud, and conservation projects.

The *enkiguena* can be understood as the primary institution for decision-making within Maasai society. There are, of course, different types of meetings that encourage different kinds of participation and levels of agreement or contestation and thus different decision-making practices. At the broadest level, there are two types: those that call together people to make a joint decision on a matter that concerns them all equally, such as a village development project or an age-set celebration; and meetings that are called to arbitrate between two disputing individuals or parties, such as clan disputes. For the latter, the individuals involved usually rely on their *ilaigwenak* to arbitrate their case for them, similar to going to court and hiring a lawyer.[6] The principles governing the different *enkiguena* are the same, albeit with differences in the type of consensus that is reached, as discussed more below.

There are three primary principles underlying the *enkiguena* structure that I argue make it a more fluid space to enact multiplicity and thus an ideal diffraction apparatus. First, the discussion is opened by naming *only* the problem at hand (e.g., the *issue* "concerning" the dam). There is no mention of possible solutions within the problem statement itself or by the person who opens the meeting (e.g., to vote if we should place the dam at location X). Second, *everyone* at an *enkiguena* has the freedom (theoretically) to speak and to be listened to; there are no rules constraining his/her contribution. And third, a meeting is finished when, and only when, a "consensus" has been reached. But what is a consensus? Spencer (2003, 25) described it as an ending that is "sufficient to stifle further protest." It is a process that is not adequately described with the English word "consensus." I will address this in more detail below. First, I'd like to explain the general setting of an *enkiguena* and discuss how the first two principles play out, as observed in the *enkiguena* chapters.

An *enkiguena* is usually held under the shade of a large tree, though it is becoming more common to hold meetings inside (e.g., village office buildings, vacant school rooms). After a blessing from an elder, the chairman of the meeting will explain the nature of the problem. If the case involves a feud between two people, they will both have their chance to present their views (Saitoti 1980). If it is a government meeting, the minutes may be read from the prior meeting. If it is a continuation of an issue previously discussed, the prior meeting is summarized. If the meeting brings together people from far away, they are asked to share news from home. Regardless of the issue being debated, *the meeting starts by stating the problem (or issue) only*, and the floor is opened for dialogue. Everyone has a chance to stand up and speak if they have something to say and the courage to speak to the crowd. In certain circumstances, visitors are expected to contribute as "objective outsiders" or assumed "experts" on a given problem.[7] When someone wishes to speak, they stand up in the center of the circle, where they can address the entire crowd, turning to look in different directions as they talk. *Ilaigwenak* hold their *olkuma* when speaking, as a sign of their respected status. Other men hold on to their walking stick, leaning on it authoritatively, clutching it nervously, or confidently holding it against their back, as they turn to speak to the crowd. During my time in the field, women in *Emanyara* still spoke while sitting, which I was told was the tradition, unless a man stood at the same time (which I saw occur in Kitengela). However, in Longido, Simanjiro, and Ngorongoro, I saw women stand up and speak confidently at meetings.[8] At government and NGO meetings, women will often be called on to speak. All others must request a turn. There are no rules governing who can speak; the chairman for the meeting just makes sure that everyone who wants to speak has their chance.

At an *enkiguena*, each speaker speaks until they are finished, regardless of how long this takes; then and only then does another stand to speak. The one who speaks does not need to respond to, or in any way address, what the last speaker said; it is simply their turn to explain their story, just like when "eating the news." However, to strengthen their words, there is often reference to what others have said. When speaking, there is no constraining etiquette the speaker must follow; they are free to speak their concerns, voice their anger, show their lack of interest in the topic being discussed, and even insult a prior speaker, as long as it is done during their turn to speak. When there is general disapproval for what a speaker is saying (especially if they are drunk), loud, abusive comments are often blurted out at them while they are speaking to remove them from the "stage." Negative words or interactions exchanged at an *enkiguena* are supposed to be left at the *enkiguena*. For the most part, everyone's experience or knowledge is respected and considered relevant, which means that a meeting can take all day, much gets repeated, and the conversation may go in unexpected directions. This process was explained by a Maasai junior elder to his *mzungu* (Swahili: European; pl. *wazungu*) guest who was clearly confused trying to follow a meeting that was being conducted in Maasai style (*ya Kimaasai*):

> We do things the Maasai way. We do not know how to make things short, like you *wazungu*. We can take a very long time, but it is like this: one person goes into detail, another makes an error, another goes far off the topic, and then we return right there. If you try to have ten agenda items in one meeting, [it is not possible]. It is not like those [meetings] of *wazungu*, or even . . . those others who have developed. You can have only two agenda items and still it will take a very long time. Until most of the people present have stood [and spoken].

An individual can stand to speak multiple times, with something new to say each time, as the dialogue progresses, twists and turns, and a "consensus" is constructed. It is only when nothing new is being said that the chairman of the meeting may try to prevent someone from speaking again or may cut short the long-winded words of an elder. At this point, the chairperson will try to see if there is agreement on a "consensus" by asking something like *kirukoke* (we have agreed), *kituningoki* (we have heard/listened to each other), or simply *kindipa* (we have finished).

So how do they construct a consensus? There are no choices put forth, and there is no voting. The dialogue rarely follows a linear path. It circles around and meanders in different directions as speakers contribute new ideas, knowledge, and opinions to the topic at hand. People will often draw on memory and discuss how a similar problem was tackled in the past, what they decided then, and if that is relevant today. The different words slowly piece together a collage, or as Spencer suggests, "an imaginative synthesis" (Spencer 2003). The "synthesis" is imaginative in that there is no formal construction of a "compromise." Imagine, for instance, a meeting regarding an age-set fine. One speaker suggests the age-set be fined ten bulls and five calves. Another speaker argues against livestock contributions, demanding a fine of cash and alcohol. Others scoff at this and recall the time when cattle only were used for fines and the *ilmurran* knew how to behave. Several speakers argue against a fine and push for forgiveness. No one suggests that a compromise be met between the different extremes that will please everyone. Yet as more people speak, it becomes clear that a fine is necessary (they have always done so in the past) and what an appropriate fine should be (today things are different, money is easier than cattle). Most people believe the fine should be some combination of cattle and cash and alcohol. Various possibilities are suggested, with different cohorts pushing for different things until a statement is made that encapsulates enough of the variability expressed and provides a solution agreeable to all. The contributions of outside guests are considered, and the fine is lowered further. All are happy because their voice was heard and no one voice dominated the debate or predicted the outcome. The final agreement may not reflect the wishes of all, but it is *acceptable* to all. It will be final.

The consensus is not reached magically. There are inner workings, key players, skilled arbitrators, and decisions about whom to trust and whom to respect. There are often premeetings held by various cohorts to strategize how best to argue their point, which involves deciding who should speak and how. There are individuals respected for their wisdom and knowledge who do not normally speak at meetings. Such people, however, often consult others prior to the meeting, or even during a meeting in private side discussions (Maa: *engilipata*, often translated as chamber). Sometimes such individuals will speak up and play a key role in the building of a consensus. One such elder in Oltukai was one of my most valuable interlocutors. He was one of the most knowledgeable men in the village, also kind, easygoing, and aware of everything that was always going on around him. He did not, however, regularly speak at meetings. It was not his style, he told me, and he hated politics. As a fellow acquaintance explained, "He sits and listens quietly, listens to everything that is being said and digests it all. If he chooses to speak, he will sum up all that has been said by the various speakers, make connections others have not seen, and bring the meeting closer to a consensus."

Maasai can deliberate all day long until a consensus is built/enacted. The chairperson will often summarize the conclusion of the discussion and (if relevant) state the fine as set down by Maasai law or decided upon in the meeting, set the schedule of events (or payments) discussed, or otherwise plan for a follow-up meeting. An elder will often bless the consensus, and the meeting is closed. Sometimes, an entire day is not enough time to reach a consensus, and a meeting will reconvene until one is reached. Sometimes more side deliberations are needed. If a consensus cannot be reached even after several meetings, then an *olaigwenani* will be called on to decide. When this occurs, rather than saying "we have all agreed" or "we have all listened to each other," people will say that the meeting or the decision has been "cut," indicating that a decision has been made (from above).[9]

The pressure to come to a consensus confirms the unity ideal upheld by Maasai. It is markedly different than the process of voting and majority rules. This was clear when talking with people after meetings. In Kitengela, people regularly discussed agreeing with a consensus but wanting more in terms of ongoing negotiations. In such instances, the end of the meeting was the enactment of a new set of discussions. In Oltukai, people often spoke about the various twists and turns a meeting took to get to the consensus and what that meant. Different meetings lead to different types of consensus building. A community meeting (e.g., village, age-set) will often strive for a true consensus as a sign of unity within the defined "community," while the consensus at an *enkiguena* involving a dispute may look more like an agreed arbitration between disagreeing parties. Both types are respected as the final word because they are created through the process of debate; even if it is not deemed to be preferable to all, it is to be respected by all.

A consensus does not represent a singular (cohesive, complete) Maasai viewpoint, but rather the hanging together, or the enactment of multiple contributions from partially connected participants. The participants are partially connected in that they are all at once "Maasai," but they are women and men of different age-sets, wealth, clans, and status within Maasai society, reflecting different loyalties, knowledge, expertise, and experience, and commanding different degrees of respect or *enkanyit*—both within the *enkiguena* and society more broadly.

Enkanyit and the Changing Politics of Participation

Enkanyit is a Maasai word which generally translates as "respect," "good manners," or "decency" (Mol 1996, 17; Hodgson 2001). *Enkanyit* can also be translated as "obedience" or "deference" to structural superiors (Talle 1988) and is the general principle guiding Maasai social interactions and mediating power dynamics. *Enkanyit*, enacted *as both respect and fear*, strongly mediates participation in Maasai meetings. It operates across structural divisions of age, gender, clan, and wealth among Maasai and with outside "experts" or politicians. These divisions, covered briefly in the introduction and displayed in the *enkiguena* chapters, are not static, but have been shifting over time and in relation to each other. Divisions by clan, for instance, have increased dramatically within Maasai communities over the past few decades, with clan leaders (*ilaigwenak le nkaji*) multiplying in numbers and carrying with them the power of the *olkuma* and the threat of the curse that comes with it. At the same time, *ilmurran* and women are gaining power through education, government leadership positions, involvement in church, and NGO activities to shift relations of *enkanyit* based on age and gender. In this section, I briefly outline the ways in which *enkanyit* works through these categories of difference to mediate power within Maasai society and within an *enkiguena*, and how it is changing.

AGE-SETS (*OLAJI*)

Mejool emurt endukua. The neck cannot go above the head, even for a day; youth cannot go ahead of the elders, they must respect the elders.

Don't dance in front of the nose of a lion; it will bite you. Your father is the lion; you need to respect him.[10]

The age-set system provides multiple places to cement relations as well as to divide groups—between elders and *ilmurran*, junior and senior *ilmurran*, adjacent and alternate (*ilpiron*-related) age-sets. Historically, a "parallel overlap" in adjacent *ilmurran* groups assured that there was a "standing army" of warriors if needed (Waller 1979, 172). Today, the overlap ensures a supply of labor for herding, watering cattle, and engaging in wage-labor pursuits to provide for the family. It also enables knowledge transfers, with junior *ilmurran* learning from their seniors everything from how to plait their hair, throw spears, and slaughter and skin a cow, to lead an *enkiguena* and hunt a lion. For lion hunting is a way in which the *ilmurran* collectively prove they can protect their community. There is often a rise in lion hunting toward the end of an age-set overlap, as one age-set seeks to prove their competence and compete for status and respect (Goldman, Roque de Pinho, and Perry 2013). Conflict has always been rife between junior and senior *ilmurran* over the privileges and responsibilities associated with the warrior grade. While the animosity fades as men become elders and collaborate in community affairs, it never completely disappears. Age-set conflicts continue to define interpersonal relations throughout much of a man's life. They contribute to village politics and governance disputes among the expanding Maasai NGOs (Hodgson 2011; Igoe 2000), where younger age-sets use education and access to funding to challenge the elders' traditional authority, and adjacent groups compete with each other over positions of power.

Contrasting with the animosity between adjacent/consecutive age-sets, there is a supportive, father-son respect between alternate age-sets, institutionalized with the firestick (*olpiro* sg., *ilpiron*, pl.) relationship. The name refers to the kindling of a ritual fire that the senior age-set performs, which brings the junior age-set "to life" as *ilmurran*. *Ilpiron* elders demand respect, and they control the ceremonial progression of the *ilmurran* age-set, deciding when a new age-set should be opened, when it is time to perform the *eunoto ceremony* (to gain senior warrior status and historically to be permitted to marry), and when it is time to perform the *olng'esher* ceremony for *ilmurran* to officially become elders. As such, the firestick elders officially limit *ilmurran* access to wives, cattle, and political decision-making.[11]

Much of this has changed dramatically over the last several decades with a waning in the power of the *ilpiron* over the *ilmurran*, as many families depend on the financial contributions of *ilmurran* who may work in town or in the livestock or gemstone industries. Today, many *ilmurran* marry before *eunoto*, act like elders before *olng'esher*, and rise to positions of power within local and regional government structures. Yet they do not have the power to bless and curse until they become elders, and even then, the elders above them hold this power over them. The power of the curse cannot be overstated; some scholars have argued that it is what helps elders maintain authority and control (Hodgson 2001; Spencer 2003; Talle 1988). While the use of the curse is rare, Waller argues that it symbolizes the "ultimate authority of the elders" over the *ilmurran* (Waller 1979, 184) and is even stronger and more dangerous when associated with clan ties, or with particular ritual leaders such as an *oloiboni* or *ilaigwenak*.

Age-set affairs during the *ilmurran* period are dealt with primarily by the age-set *olaigwenani*, who is seen as a spokesperson for his age-mates. As such, leadership qualities are strongly linked to knowledge, the ability to both command and give respect, and being a good speaker, which includes speaking, listening, delegating, and providing others the opportunity to speak. As one of Waller's informants expressed it,

"The job of the *olaigwenani* is *enkiguena*" (Waller 1979).[12] The power of an *olaigwenani* is associated with his capacity to curse the entire age-set, embodied in the *olkuma*, which he holds as a sign of his title. Yet this power wanes as the age-set graduates into adulthood. Today, the power of the *ilaigwenak* title has been transformed with the expansion of clan-based *ilaigwenak* (*ilaigwenak le nkaji*).

CLANS (*ENKAJI*)

In addition to age-sets for men and *esirit* (circumcision groups) and general age-grades for women, Maasai are also united and divided along clan lines. The term *enkaji* means house, and refers to the larger overarching moieties (*Narok-kiteng'*, the black cow, and *Nado-Mongi*, the red oxen), which encompass various clans and subclans. It illustrates the strength of clan affiliations *as home*, particularly when traveling, where clan associations unite Maasai across space. However, at the smaller scale of villages/*enkutoto* or even *olosho*, clan affiliations can divide Maasai, leading to antagonistic and competitive relations. Most of this antagonism is left behind during *enkiguena* negotiations, yet it can be ignited by the words and actions of clan leaders, *ilaigwenak le nkaji*.

Clan-based *ilaigwenak*—old and new—are quite different than the age-set ones. Many are directly linked to *siasa*, the Swahili word that Maasai use to refer to the politics associated with elected and appointed government positions. The word implies what many Maasai see as the negative aspect of such politics—greed, lies, and corruption, as people make political promises to get votes and then gain privileged access to resources once in positions of power. Many of the clan-based *ilaigwenak* are now seen as closely associated with *siasa*. During the time I was in the field, I saw these new *ilaigwenak* proliferating rapidly (from one in each village at the start to more than four). New *ilaigenak le nkaji* were running campaigns for their positions at the village level, and then *ilaigwenak le nkang* [of the *enkang'*] were being elected for individual clans and homesteads. And there was discussion of a third type of leader: *olaigwenani lo losho*, leader for the whole *olosho*. These new *ilaigwenak* insist they are striving to unite Maasai and strengthen their capacity to speak for them as a group. They argue for the need to mimic the government system of decentralization and have leaders at every level (e.g., village, district, etc.) so that they can work with government-based leaders and gain respect. Many Maasai I spoke with suggest that rather than uniting Maasai the new *ilaigwenak* were fueling clan-based politics. Since they receive an *olkuma*, and thereby possess the power of the curse, it is hard for other Maasai to challenge them. In this case, *enkanyit* has become more associated with fear, but not always in line with respect. When it comes to an *enkiguena*, the *ilaigwenak* can dominate a meeting and try to steer the course of the discussion. However, if they do so in a way that undermines respect, they can be scorned and their power questioned.

Despite these new challenges, *ilaigwenak* as a whole tend to garner more respect within Maasai communities than elected leaders, which led one organization, Ujamaa Community Resource Trust (UCRT), to develop the community leadership forum, to support them. The project seeks to formalize the *ilaigwenak* institution and build the capacity of leaders to support communities in rights-based disputes over land and resources claims. The community leadership forum also challenges the customary structure of the *ilaigwenak* institution by facilitating a separate women's leadership forum, as well as the inclusion of women in the larger leadership forum (Goldman, Sinandei, and DeLuca 2014; Goldman, Davis, and Little 2016).

While women do not have official age-set leaders, there are informal leaders of various kinds—elder women with a great deal of knowledge of "the way things used to be," as well as formally educated young women who can read and write in Swahili. Today both types of leaders are being formalized as *engaigwenak* (feminine of *ilaig-wenak*, traditional leader) through the community leadership forum work of UCRT. Yet even without this formalization, women have always had their own ways of participating in meetings that were previously seen as the purview of men. This is perhaps best embodied in the term *olaigwenani lol-choni*—the spokesman/leader of the bed. The term describes the behind-the-scenes role that women have always played in decision-making processes when a meeting failed to reach a consensus and the men would go home and discuss the issue with their wives/mothers. The women would then tell the men exactly what to say when they returned to the meeting to settle the dispute. This was often described in a way that suggested the decision was easy for the woman, who often scolded the man for not seeing what was so clear. The man, upon returning to the meeting, would say that after "sleeping on it," the "*olaigwenani lol-choni*" (of the bed, i.e., his dreams) told him he should say the following, and he would then repeat what he was told by his wife (or mother). All present at the meeting would know that it was the wise words of a woman that lay behind the man's decision, but this was left unsaid.[13]

> **The missing Enkanyit at the meeting:** It was December 2006, and I was just starting to conduct research in Kitengela. I had come with a *Ilkisongo* Maasai from Tanzania to help navigate the new terrain, and together with our local contact, we walked up to join a meeting that had already begun. The gathering was small, but there was a sizeable group of women present, who sat behind the tight circle of men. We watched as one by one, junior and senior elder men

stood up to speak in highly animated tones, swinging their *ngudi* (walking stick) around at those gathered, or holding it firmly in their hand pointing it out at the crowd. Both gestures denoted a sense of power and authority, if not intimidation. They were discussing their outrage about a large water project that had been proposed for the area against their knowledge. They seemed quite upset and wanted to fight the project. There was a consensus that Maasai knew how to fight a war and that was what they should do. It did not seem as if there was much space to disagree with this point, since the men sharing this view spoke so strongly, although the chief, who was chairing the meeting, did say a few times that if there was anyone who wanted the project (rather than fighting a war against it), then they should speak out. At one point, the chief stood up and asked the women to speak. They seemed to be preparing, talking among themselves, but soon enough a man stood to speak, and the chief did not stop him. After that, the women refused to speak, despite complaints and continual urging by the chief. He stated quite angrily that he knew they could speak and had thoughts, for they had just succeeded in having their own meetings to remove a village problem (men selling illegal liquor). Why then, he asked, could they not speak now, at this meeting, about this issue? The women ignored his pleas, and the meeting soon ended. After the meeting, the women gathered for their own meeting, and I went to join them. When I asked them why they had refused to speak at the meeting, they said it was because they were not informed about the issue. They had been called to the meeting at the last minute, had arrived late, and had not been told enough about the issue. They were not prepared. They assured me that they would be prepared and ready to speak up at the next meeting. They then continued with their own meeting, which was about keeping illegal liquor out of their community.

CHANGING GENDER RELATIONS

In the story above, it was not just the presence of *enkanyit* that inhibited the women's participation, but the absence of it—the men did show respect by informing them about the meeting on time or allowing them time during the meeting to prepare a joint statement. Having the agenda ahead of time would have been helpful. This enables women to talk among themselves and select certain women to speak for them. There are always certain categories of women, for instance widows, the wives of very old (retired) elders, and the mothers of respected leaders, who are usually free from the constraints of *enkanyit* at meetings and able to speak openly. Yet often it is the younger educated women who can follow the meeting better. And there are individual women who are not afraid to speak in front of men, just as there are men who tolerate or even take pride in their smart and outspoken wives. But there are of course also women who remain fearful to speak out at an *enkiguena* and may indeed face the threat of physical violence at home if they do.

Women's formal participation in meetings has been changing rapidly and varies across Maasailand. While in the field in 2002–4, I did not see women in *Emanyara* participate in the *enkiguena* of age-sets, clans, or male elders. They did, however, have their own meetings, which often occurred at night, under the light of the moon, when they were freed of their many daily responsibilities. Women's meetings were often in preparation for a spiritual pilgrimage (*olamal loo n-kituaak*) to the mountain of God (*Oldoinyo Lengai*) or to an *oloiboni* for fertility and rainfall blessings. Such meetings generated a great deal of respect and fear (*enkanyit*) from men, who dared not resist their wives' permission to attend the meetings and supplied all that was asked for (e.g., slaughter animals). Women also attended government meetings and those called by visiting NGOs, although in *Emanyara*, less frequently and enthusiastically than the men, at least in the beginning. In later years, women became more involved in meetings of all kinds, at first due to frustration over their own village government and then through increased involvement with NGOs' activities (Goldman and Little 2015). They initiated their own meetings related to work groups they were in, problems in the village (drunkenness and land sales), and even to challenge the local member of parliament over the ownership of the Manyara Ranch (Goldman, Davis, and Little 2016).

Over the past two decades, women have been speaking more freely in meetings of all kinds across Maasailand. In addition to having their own meetings, they are more regularly attending the "meetings of men" and speaking out, both at the meetings and after them, about what they heard and what they think. In Tanzania, some of this is related to the work of NGOs and learning that if government decisions are made without them, it is against the Tanzanian law. A political dispute in Oltukai in 2004, regarding the Manyara Ranch Steering Committee, was upheld by women who refused to acquiesce, even as the men finally did. Men, women explained to me, would give in to a decision they disagreed with because of their fear of losing popularity, of angering an age-mate or an elder they respected, and of decreasing their opportunities for good reciprocal relations down the line. They themselves, the women argued, did not have such fears and were more likely to stick to their argument once they had the courage to speak it. Similarly, in Simanjiro, women were the most outspoken opponents to the creation of any new conservation area in their villages, and they spoke loudly and defiantly at meetings, particularly the elder women. Another way in which women in

Emanyara have shown their strength is to show their disapproval of a consensus from a meeting that they did not attend or at which they were not properly consulted by "voting with their feet" at subsequent meetings related to that decision by leaving the meeting early or not showing up at all.[14] Men can also use this mechanism to show their disapproval for the way decisions are being made (i.e., not in line with the consensus ideal), and they did so with village government meetings in Oltukai in 2003. By boycotting meetings, they showed their disapproval for the way the meetings were being conducted—that is, not along the *enkiguena* ideal. For while silence is often interpreted as approval/agreement with a consensus, absence is not.

ENKANYIT AND OUTSIDERS

Enkanyit also plays a major role in interactions between Maasai and outsiders. Respect for Maasai views, knowledges, and world-making practices is essential for their participation at meetings. If they feel their input is not respected, they will often remain quiet. At the same time, when a meeting is held in a manner with which they are unfamiliar, and the organizer(s)/leader is someone whom they respect or see as being in a position of authority, Maasai participation is often constrained, as shown in the interlude before this chapter. I saw this occur often when outsiders would come into a Maasai village to hold meetings, even from Maasai NGOs. They would nearly always convene the meeting in a Western-style format—sitting/standing up front, explaining multiple agenda items that nearly always foreclosed debate by proposing a way forward and asking for feedback. For many Maasai, this literally left no space to participate. If Maasai consistently feel like they are not being respected (for their knowledge and opinion), then they are likely to back out of the relationship altogether, or demand changes to it. For example, as discussed in chapter 5, when Maasai in Oltukai began to see that AWF was not being honest in their relations with them regarding a new project, but "playing tricks" and avoiding open dialogue and discussion, they refused to participate in the project.

An Experiment: Holding a Meeting Enkiguena *Style*
Toward the end of my time in the field in 2005, I began talking with Maasai about my interest in the *enkiguena* and about the possibility of changing the structure of the Manyara Ranch steering committee meetings to follow the structure of a "Maasai-style" *enkiguena* to create more space for them to participate. Steering committee members agreed that this was a good idea, but they were skeptical that it would change much. It would help, they said, but only in a small way. "What did it matter how the

meeting was structured?" they asked, if in the end they had no power? "We are only puppets," one man insisted, being pulled by political powers higher up. They argued for the need to have more *control* and the need to see benefits from the MR. That, they argued, was more important than a transformation of the meeting style. Yet they were excited about trying to change the meeting structure and spoke positively about it at the next meeting, which was run as an *enkiguena*. I spoke with other Maasai, who, like myself, were involved as observers and liaisons between Manyara Ranch and the communities. They saw the inherent value of the meeting shift. Yes, it was just a start, but it was a big gesture. It would enable participation. It would enable power shifts. It was a necessary component of any future democratic management for the area. It was a sign of good faith.

But, as to be expected, the situation was extremely complex. The power dynamics and politics involved were not only those associated with the steering committee and Manyara Ranch management but also between the steering committee and their constituents, Maasai villagers. The committee needed to be changed before any progress could be made between the villagers and the MR, and this had nothing to do with the meeting style. When the villagers tried to remove the committee, they held meetings, many meetings, *enkiguena* style. These meetings were participatory, even including women in large numbers and strong voices. The women were angry and demanded change. They openly challenged "consensuses" made at meetings where they were not present and succeeded at reopening the dialogue in new meetings. But in the end, the women, together with the men, agreed to a decision that I knew they did not fully agree with. They agreed to keep the committee in place. I was confused and disappointed. I did not understand. Even the ranch management was bothered by this decision and took the agreement to be "Maasai politics" as usual, or worse, to be their complacent bowing to internal power relations.

Neither of us really understood what was happening or grasped the complexity of the situation. Yes, there were internal power relations. Those in power did not want to leave and fought hard for their right to stay. But it was the smart ones—those good at speaking, those who had that perfect combination of *eng'eno*, respect, good speaking abilities—who won. Their victory was related less to structural power dynamics than to their ability to steer the meeting and affect the consensus. Those who tried to use structural power only, as associated with wealth or a government position, not only failed, but were criticized and made an example of bad behavior, of what should not be done. In the end there **was a consensus**. People decided that it was more important to fix social relations in the village than replace the committee. They were willing to allow the committee to finish its term, to ameliorate conflict in the village. This was not a cop-out or a compromise, it was an agreement, it was a consensus. They needed to trust each other, to trust their unity, to build a future together. Many villagers, particularly women, were extremely happy about this outcome.

Sometimes a consensus may seem contrary to the end goal but is supportive of another goal. The open structure of the *enkiguena* means that the diversity of opinions remains known (despite a consensus being formed), the multiplicity (and disagreements) not erased, and the power dynamics exposed. Power dynamics exist at all levels and are used for various means. But they work in complex ways and are not all encompassing. The very ability for the above sequence of events to occur was tied to the replacement by villagers of their government leaders in one village. In the other village, there was a strategic mixing of the various aspects of power—an elected government politician who was also an *olaigwenani*, an appointed politician with education and well-schooled in local politics, and a very wealthy *oloiboni*. Together they covered three realms of power—that associated with divinity, government, and traditional leadership. They also covered three age-sets: from junior, to senior, to retired elder. However, they were most powerful when their triad also included other elders. Elders respected for being honest and smart, elders who were *mpole* (kind, easygoing), elders who were trusted. When they did not include the elders and the *ilmurran*, they were recognized as powerful but not respected. And it was well recognized that they no longer spoke for the community. People did not attend their meetings. And they were replaced a few years later. So yes, power is everywhere, and it is everywhere contested and refracted.

Conclusion: The Enkiguena in Theory and Practice

The discovery of multiplicity suggests that we are no longer living in the modern world, located within a single *episteme*. Instead, we discover that we are living in different worlds. These are not worlds—that great trope of modernity—that belong on the one hand to the past and on the other to the present. Instead, we discover that we are living in two or more neighboring worlds, worlds that overlap and coexist.

—LAW AND MOL 2002, 8

Despite the *enkiguena* ideals, the ability to speak up at meetings is related to many factors, and linked to overlapping and changing social relations, terms of *enkanyit*, and power dynamics across age, gender, clan, class, and leadership status. Why then propose it as a tool for participatory dialogues, a diffraction method for data presentation, or even a decolonial theory for encouraging multiplicity? As explained above, I believe that the *enkiguena* ideals do provide guidance for theory and action, and that power is never complete but always shifting, diffracted, and contested. Following the above quote by Law and Mol, the *enkigeuna* enables a view into multiplicity that does not demand simplicity. It does this with the set of guidelines described above, but also by giving power to the spoken word. Power of oratory skills (perhaps not best displayed in my writing, but clearly in use by Maasai in practice), power of repetition and multiplicity. How things are said matters. Words matter. Tone matters. Storytelling matters. And it should for all of us—in how we conduct "participatory" meetings and how we tell stories and write our academic books.

Choosing to write in an *enkiguena* style not only changes the power dynamics at play and begins to decolonize the conversation, but it helps to increase "the possibilities for cooperation while respecting difference" between knowledge historically categorized hierarchically (Verran 2002; cf. Harding 1988; Hobart 1993; Sletto 2005). I argue that such a dialogue enables a more inclusive and sincere participatory setting. It also enables a more rigorous engagement with knowledge—defined scientifically or otherwise. For it is the dialogic mixing of different knowledges that contributes to successful knowledge creation, even *within* science. As pointed out by Star (1991, 46, cited in Turnbull 2000, 10),

> Scientific theory building is deeply heterogeneous: different viewpoints are constantly being adduced and reconciled. . . . Each actor, site, or node of a scientific community has a viewpoint, a partial truth consisting of local beliefs, local practices, local constants, and resources, none of which are fully verifiable across all sites. The aggregation of all viewpoints is the source of the robustness of science.

The *enkiguena* enables a more open process of theory building through diffraction across multiple ways of knowing and being in the world, including those historically Othered, ignored, or rejected as invalid.

Conclusion

Knowing and Being with Nature Otherwise

HAVE TRIED in this book to cover a lot of ground—literally and figuratively. Literally, I have taken you across Maasailand from the Kaputei plains and Loita hills in Kenya to the Kisongo and Simanjiro plains in Tanzania, always landing in *Emanyara* for detailed excursions in place. Figuratively, we have moved through the ongoing enactment and reenactment of boundaries across space, time, ontologies, and epistemologies—including shifting Maasai sociospatial relations, colonial boundary-drawing practices, wildlife movements, and ongoing conservation planning. Now, after covering all that ground, where do we end? It is my goal in this chapter to not necessarily close the book as in a final ending, but rather to create some sense of closure as in a parting of ways—a relational process. Perhaps a good place to start is to look at all that has passed, between the preceding pages and over time—in the academy and on the ground—since this work began.

Since the work for this book began, things have progressed within the academy, moving discussions beyond epistemology toward ontology, from postcolonial recognition of difference toward decolonial theory building, writing, and activism. All of these have created not only the language but also the momentum for taking different ways of knowing and being with nature seriously in theoretically nuanced and rigorous ways. On the ground, critiques of community-based conservation have continued, with a growing concern for the rights of Indigenous communities. On the other hand, ecologists have pushed to build more boundaries to protect an increasing amount of nature (Hutton, Adams, and Murombedzi 2005; Büscher et al. 2017). Conservation has become even more militarized (Duffy 2014), using drones to "see from above" and police boundaries below (Lunstrum 2014). And scholars, activists, and NGOs have promoted payments for ecosystem services as the win-win solution for all—supporting local communities for protecting nature, while keeping nature valuable with a price tag. Where does this book sit amid all these developments? Many of the on-the-ground developments end up building more boundaries or reifying existing ones (nature-society, science-Indigenous knowledge, conservation-Indigenous rights), whereas the academic debates are often (though not always) removed from on-the-ground struggles and practical action. I hope that the approach I have taken in this book, particularly my use of the *enkiguena*, provides a tangible methodological tool, a diffraction device, and at the very least an honest attempt to recognize difference and work across boundaries in ways that do not reify them, or ignore them, but instead opens up space for new ways to see, write, and explore nature-society relations, which I argue is key to moving beyond the "communities" *or* "conservation" impasse.

The *Enkiguena*

My use of the *enkiguena*—the Maasai meeting—as a theoretical framework, narrative device, and methodological tool of diffraction was in many ways fictional and hopeful. Taking what is so central to Maasai society and making it do some work to build the power-charged conversations between multiple situated knowledges (among Maasai and conservationists) and enactments of truth that Haraway (1991) argues is the future of responsible (social and ecological) science.

As such, I am proposing the *enkiguena* for practice and theory building. I suggest that it enables more space to diffract and expose power than other potential (re)presentation formats/frameworks. Additionally, using the *enkiguena* to debate conservation science with Maasai knowledge contributions powerfully disrupts existing power dynamics that privilege Western ways of knowing, being, and narrating nature-society relations, and contributes to efforts to *decolonize conservation dialogues*. For how we tell stories about the world matters. Scientific practice itself, as Haraway reminds us (1989, 4), "may be considered a kind of storytelling practice—a rule-governed, constrained, historically changing craft of narrating the history of nature." In presenting my research findings as an *enkiguena*, my intent was to *create narratives* that keep the "history of nature" open for debate and invite the reader to participate in the enactment of new sets of relations, contestations, and discoveries. It is an attempt to *decolonize conservation* practice, storytelling, and theory building, by building on an Indigenous storytelling practice.

Social scientists working with Indigenous communities have long argued for the need to build "dialogic" or "synergist" dialogues between and among different knowledge spaces (Gustavo 1996; Semali and Kincheloe 1991). In doing so, they were interested in avoiding the primacy of one knowledge expression (i.e., science) over others, as well as the essentialism of any particular "type" of knowledge (i.e., Indigenous knowledge). Yet there was still the risk of colonizing knowledge by extracting pieces of knowledge or "TEK" from communities, people, and processes (Simpson 2004). Others have argued for the need to move beyond conversations of multiple epistemologies to create ontological openings (de la Cadena 2015), which demand translations across worlds, or for a political ontology that decolonizes knowledge and creates new stories of globalization (Blaser 2010). My proposal for an *enkiguena* builds on these contributions—to find new ways to tell stories to create ontological openings, while challenging historically situated epistemological hierarchies associated with the colonialism of people, nature, and knowledge. In doing so as a non-Indigenous scholar, I recognize the risks involved. I do my best to minimize these risks by suggesting a Maasai Indigenous format to display Maasai words along with those who have historically dictated the format, and by checking along the way and collaborating with Maasai friends, interlocutors, scholars, and activists.[1] In doing so, I take seriously the words of caution put forth by Zoe Todd (2016, 18) but also see it as a call to (ethically responsible) action:

Indigenous peoples, throughout the world, are fighting for recognition—fighting to assert their laws, philosophies, and stories on their own terms. When anthropologists and other assembled social scientists sashay in and start cherry-picking parts of Indigenous thought that appeal to them *without engaging directly in (or unambiguously acknowledging) the political situation, agency, legal orders, and relationality of both Indigenous people and scholars,* we immediately become complicit in colonial violence.

Possibilities for Managing Nature Otherwise?

In light of the above quotation, I am interested in more than creating a rhetorical tool or narrative device. I am also interested in the *enkiguena* as a political tool to decolonize participation and bring multiple ontologies into dialogue. This is particularly relevant now, at the latter part of the twenty-first century, when new possibilities for conservation are being proposed and negotiated alongside international recognition of and interest in Indigenous rights, knowledge, and politics, and a growing (academic and activist) anti- and decolonial movement.[2] It is also a time, perhaps most importantly, of growing resistance from Maasai to the politics of knowledge as usual. Maasai are learning the tools of the trade, arming themselves with Western education (the power of the pen), and contesting conservation knowledge claims from multiply situated positions that draw simultaneously on global Indigenous rights movements, Western education, pastoralist production needs, and claims to land for their livelihoods (herding and farming). In Loliondo, Maasai have used political capital, digital media, NGO strength, and conservation enterprise connections to demand rights to their land, and to do conservation otherwise, in ways that include Maasai, their knowledge, and their livestock (Gardner 2016a). In the Manyara Ranch, Maasai have fought for changes to the board and management structure to ensure they have a stronger voice in management decision-making. Yet at the same time, community-based conservation in both Tanzania and Kenya is being redefined in ways that continue to draw new boundaries around nature and society and alienate communities from "nature."

MANYARA RANCH

The Manyara Ranch is steeped in the epistemological and ontological politics discussed in this book, while also enmeshed in party politics of the state, international conservation politics, and local-regional politics of control.

In 2016, after the former chairman of the board of the TLCT (in charge of the MR), lost a bid for the presidency, the Tanzanian prime minister revoked TLCT's contract for the MR. At the time, villagers reported with much hope and pride that the MR had been returned to them. However, doubt grew as district government officials stalled on negotiations and demands from Maasai that they participate and see the land title. The truth was expressed quite clearly in January 2017 by the district commissioner (DC) at the First Manyara Ranch Stakeholder Meeting, where he reminded everyone of the "primary value of the Manyara ranch [sic] which is a corridor for wildlife." He firmly stated that "as a DC, I will not allow Manyara ranch [sic] to die and this is the same sentiments from the President." To that end, he made it clear where control/ownership in the ranch resided: it was "government property" and the "*beneficiaries* are the two villages of Oltukai and Esilalei" (emphasis added). He explained that "the Prime Minister handed the title for the corridor to the District council with clear objectives of maintaining the corridor."[3]

It seems the title has merely changed hands from TLCT to the district, with conservation politics maintaining the strengh th of the MR as a corridor. Villagers are still "beneficiaries" rather than "owners," and AWF is still in charge of management and fundrasing, with the help of another NGO, Honeyguide, which runs the antipoaching units. Yet some villagers, who are aware of the details, place hope in the new MR board for real change. While chaired by the district executive director, the board contains four village representatives (as opposed to the prior one), including the two village chairmen and two women. Maasai see this as providing an opening to run the MR differently, with the involvement of a fired-up and highly educated youth and junior elder population and the inclusion of women. It remains to be seen how they will navigate the boundaries and succeed at doing conservation otherwise in the MR.

A Strategic Tending to Complexity

What does this all mean for building participatory dialogues—on the ground in MR and elsewhere (where power dynamics are complex, diffuse, and shifting) and in scientific dialogues where multiplicity is frowned upon and singular explanations sought? How can we talk about diffracting multiple ontologies and epistemologies, or ways of being with and knowing nature, as more than just a "postcolonial moment" (Verran 2002), but a strategic shift away from simplicity toward engaging complexity and multiplicity (ecological, social, epistemological, ontological). Such a shift would be strategic on many levels: for communities and knowledges usually Othered and made peripheral; for ecological complexities that are usually smoothed or dismissed (as outliers); and for people (and animals) whose lives have been impacted by boundaries that they themselves played no role in enacting, but which today they must contend with and often cross.

This is not just an academic question. Smooth data is used to formulate conservation projects that then create smooth and simple ecologies and communities on the ground, the outcomes of which we are all familiar with—wildlife conservation corridors, community conservation areas, national parks, and "beneficiary" communities. The unexpected (and often undesirable) effects can be seen along abrupt, hard national park boundaries (Botkin 1990) and within disgruntled communities in CBC projects—communities that may once have allowed wildlife to graze in their pastures with their livestock but now shoot wildlife that enter their farms and scare them off pastures.

I began this book by disrupting the story of Maasai as "Indigenous custodians of wildlife" as more complex and multiple—they can be, if they want to be, if they see a benefit in it, if they have control over the situation, if they are allowed to be *on their own terms.* This final point is important. For how can people be expected to be "custodians" over something that they are alienated from and not recognized as knowing about? Without contributing their own knowledge, expertise, and ways of *being* with wildlife and nature, Maasai are merely being asked to babysit the wildlife of the state. The same can be said for the growing interest in ecology over the past decade of "Indigenous/traditional ecological knowledge," (TEK/IK), which has rightfully been critiqued as an ongoing colonialization of knowledge, this time masked in the language of "co-management" or "inclusion" (Nadasdy 1999, 2005; Simpson 2004). Yet decolonial, Indigenous, political ecology, STS and feminist scholars suggest there are other options—options for getting on with difference in ways that do not reinforce colonial knowledge hierarchies.

I have tried to show in the preceding pages that Maasai have much more to contribute to conservation debates than as passive receivers of CBC benefits, as babysitters for government wildlife, or even as a source of TEK. I also tried to expose the complexity of the situation—cultural, social, political, and ecological—and to create ontological openings for knowing and being with nature otherwise. I hope that I have succeeded in showing that complexity matters, in the various ways mentioned above, and that smoothing it, trying to make it "stay put" in simple containers (e.g., wet and dry season months, corridors), is to risk losing what is so valuable in the first place—the continued existence of wildlife, with people and livestock, in village lands, outside of national park boundaries. And that the only way to really understand, to really capture this complexity (ecological and social) is to expand our understanding of what counts as method and what is seen as valid knowledge and valid ways of being with nature. This involves challenges which are epistemological (which knowledge counts?), ecological (which ecological relations are we concerned with maintaining?), and ontological (what worlds do we want to support?), which will determine what kind of future natures are constructed—ones confined to protected patches and landscape corridors, or ones based on multiple and complex relations between people and nature.

As discussed throughout this book, current conservation interventions in the TME attempt to smooth out complexity and create singular solutions, alongside singular accusations of politics as usual. Corridors are recommended to protect wildlife movements (i.e., manage boundary transgressions). Standard participatory methods and awareness trainings have been used to incorporate local communities and build local support. Yet Maasai have argued that these are not the right solutions; that wildlife cannot be separated from livestock, from homesteads, from people; that corridors and zone-based planning for wildlife protection just make no sense. They also argued that they, the residents of the area, knew where the wildlife like to go and what their needs were, perhaps more so than the scientific "experts." Villagers requested more information, challenged the "corridor" concept, demanded a more participatory process. Throughout all of this, many of the villagers most actively involved in the discussions were consummate boundary crossers. They used Maasai knowledge from home and spoke as "Indigenous caretakers of wildlife"; they drew from wildlife science gained in officially recognized institutions; they defended the importance of their farms, while promoting the importance of protecting "grazing areas" for wildlife and livestock. They were cautious of the politics of land and conservation and spoke proudly about their new conservation tourism venture in their village.

I have suggested that one way of showing/narrating, rather than smoothing out, this kind of multiplicity and complexity was through the structure of the *enkiguena*. I also proposed the *enkiguena* structure as a way of addressing the politics of participation while simultaneously engaging in the politics of knowledge—by diffracting different knowledge contributions, along with different ways of being with nature. Of building dialogic conversations and deliberative practice. It is, if you will, a context where the types of multiple vision employed by Maasai can be expressed alongside the insights of others (scientists, conservationists) working in the area—without having to define "Maasai" knowledge as a coherent singularity. It brings to light the multiple possibilities for being with, knowing, and talking about nature otherwise and thus illustrates what "multiple ontologies" looks like with a decolonial sensibility for the future of nature conservation (Collard, Dempsey, and Sundberg 2015).

Creating openings for knowing and being with nature otherwise is an ethical undertaking with immense political ramifications for managing nature otherwise as well. These ramifications are starting to play out in Tanzania and Kenya. Kenya has instituted a nationwide conservancy program where nature can be managed by a community, private landowner, or NGO. There was much hope and skepticism associated with this new legislation. Unfortunately, much of the hope is beginning to wane as traditional boundary-drawing practices are leading to increased alienation of Maasai lands for wildlife conservation led by outside conservation NGOs. In Tanzania, the grassroots organization UCRT is working with Maasai communities to change the way that NGOs work on conservation in pastoralist (and hunter-gatherer) lands—in ways that respect Maasai needs to manage the land as a community through community land rights titles. Drawing on the definition of customary rights in the Tanzanian land law, they are promoting the use of a legal tool referred to as the CCRO—Certificate of Customary Rights of Occupancy—to secure *communal* rights over land. This is a way to formalize village rights to land that can be held in common without the risk of appropriation by outside interests. A powerful tool, CCROs had not previously been used for communal rights. UCRT is drawing on funding from The Nature Conservancy to ultimately challenge the way land should be managed—namely by communities rather than outside investors—and conservation achieved—by including Maasai and their livestock rather than excluding them.[4]

UCRT is also working with Maasai villagers in the TME, who are fighting for resource rights, and for recognition on conservation management boards as educated and traditional leaders, as men and women, young and old. As Maasai struggle to gain a voice regarding management of the MR, along with other lands targeted for conservation (see preface), the arguments made in this book matter. They matter because as local and global politics play a large role in determining the management of various pieces of Maasailand, conservation interests continue to prevail, and Maasai NGOs continue to gain strength. Those of us committed to ethical change, social and ecological justice, and *conservation otherwise*, need to push for fundamental shifts—beyond debates between fortress and community-based approaches—toward an appreciation of the multiple ways in which nature can be known, narrated, and enacted and conservation landscapes made otherwise.

Appendix

Maasai Animal Taxonomy

A. Ilcang'it (olcang'ito sg.) (herbivores)

1. Gazelles (*enkoilii; inkoiliin*)—Not afraid of people; many in the village lands.

   a. *En-kolii* (one group—same origin/nature)

      i. Thompson's gazelle (*enkoili minimin*)

      ii. Grant's gazelle (*olwargas; ilwargasin*)

   b. Impala (*oloubo; iloolubo*)

   c. Dikdik

      i. Duiker (*emarujamuro*)

      ii. Dikdik (*erongo; irongon*)

      iii. Reedbuck (*olpua; ilpuai*)

   d. Klipspringer (*enkine oo soito; enkineji oo soito*—the goat of the stones)

2. Eland (*osirua; isiruai*)—There used to be many; they were chased away by hunters. Don't like to be in places with people.

   a. Eland (*osirua; isiruai*)—mountain areas, open plains, places without people

   b. Waterbuck (*osiram; isirami*)—mountain areas, open plains, places without people, bushed/forested places

   c. Oryx (*olkimosorogi; ilkimosorok*)—mountain areas, open plains, bushlands

   d. Hartebeest (*olkonde; ilkondin*)—grassland, wooded grassland. Likes to be near termite mounds; eats grass.

   e. Kudu

    i. Lesser kudu (*Olominguni*)—likes *pori* (bush savanna, like *Oremit* and in the dry riverbed), eats grass and dicots. Doesn't drink much water, so it can stay in dry country.

    ii. Greater kudu (*olmaalo; ilmaalon*)—likes mountainous areas

They are the same family. Differences include the names, the colors, and the horns being a little different.

3. Donkey/zebra

    a. Zebra—*oloitiko; oloitikoishi*

    b. Donkey—*osikiria; isirikon*

    c. Horse—*embarta; imbartan*

They are the only of the *Ilcang'it* that do not ruminate. They like grass plains, and the bush, all places, wherever they can get grass.

4. Buffalo (*Ilarroi* [*olarro* or *olosowuan; inkosowuani*]), wildebeest (*Oingat* [*iigati*] [*engati*]), cattle (*inkishu*)—The difference is in size only. They all eat grass. Buffalo eats more because it is bigger, and it doesn't get full quickly. Wildebeest only stay in open grass areas, and the other two will enter the bush. And buffalo particularly like the bush.

5. Elephant and so forth—They have similar skin. If you look at them from afar, they resemble each other. And they all like places of mud. The differences are in the teeth (tusks) and the horns. They love the mud because they don't have hair, so their bodies get very hot.

    a. Elephant (*Olkancaoi; ilkancaoni* or *olcang'ito sapuk*)

    b. Rhinoceros (*emuny; imuni*)

    c. Hippopotamus (*olmakau; ilmakaun*)

    d. Pigs

        i. Wild boar (*olkupe*)

        ii. Domestic pig (*engaruwe*—Swahili)

        iii. Warthog—*olbitir; ilbitiro*

6. Giraffe (*olmeut; ilmeuti*), camel

    a. They like trees and dry country, but with trees. They don't like cold places. They eat trees, dicots, and grass—but with trouble, because they are so tall. But if there is fresh grass, they will eat it.

7. Rabbit—*enkitejo; inkitejon*. In a class by itself, others that resemble rabbits are carnivores so do not belong to *olcan'it*.

B. *Ing'uesi*—Dangerous animals

1. *Olowuaru*—the large predators

   a. Lion (*olng'atuny; ilng'atunyo* or *olowuaru sapuk*—the large carnivore)—the leader of the carnivores
       i. *Olng'aririma*—Tan, with a long mane, they are very mellow and cannot kill people; they will eat a spear.
       ii. *Oldiamingish*—Has no mane, has a white behind, and is redder in color. Is much smaller but more fierce (Mol 1996: *Olng'arurumi; ilng'arurum*).
   b. The spotted carnivore (*olowuaru keri*)
       i. Cheetah—*Olowuaru la cang'it*. Has color like a giraffe, but it is not seen around here.
       ii. Leopard—*olowuaru oti* (small lion). They like rivers, bush/forested places where they can hide. Eat bushbuck, gazelle, goats.
       iii. Serval—*engirasi*. Eats goats, birds (francolin and guinea fowl).
   c. Wild dog—(*Osuyiani; ilsuyian*)
   d. Hyena—trouble animals. No other animal as bad as the hyena. It can finish all the animals in an *enkang'*! Same as family Hyaenidae.
       i. Spotted hyena (*Olng'ojine / ilng'ojiniaa*)
       ii. Striped hyena—*Nemelil*—small
       iii. Aardwolf—but confusion over its name—whether *nemelil* or *olng'*
   e. Jackal (*Enderah* [*enderai*]/*enterrash; interrashin*)
       i. Jackal—includes all three types; they differentiate by description like color.
       ii. Fox—*esiro; isiron*
2. Smaller carnivores
   a. Skunk (*orpilis*—also sometimes used for mongoose)
       ii. Honey badger—*narok kahauke*—very fierce
   b. Mongoose—*olcuki* (sometimes cervit)
       i. Striped mongoose (*enkisheren; inkishireni*)
       ii. Mongoose—*olcuki*—They are all the same. They will all enter different places, sometimes in the trees, sometimes in the rocks, sometimes in the holes, but they don't differentiate between them.
   c. Large-spotted genet—*osimingor* (but this is on the side of the leopard)—Not easy to see, but it is in the river (*Lolgabolo*).
3. Snakes (*olasurai; ilasuriaa*)
   a. Snake (*olasurai; ilasuriaa*)
       i. All snakes
       ii. Python (*entera; interai*)
   b. Lizards (Agama lizard [*oloiriiri; iloiriir*])

    c. Gecko—*oloitirtir*

    d. Lizard—*olmaima; ilmaiman*

    e. Chameleon—*kotorangi*—think they have poison like snakes, all the same

    f. Crocodile—*olkinyang'; ilkinyang'in*

4. Tortoise

    a. *Olekuma*—It eats grass, beans.

Glossary of Maa and Swahili Terms

NOTE ON SPELLINGS: Maa is primarily a spoken language with a great deal of variety in dialects across sections. I draw from Mol (1972, 1996), with modifications made for Kisongo pronunciation with help from Maasai in my field site and from Hodgson (2001).

Maasai words are gendered.

Masculine singular: o/ol/or   Masculine plural: i/il/ir

Feminine singular: e/en/er   Feminine plural: i/in/ir

Often a feminine version of a word implies it is smaller (e.g., *en-keju* as stream and *ol-keju* as river), or that it is unknown (e.g., *en-tim*, forested bush, *e-weuji* as place). In this table I remove the hyphen for ease of reading and to match the words as they appear in the text.

Maasai word (sg./pl. or fem./masc.) and English translation

Arriya	Skilled, talented, expert
Ee pae	Of course
Emanyata; imanyat	Special homestead for warriors (warrior "villages")
Empoor; impoorri	Hard ground where grass won't grow "stony place, eroded land" (Mol 1996, 336)
Engudi	Walking stick
Eng'ues; ing'uesi	Dangerous wildlife
Enkaji; inkajijik	House; houses

Enkang'; *inkang'itie*	Maasai homestead; *boma* in Swahili
Enkanyit	Respect
Enkeju; *olkeju*	Stream; river
Enkiguena; *inkiguenat*	Meeting(s)
Enkishomi; *inkishomin*	Clan; subclan; also family gate of the *enkang'*
Enkop; *inkuapi*	Country, land, soil, world
Enkutoto; *inkutot*	Corner, nook, Maasai sociocultural spatial unit of organization
Enkung'u (fem.); *olkung'u* (masc.)	Knee, small uplifted place; large uplifted place in the landscape
Entim	Heavily forested places; "wilderness" or "the bush" (*pori* in Swahili)
Eronjo	Temporary homestead put up for seasonal grazing
Esiangiki; *i-siangikin*	Young circumcised woman; new bride
Esirit	"Company of warriors, group, band, companionship" (Mol 1972, 374); men or women circumcised together or at about the same time
Eunoto	"The planting" ceremony where junior warriors become senior warriors. After this they are permitted to marry.
Ilmoruak	Elders
Olaigwenani; *ilaigwenak*	Spokesmen (age-set and clan based)
Olayioni; *ilaiyok*	Boy; boys
Olcang'ito, *ilcang'it*	Wildlife, nondangerous animals
Olkuma	The black club used by *ilaigwenak* as a sign of their leadership status
Olmaasinta	A Maasai, sometimes used to refer to "original/real" Maasai
Olmurrani; *ilmurran*	Warrior(s)
Oloiboni; *iloibonok*	Ritual expert; spiritual leader; medicine man, prophet, diviner
Olosho; *iloshon*	Section, "nation," "country"
Olpayian; *ilpayiani*	Elder, married man, husband (also *olmouro*; *ilmoruak*)
Olpiron; *ilpiron*	Firestick elder(s)

Olpura; ilpurai	Bare spots in the ground without grass
Olpurkel	Dry lowlands (perennial water sources, grasslands)
Oltim	Large branch used to close off the gate of an *enkang'*
Oosho; o yie kake	Exclamation of surprise or emphasis
Orpul; ilpuli	Meat feast (mostly for *ilmurran*)
Osero; iseroi (rarely used in pl.)	Places filled with bush/shrub (wild places, *pori* in Swahili)
Osupuko	Uplands (cool, wet, permanent water available)

Swahili word and English translation

Boma	Maasai settlement, *enkang'* in Maa; this word is used by many English and Swahili speakers
Korongo	Seasonal river, ditch
Mtaalamu/wataalamu	Expert(s), specialist(s)
Pori	Bush, scrublands, "wilderness" areas
Ramani	Map; used by Maasai for "boundary"
Shamba(s)	Small cultivated field(s)

Notes

Preface

1. And personal conversation with Alan Rodgers, 2003.

2. Oakland Institute. 2019. "UNESCO and Tanzanian Government's Plan Threatens the Continued Survival of the Maasai." Accessed Octrober 20, 2019. https://www.oaklandinstitute .org/dividing-ngorongoro-conservation-management-resettlement-plan. All subsequent information regarding the new plan comes from this site.

3. Ministry of National Resources and Tourism, United Republic of Tanzania, 2019. "The Multiple Land Use Model of Ngorongoro Conservation Area: Achievements and Lessons Learnt, Challenges and Options for the Future." Final Report. Dodoma. Game Controlled Areas are the primary location for tourism hunting but are also occupied by Maasai villages.

4. UNESCO World Heritage Centre. n.d. "The World Heritage Convention." Accessed October 21, 2019. https://whc.unesco.org/en/convention/.

Introduction

1. Throughout the book, I use pseudonyms unless otherwise noted.

2. Maa is the language spoken by Maasai and other related groups (Il Samburu, Ilarusa [Waarusha], and Ilparakuyu).

3. My use of the word *enactment* draws mostly on the work of Karen Barad (2007) but also that of Annemarie Mol (2002), who argue realities are enacted alongside knowledge production practices.

4. Interview, 2008.

5. See Igoe 2017.

6. See the work of Jim Igoe, Dan Brockington, and Rod Neumann, among others.

7. In Africa, the term *Indigenous* is utilized by groups, like Maasai, who have been historically marginalized economically, politically, and culturally, by colonial and postcolonial states. Their

Indigenous status provides a powerful platform for building global alliances, particularly in relation to livelihood challenges and land dispossession (Hodgson 2002; Igoe 2006).

8. Maasai historically viewed wildlife as "second cattle" (Western 1997), hunting only in times of extreme need, otherwise shunning it as something only the poor (*ildorobo*) without cattle do. Today, many Maasai eat game meat when given the opportunity, but hunting for meat is still culturally unacceptable for many, though this varies by sections (see Roque de Pinho 2009 for game eating among the Matapato section of Maasai in Kenya).

9. For more on the historic cohabitation see Deihl 1985, Collet 1987, Parkipuny and Berger 1993.

10. This includes Amboseli, Tsavo, and Nairobi National Parks and Maasai Mara Game Reserve in Kenya; Serengeti, Manyara, Tarangire National Parks, Ngorongoro Conservation Area, and Mkomazi Game Reserve in Tanzania.

11. These scholars and activists have linked Maasai struggles to those of Indigenous people globally (Hodgson 2011), where similar processes of dispossession have occurred and continue to occur.

12. Leanne Betasamosake Simpson (Simpson 2017) refers to similar practices by the Nishnaabeg people in Canada as resistance, by continuing to go to the places they have always gone (to hunt, camp, ceremony, etc.).

13. *Boma* is a Swahili word often used by Swahili and English speakers to refer to a Maasai settlement, and more broadly means enclosure. The Maasai word is *enkang'* sg., *inkang'itie* pl., and refers to groupings of houses (*enkaji* sg.; *inkajijik* pl.) with one or more shared livestock kraals, usually encircled with a thorn fence (*esita*). I mostly use the Maasai word and alternate with the English words *home*, *settlement*, and *homestead*, depending on the context. I use the word *boma* when it is used in the literature or would be used by the speaker.

14. My commitment here resonates with the work of Nishnaabeg scholar/activist Leanne Betasamosake Simpson (2017) and feminist scholar/activist Richa Nagar (2014, 2019), who both work across boundaries of activist/scholar to challenge knowledge production hierarchies while engaging in activist practice.

15. This is his real name. He tragically passed away in 2013 and played an essential role in my research and life in Tanzania. He gave me permission to use his name in an earlier version.

16. As a former state-run cattle ranch, the MR still maintained herds of cattle, even after it became a conservation area.

17. As noted in footnote 13. I use *enkang* to refer to a Maasai homestead.

18. Maasai use this term to refer to non-Maa speakers and farmers.

19. Stated by a Maasai junior elder in Oltukai; also heard throughout East Africa in relation to the value of wildlife. See the documentary film *Milking the Rhino* (Simpson 2008).

20. This is a Swahili word that is used to refer to white people throughout East Africa, though its original meaning is "those that circle around" or "wander around," and seems to have been first used to describe explorers who were thought to wander around aimlessly.

21. WMAs were introduced in the Wildlife Policy of 1998 as community-run conservation areas for villages, though they mandate the involvement of NGOs and have been heavily critiqued for coercive and exclusive procedures. See Benjaminsen et al. 2013, Goldman 2003, Igoe and Croucher 2007, and Kicheleri et al. 2018.

22. See for instance Anderson and Grove 1987, Brockington 2002, Igoe 2004, and Neumann 1998.

23. Nagar (2019) complicates the various ways in which storytelling can be brought into academic texts.

24. "Partial connections" (Haraway 1991; Strathern 1991) refers to the coexistence of multiple identities that are related and can be political (e.g., different social identities or political commitments), material (e.g., animal-human-machine), or representational (e.g., between fact and fiction).

25. Unlike Ngugi's novels, which even when translated into English maintain the metaphors/proverbs central to Kikuyu communication, the *enkiguena* I produce does not. And as a non-Indigenous scholar I am not embedded in these forms of storytelling in the way that Smith and Simpson discuss.

26. I also take seriously her caution to keep translations open and negotiable, for "when a project of translation assumes that it can render transparent the meanings of complex lives or struggles, it not only consumes the other, it also annihilates that which has been othered" (Nagar 2019, 29).

27. When I started, I was single and without a child, which upset many of the Maasai women I befriended. There was much joy when I returned with my husband and child in 2013 and another child in 2019.

28. Discussed in detail by Goldman (2018) and referenced in the following chapters.

29. Recent scholarship suggests less rigid groupings than previously assumed (Waller, personal communication, 2017). I suggest the problem is an ontological one, exposing differences in boundary-drawing practices. For while Maasai do draw social and spatial boundaries, these have always been more fluid than the boundaries that westerners sought to find and demarcate.

30. The word *enkutoto* translates as a corner/nook/section of a region, as in "your neck of the woods" (Saning'o Milliary, personal communication, November 2005)—the corner of a Maasai house where firewood is kept; the corners (or nooks) in mountains and bends in a river; and corners in the landscape, where clusters of homesteads or bomas constitute a neighborhood, or a (loose) social unit.

31. *Olgilata/ilgilat* is the Maa word for clan, though the more common term used was *enkishomi* (*inkishomin*, pl.), which stands for subclan, but also an individual family's gatepost within an *enkang'*.

32. For a critique of this, see Goldman et al. 2013 and 2010.

33. In terms of extramarital affairs, this plays out differently on a case-by-case basis. Some men have absolutely no tolerance for any extramarital affairs of any kind by their wives. Yet social norms dictate that relations with those of the same age-set of a woman's husband are allowed, while those of the age-set below are forbidden. Usually the clan and the general temperament of the lover will also come into play, as the affair may produce a child which will legally belong to the husband.

34. At *Eunoto* junior *ilmurran* need to have their heads shaved by their mothers to become senior *ilmurran*. At *Olng'esher*, senior *ilmurran* need to have their heads shaved *by their wives*, forcing many Landis in 2003 to rush arranged marriages, particularly if their only wife was not allowed to participate because she slept with a junior *olmurrani*. After *Olng'esher*, a second cere-

mony occurs where one or more of the wives of the graduating age-set feeds the men meat, officially putting an end to the taboo that forbids men of the *ilmurran* age-grade to eat meat seen
by women. In this way and others, wives play a strong role in mediating age-set relations—in
both ritual and daily practice.

35. For many Maasai sections, there has also been an *oloiboni* associated with each age-set,
needed for all the official age-set rituals to occur, some of which persist today. In addition to
these, there were other *iloibonok* across Maasailand consulted by *ilmurran* and others for medicine and divination, with some seen as more powerful than others. While age-set *iloibonok* need
to be from the Ilkidongi clan (*Orok Kiteng* Moiety), where most *iloibonok* come from, there have
always been exceptions, with the most powerful *oloiboni* in *Emanyara* being Ilaiser, rumored to
descend from a different ethnic group (the Kikuyu) in Kenya.

Chapter 1

1. From a meeting in Esilalei Village where the role of the Manyara Ranch within the global
discourse of biodiversity conservation was explained to villagers.

2. Director of the Africa Program for the Frankfurt Zoological Society since 1983.

3. Interview, November 31, 2003.

4. All place-names used in this chapter can be located on map 3. Chapter 2 provides a
detailed tour of the place-names for the study area.

5. Interview, October 2003.

6. *Alare* is also Maa for "year," illustrating the importance of rain to Maasai seasonal cycles.

7. This refers to different researchers on the same study, who worked together and separately
producing different types of data. In the following statements, I attempt to show this internal
similarity and difference, as related to different scales.

8. This statement is fabricated, reflecting ongoing frustration on this issue by village government.

9. Throughout the *enkiguena* I use direct quotation marks when the statements are direct
quotes from interviews or from written texts, and then cite appropriately.

10. The maximum number of cattle/km was 64.4 in January 2001 (Tarangire-Manyara Conservation Project [TMCP] 2002b, 27).

11. From comments heard often when discussing wildlife in casual conversation, in response
to interview questions, or related to research findings.

12. An *olkuma* is a specially carved club usually made from ebony and often covered in beads,
that only men with special status (traditional leaders, spiritual healers) are permitted to carry.

13. From a group interview of eleven junior and senior elders from Esilalei, ranging in age
from early to midthirties to eighty.

14. Rainfall data from Clive Jones, TLCT.

15. Recognized by the Maasai men I was with as poaching tracks from the pattern of the tire
tracks, circling around in a fast way.

16. This statement is fabricated for the sake of dialogue.

17. When a man wants to point to the truth of what he is saying, he will say "*enkerai*" (my
child), as in "It is as true as the fact that I won't sleep in my daughter's house." A woman, on the
other hand, says "*papai*" (my father), with the same connotation. This reflects the strength of

incest prohibitions which forbid *all* social interactions, including eating together, talking in a casual manner, or even sleeping in the same house (as well as sexual relations) with someone from the same age-set as a woman's father or a man's daughter.

18. He has published several articles that advocate particular conservation agendas with little or no scientific backing, clear bias, and unscientific tone (Prins 1987, 1992). I draw on these for the tone of his statement here.

19. Interview with this Makaa elder in Esilalei, November 23, 2003, drawing also from conversations with him and others at other times.

20. Interview, November 8, 2003.

21. An educated elder, also a traditional clan leader and a former political leader, he wields a great deal of respect.

22. Group interview comprised of six Landis, two Makaa, December 2003.

23. Both these names refer to the same area. *Oloyeti* is the grass that grows there, while *Emborianda* refers to crusted soil that forms when the lake recedes.

24. He never went to school but is fluent in Swahili. His father is an *oloiboni*, and he is the oldest son, inheriting his father's position and learning his skills.

25. Group interview, December 10, 2003; these words are from a well-respected elder, often chosen by the women to accompany them on their pilgrimages.

26. Tarangire-Manyara Conservation Project (TMCP) 2002b.

27. Interview, October 5, 2003.

28. Maasai often see wildlife while herding, as discussed in more detail in the next chapter. See table 6.

29. Interview, December 7, 2003.

30. Interview, October 2003.

31. While the mapping process of the study area discussed in the next chapter began by getting contributions from all groups, the final maps reflect a male bias, as they were completed as a collaborative effort between myself, my (male) assistant, and other educated men. This comment illustrates the different knowledge women have, particularly regarding water sources.

32. Interview, July 2003.

33. It also useful to look at densities by transect. When we do this, we see that the highest abundance for a single transect was in *Oremit* (T5) in April with a density of 61.5 wildebeest/km^2 and 44.7 zebra/km^2. These numbers represent mostly animals in *Oloyeti* by the lake.

34. From data collected and recorded as "opportunistic sightings."

35. Interview, October 16, 2003.

36. The Arusa tribe are also Maa speaking but agricultural and were excluded from Maasailand by British tribal distinctions. With independence they were able to call on kinship, clan, and age-set relations within Maasai communities to access land (Hodgson 2001; Spear 1993, 1997) and spread rapidly into the Maasai plains west of Arusha Town. While in the field, I would regularly drive from Arusha town to Olutkai Village and was constantly reminded by elderly Maasai that this entire area used to be "Maasai," but now it was Waarusha. As a result, there was a great deal of mistrust and contempt for people that Maasai referred to as Waarusha, despite a great deal of intermarriage.

37. An individual from a group interview, October 2003.

38. A group interview comprised of six Landis, two Makaa, December 2003.

39. Group interview with Korianga, Esilalei, 2002.

40. The land the *enkang'* is on belongs to the Tanzanian Army (JKT). The family had a memorandum of understanding (MOU) to be on the land, and AWF was trying to sign an MOU with the Tanzanian Army to protect this portion of the Losimingori Mountains.

41. Whenever the wildebeest were not in the village, I was nearly always told they were in Selela, if they weren't thought to be back in the park.

42. Group interview with women, October 7, 2003.

43. This woman once spoke with me about the problem many women had participating in meetings. Elder women, like herself, were free to speak and not afraid of anyone. Yet they often had trouble following the meeting, as they were old and their hearing and sight not good, or they were not able to follow some of the current politics. The younger women could hear and see everything but were often without the freedom or courage to speak.

44. Group interview, December 10, 2003.

45. Wildebeest are the only African ungulate to breed at only one time of the year, at the optimum season (rainy season). All birthing occurs during the rains, and 80 percent of the calves are delivered in three weeks (Sinclair 1983).

46. This is not a direct statement but draws from conversations with male and female elders and younger men.

47. Combination of words from MN during a trip to LMNP and other times, as he was one of my regular interlocutors.

48. Direct quote from this man, which he explained as meaning "talk to those who are from this place; they may know something you do not, even though they are not 'educated' people."

Chapter 2

1. See (Bryan 2009, 2011) for the complex politics involved in producing "Indigenous" maps.

2. I shared my maps with Maasai organizations and village governments, unfortunately to little effect. The dominance of standard land-use planning techniques combined with the limited availability of training and technologies means that land-use planning continues as usual.

3. Cardinal directions do influence Maasai spiritual practice, with north and east seen as more auspicious and thus faced when praying. House [*enkaji*] and homestead [*enkang'*] entrances also face north and south (Hodgson 2005). Yet cardinal directions were not used to talk about movements through space; place-names were.

4. *Olkeju* (masculine): river; *enkeju* (feminine): stream.

5. Drawing from Loth and Prins 1986 and Mwalyosi 1981.

6. This is a generalized Swahili term I heard used for annual grasses. Individual grass species have specific names in Maa.

7. Most references to this tree identify it as *Commiphora africana*, which is another similar tree that Maasai call *Enchilichili*. I thank Jeff Worden for pointing this out.

8. During a visit to this area in 2018, I found this area barely recognizable. A local resident explained that during the heavy rains a few years prior, an elephant died, fell into the river,

and clogged it. This forced the river to flood into multiple pathways on the land, eliminating *embarimbali* entirely.

9. These are redug every year, the locations of the wells are known and family/clan owned, providing water for the entire dry season.

10. Lembeti refers to a common plant that I was unable to identify.

11. Interview, Seuri Elder, June 2003.

12. While there are other trees used as toothbrushes, *Oremit* is known for its special anti-septic properties and is valued for other medicinal purposes as well, particularly for purging.

13. The word *olotoro* is used throughout Maasailand "indicating the storage of water" (Mol 1972, 51).

14. Interview, Makaa Elder, Oltukai, November 2003.

15. A family is defined as a man, his wives and all dependents, or in rare circumstances a woman and her children and extended family. Multiple families often share one *enkang'*, though in recent years there has been a shift toward smaller homesteads.

16. Maasai in Kakoi subvillage were not officially allowed access to Manyara Ranch, as they did not belong to any of the "stakeholder" villages. Their negotiated access through Maasai in Oltukai was viewed as illegal, though they are in the same *enkutoto*. On the other hand, the creation of a WMA in Minjingu Village affected Maasai in Oltukai who regularly used the area for grazing but were not included in negotiations.

17. Contemporary administrative boundaries in Maasailand reflect a long history of bound-ary drawing that began during the colonial period and is covered in more detail in chapter 4.

18. Personal communication, UCRT director, November 2017. See http://www.ujamaa -crt.org/.

19. The *Wa-* is a Swahili prefix used to connote people with an (m-) prefix, the singular, thus Waarusha being the tribe, and Mwarusha an individual of the tribe. I use this form to differentiate from the town, Arusha, and because it is commonly used in this form by Maasai.

20. As Maasai say, for Waarusha in particular, those who have recovered (Swahili: *aliopona*).

21. There was one Barabaig resident in Oltukai, whose presence was hotly contested.

22. Of which, 202 were under five years old. United Republic of Tanzania, 2002 Population and Housing Census.

23. Of which, 471 were under five years old. United Republic of Tanzania, 2002 Population and Housing Census.

24. *Enkang'* counts come from Manyara Ranch data collection, 2002. A repeat survey in 2005 reported forty-seven *inkang'itie* in Oltukai and one hundred in Esilalei.

25. Government of Tanzania Census Data.

26. Calculations of livestock units per capita is common (Ndagala 1992). Maasai use live-stock units per "house" [*enkaji*], meaning a wife and her children and this unit of analysis is utilized by Potanski (1999) and McCabe (2003).

27. Also, personal observation.

28. The area was designated as the first "heartland" by AWF; see https://www.awf.org/news /introducing-african-heartlands, accessed May 12, 2020. The region has also been referred to as the Manyara-Tarangire Complex (LEAT [Lawyers Environmental Action Team] 1998); the Masai [*sic*] Ecocomplex (Mwalyosi 1991), and the Masai [*sic*] Ecosystem (Prins 1987).

29. Numbers come from an AWF funding document obtained in 2002. Since that time, many new villages have been delineated.

30. AWF website, https://www.awf.org/news/manyara-ranch-corridor-and-more, accessed May 12, 2020.

31. See conclusion for updated status of MR.

32. Pasiansi Wildlife Training Institute, run by the Ministry of Natural Resources and Tourism, Wildlife Division of the TZ government, http://pasiansiwildlife.ac.tz/.

33. See Goldman 2018 for more detail.

34. Spoken by Maasai senior *ilmurran* during *Orlpul*, Tanzania, 2003.

35. Place-names are linked to stories and knowledge. See Verran for discussion of the importance of place names for aboriginals in Australia (Verran 1998). See Basso for a discussion of place names for theWestern Apache in the United States (Basso 1996), where they are connected to dreamscapes, ancestors, and moral teachings.

36. This resonates with what Leanne Betasamosake Simpson writes about her own people, the Nishnaabeg of Canada: "Our intelligence system is a series of interconnected and overlapping algorithms—stories, ceremonies, and the land itself are procedures for solving the problems of life. Networked because the modes of communication and interaction between beings occur in complex nonlinear forms, across time and space" (Simpson 2017, 23).

37. From a conversation with an elder, whom I saw taking his young boys to the wells where he waters cattle and asked what they were doing. "They are out learning!" he said, sparking a conversation about the process.

38. It was common for elders to know nearly all grasses in the area and which animals consumed it (e.g., cattle, goats, zebra).

39. Joana Roque de Pinho, personal communication, 2018.

40. Maasai interlocutors often translated this in Swahili as *akili*, intelligence (wisdom is *busara*), yet they often used the word in line with an understanding of wisdom.

41. See Goldman 2018 for a detailed discussion of the epistemological and ontological challenges of these methods.

42. Total aerial counts were also used by the FZS and the Tarangire Conservation Project and are presented with SRF data by Tarangire-Manyara Conservation Project (TMCP) 2002b in the *enkiguena* chapters.

43. The Italian Istituto Oikos initiated the Tarangire Manyara Conservation Project (TMCP) with TANAPA to produce multiscalar data of wildlife for the TME. They combined sample and total counts and averaged across months and years to display levels of abundance of species by season, radio-collared a small sample of animals (twelve wildebeest, thirteen zebra, and seven elephants), and conducted road transects.

Interlude I

1. Steering committee meeting, Manyara Ranch, September 26, 2003.

2. Edward Lowasa was still the member of parliament for Monduli district and chairman of the board (of the TLCT) at the time. He became prime minister of Tanzania but was forced to resign on corruption charges.

Chapter 3

1. The beginning of this chapter draws directly from a meeting that occurred in Oltukai Village on October 15, 2003.

2. Corbett passed away in 2009, and his company Corbett Bishop Safaris was the first tour company in Oltukai.

3. These are the direct words spoken in Swahili at the meeting. I translated the meeting dialogue into English (from a recording). Most of the words spoken in Maa were translated at the meeting out loud, and I also had an individual translating to me, which I wrote down. I draw from both sources.

4. Direct words from the meeting.

5. The original meeting had a second agenda item for "collection for the school together with that requested by the district for the police *banda*." I have reframed it for the purpose of this chapter. The second agenda does not draw from actual meeting material but is constructed from interviews, observations, and written texts.

6. This individual often criticizes what he sees as unnecessary talk at Maasai meetings. He likes to be efficient and move quickly. But he is also very diplomatic, making sure all opinions (even oppositional ones) are expressed.

7. He says as someone who claims to be interested in participatory methods. Yet he never questioned why women were never present at any of his previous meetings or on the trips to select a dam site.

8. For bureaucratic reasons and disagreements with MR management, dam construction did not occur until 2005/6, after more than two years.

9. Statement made at the meeting, with final sentences reflecting comments made during later conversations.

10. I combine statements made by the speaker and those of others during the time that the land committee was looking for an appropriate dam site.

11. Conversation with a man of Landis age-set, September 30, 2003, echoing the comments of many others.

12. This statement reflects the impatience outsiders often show with the slow pace of Maasai deliberations. In this case the deliberations were longer than usual because of a lack of engagement by the village government with their constituents.

13. Statement made at the meeting.

14. Statement made at the meeting.

15. Ololosokwan is a village north of Serengeti where Maasai have been involved in tourism activities to profit from the large numbers of wildlife on their lands. Recently the Tanzanian government has renewed attempts to take the land and evict Maasai (see Gardner 2016).

16. From a conversation with Corbett and written reports proposing plans for the new Oltukai Trust created after the campsite was established to promote wildlife conservation, improved land-use planning, and appropriate development in the village.

17. Based on ongoing conversations with "MN."

18. Magadi refers to the "salty" quality of the water, characterized by high levels of trona, a hydrated sodium bicarbonate carbonate $(Na_3HCO_3CO_3.2H_2O)$.

19. This is for those women from Oltukai only. They go with donkeys for water a couple times a week. It is over 6 km away.

20. The first part of this statement comes from a discussion with a woman about the dam (September 2003), repeating similar advice provided by other women. The second half is constructed, reflecting the views of many different women regarding the hardships of water in village lands.

21. Group interview with several women from both villages of various ages, October 7, 2003, although this statement reflects mostly the words of one of the eldest women.

22. He was working for AWF at the time, in charge of the microenterprise development projects, but was also involved in the KEEP project discussed in chapter 5. He since left AWF. This statement comes from two discussions with the author, October and November 2003. I have changed the pronouns to reflect a conversation with Maasai rather than with me.

23. Oba and Katira found in the nearby village of Selala that Olpura referred to landscapes that were "highly sensitive" to overgrazing, and their soils were vulnerable to erosion. Patches were mostly dominated by annuals and usually grazed during the wet season.

24. *Imbenek* (fem, pl.) is defined by Mol (1996, 46) as "leaves." Maasai I spoke with used this term to refer to leaves and bushes/shrubs.

25. Many of the elders who were born here spent considerable time living and traveling in other locations, so it is possible he speaks from an experience elsewhere. This comes from a group interview, December 2003. Most of the words here are from the elder I describe, but the words of other junior elders contributed as well. Today there is visible overgrazing in the village that most will agree has led to changes in vegetation (more *imbenek*).

26. He is referring to the Pasiansi Wildlife Training Institute for game scouts in Mwanza.

27. Interview with game scout, October 3, 2003.

28. Interview, April 4, 2002. The early words about the youth reflect conversations with elders throughout the area.

29. Interview, November 20, 2003.

30. These villages are almost entirely populated by the agricultural Waarusha, and both have clear signs of erosion. According to Rohde and Hilhorst (2001), the roots of erosion in Kisongo are likely linked to several factors, including stock movements related to a dam built in the 1960s, agricultural conversion, and heavy rains (El Niño in 1998) after a drought.

31. Interview, May 2003. Seuri elder, Esilalei.

32. Interview, October 5, 2003. This statement also reflects the views of many others regarding wildlife use of village lands.

33. Much of this comes from Reid 2012 or other sources cited appropriately. I also worked with Dr. Reid on this project and draw from my experience with her in the field and at ILRI (2004–6) to present her views in the form of a dialogue. I use quotation marks to note when quoting the book directly.

34. She has since left ILRI to direct the Center for Collaborative Conservation at Colorado State University.

35. See in particular Ellis, Coughman, and Swift 1993; Behnke, Scoones, and Kerven 1993; Westoby, Walker, and Noy-Meir 1989; Little 1994, 1996.

36. Views presented here draw from his 1992 article. Liberty is taken to present his views in the form of a dialogue, but when his views are direct quotes, this is noted. An interview with

Mwalyosi was conducted in 2003, from which I draw loosely to elaborate the text and speaking style. His work on corridors is addressed in chapter 5.

37. Interview, July 2003.

38. Interview, June 2003.

39. From meeting in AWF office, April 2005.

40. Access to grazing land in Esilalei is based on social relations through marriage.

41. Identification by a botanist at the Manyara Ranch as *Dichrostachys cinerea*, by Gamassa (1989, 179) as *Harrisonia abyssinica*.

42. The manager voiced this concern at a meeting of researchers at the ranch.

43. Interview, July 2003.

44. This statement and the group discussion following come from a collection of interviews and informal conversations over several years regarding *endundulu*.

45. Interview with game scout, September 15, 2003.

46. Discussion during a visit to the wells, August 6, 2003.

47. This last sentence is from a conversation with a different warrior from the same *enkang'*, August 19, 2003.

48. From combined views of several different junior and senior elders at a group interview in Esilalei, December 10, 2003.

49. This last statement comes from conversations with many people in both villages. Herd boys can also control their dogs. Once out herding we saw a giraffe grazing peacefully nearby. The dog was getting ready to chase it, but I requested it be held back (so I could take a picture!) and the giraffe remained unbothered. Other times if the herder doesn't chase the animals away they will often mix.

50. There were often wildebeest around his boma, with so many in *Engusero* at the end of 2003 that people were instructed to not go out at night for fear of lion attacks.

51. This includes 280 zebra/km^2, 55 wildebeest/km^2, 25 gazelle/km^2, and 16 impala/km^2.

52. This includes 140 zebra/km^2 and 202 wildebeest/km^2.

53. The graph shows a low density for cattle in the *Bwawambili* transect. This reflects twenty-nine cattle counted right at the beginning of the transect, outside of the ranch.

54. This statement reflects complaints by villagers, observations of lions on the ranch by assistants, and predation incidents (two of cattle and two of donkey).

55. Many villagers participated in game scout training through LMNP and began unofficially patrolling the village.

56. The Maa word for cattle, *ingishu*, is often used to refer to livestock in general. The elder uses the word here to refer to donkeys to express the value of the animals lost. Donkeys do not provide food, but are used to transport food and water.

57. Interview with elder, 2003.

58. Informal talk with a Landis prior to a meeting in Esilalei.

59. Interview, August 18, 2003.

60. Interview with elder, October 2003.

61. Her work is cited often by conservationists working in this area. I draw from Voeten (1999) and Voeten and Prins (1999).

62. While these statements seem to contradict one another, they draw directly from the published work. The problem rests in the desire by the author to show competition by utilizing

words such as "likely" and "possible" in the introductions and discussions and then the need to present the findings, which suggest otherwise.

63. Interview, April 4, 2002.

64. Maasai believe the disease comes from the placenta of the new calf and avoid pastures until heavy rain washes them away. Scientists say the disease is transmitted in saliva and mucus from the nasal passages and is probably airborne over short distances (Homewood and Rodgers 1991, 183). The Maasai theory keeps them away from wildebeest during the critical period of transmission.

65. From the contributions of three different Landis at a group interview, December 2003.

66. Interview, Oltukai Village, May 2002.

67. This statement reflects ongoing causal conversations with Landis L and others.

68. Usually between 6:30 and 7:00 a.m., although sometimes we would be delayed until closer to 8:00 a.m., particularly during the rainy season when we had to walk to reach the transect as the roads were impassable by car.

69. There are certain dams that are available only for wildlife. Cattle are allowed into Manyara Ranch upon request only, and only in the dry season for grazing or to access water in the hand-dug wells in the dry riverbed. The exception is when water is available in the Mtowambu dam inside the ranch, which cattle can be granted access to. Many times, cattle cut through the ranch (and graze) on their way to the dam in Mswakini.

70. Interview, May 2003.

71. This combines the words of this elder woman and a young man from Ngorongoro, March 9, 2003.

72. Conversation with the author, February 24, 2003.

73. This statement is fabricated but draws from multiple conversations with the speaker over the years and observations of him in various types of meetings.

74. This final quote is from an earlier meeting about the campsite.

Interlude II

1. Told to the author by a junior elder, Oltukai, December 23, 2002, in Swahili, translated by the author into English.

Chapter 4

1. Elder, Oltukai Village, 2003.

2. Elder, Esialei Village, 2003.

3. See, for instance, Adams and McShane 1992, Anderson and Grove 1987, Neumann 1997, Neumann 1998, Schroeder 1999, Shetler 2007.

4. Maasai recall this period as "*emutai*," meaning complete destruction (Waller 1988) recalling the disasters related to bovine pleuropneumonia (BPP) in 1883, rinderpest in 1891, smallpox in 1892, and a subsequent famine resulting in an estimated loss of two-fifths to three-quarters of the Maasai population.

5. A ten-year, ten-million-dollar USAID project, "Ranching Associations," became the managerial unit of Maasai resource use. Maasai were lured with the promise of ninety-nine-year leaseholds on land, access to water supplies, "improved" cattle breeds, and veterinary dips. Yet only eight associations materialized (Jacobs 1978), as Maasai hesitated to replace their communal management system with a foreign imposed structure. As Parkipuny explained (1979, 147), "No Maasai will really lend a hand in keeping out the livestock of his kinsmen or neighbors from using water or dips simply because he happens to possess a title. . . . The strength of social ties . . . supersede[s] any legal regulations originating outside the ethnic group."

6. I put quotation marks around the word "use" to highlight the politics and ambiguity surrounding its definition. Land in use meant farmed, built on, or otherwise transformed, and thus often excluded land put aside for seasonal or reserve grazing by Maasai.

7. Though UCRT has tried to do land-use planning that coordinates cross-village grazing patterns.

8. The word *Eng'ai* is feminine, which can be translated as God being feminine, or as being "unknown."

9. Personal conversation with a junior elder, 2005.

10. This challenges Arhem's attempt to structurally align "domestic/home" with women and "wild/public" with men.

11. Interview, Oltukai junior elder, 2005.

12. Group interview with elders in Oltukai, December 2003.

13. For Kisongo. Among the Purko it is the opposite.

14. Kipury 1983, 32. I heard similar versions in the field and was sometimes told that the goats became gazelle, the cattle eland, and so on.

15. Maasai did not reside in LMNP but accessed permanent water sources there during emergency times.

16. At the time of finalizing this manuscript, Maasai face an uncertain future in NCA with the threat of eviction looming large. See preface and Oakland Institute report (https://www.oaklandinstitute.org/unesco-ngorongoro-conservation-area-report-related-documents, accessed October 20, 2019).

17. See Hulme and Murphee 2001 on community-based conservation. See Wright 2017; Bluwstein, Moyo, and Kicheleri 2016; and Benjaminsen et al. 2013 on specifics of WMAs.

18. Interview, 2009.

Chapter 5

1. Attempts to introduce a Swahili alternative *ushoroba* [alleyway, passageway] failed.

2. See Goldman 2009 for a detailed analysis.

3. I lived in this *enkang'* and had the privilege of talking with women as they waited to reach a critical mass, while being close enough to make sure I wasn't missing any of the meeting. The proximity of my house also meant I was the general supplier of chairs for the visitors and of tea and water for people after the meeting. In these post-meeting gatherings, I would often learn about ideas, opinions, and views that were not spoken at the meeting and why, as well as reactions to what was spoken about and how.

4. Called *Mbinyo* or *Pura*, it is distilled alcohol made from corn, sugar, and whatever the distiller can conjure up. It is extremely potent and cheap, making it a favored choice among the elders and increasingly consumed by junior elders or even senior warriors now. It is illegal but readily available, especially in Oltukai, where all one has to do is cross the river to be in a different village, district, and region, and an area populated by Waarusha, famous for making and selling the brew. This has taken a considerable toll on the social, economic, and knowledge base of the village.

5. When I was interviewing Maasai on whether they agreed or disagreed with creating a corridor in the village (after explaining what this meant if they were not aware), they would often respond (or as translated in Swahili) that *inafaa* (it is appropriate) or *haifai* (it is not appropriate) "*kutoa* corridor" or "*kutolewa* corridor." I am translating this as "to carve out." *Kutoa* means to throw away, to break off from, and *kutolewa* is the passive form of this verb (via personal communication with Magdelena Hauner, 2004).

6. I draw here mostly from his 1991 article and take liberty in presenting his views in the form of a dialogue, facilitated by an interview with him in 2003.

7. These reflect common statements made during interviews and at meetings, either by the original residents of the first three homesteads or their descendants, who have heard the story many times.

8. See also Rohde and Hilhorst 2001 for more on the growth of Mtowambu Town and agricultural expansion in Makuyuni. They suggest (19) that the Maasai-inhabited arid and semiarid plains to the east of the rift wall (the Esilalei area) have been little affected by population growth, overgrazing, or "inappropriate development," with "little change associated with pastoral activity in the agro-ecological zone during the last 50–100 years."

9. See Sinclair and Arcese 1995 for overview of shifting states between grassland and forest in Serengeti-Mara as related to rainfall, fire, grazing, and browsing (by wildebeest and elephants), and grassland-herbivory dynamics. See also Hobbs 1996, McNaughton and Georgiadis 1986, and Turner 1998 and 1993 for the various ways that grazing by wildlife and livestock impacts soil and pasture properties.

10. Interview, June 2003.

11. Mtowambu is the town bordering LMNP to the northeast; Mswakini is a village on the southern boundary of Manyara Ranch, which also borders TNP. Naitolia is another village, bordering Mswakini. Saburi is an estate east of the road; Mbulmbulu is over the rift wall, above Lake Manyara, on the way to Ngorongoro, and Serena is a hotel on the top of the rift wall.

12. These words come from an interview with Landis P in early fall 2003. I had planned an interview on wildlife-livestock relations and grazing, but he began talking to me about the history of conservation interventions. The corridor proposed by Mwalyosi would pass right through his *enkang'*. Since Mwalyosi's paper was written in 1991, it is possible it was used as a guide for the TANAPA visits discussed.

13. Interview with elder in Losirwa, March 2003.

14. From an incident that occurred on May 27, 2003, and conversation with Makaa S and the community liaison officer for LMNP who escorted him and young boy home. Reference to the cars is separate and comes from my own observations and discussions with villagers.

15. *Mweng'ati* (Maa: the bighting ones, enemy) is what the Maasai call the neighboring pastoralist tribe, the Barabaig.

16. Honeyguide was just getting off the ground as a community-based tourism/conservation organization when I was conducting the original research for this book. By 2011, they had become a dominant player in the highly militarized management of the MR and a local WMA in the TME, collaborating with AWF and state agencies.

17. Interview, October 2003. He is Mwaarusha and speaks the same language as Maasai.

18. This has since changed with the Wildlife Conservation Act of 2009 (United Republic of Tanzania [URT] 2009).

19. The new law has since been put in place but does not change the TANAPA mandate.

20. See prior chapters on conservation manager. Drawing from statements made at an Oltukai Village meeting on KEEP, April 2005. This aspect of the new wildlife law was reviewed in a draft document and explained to the village government by myself at a prior meeting.

21. Combination of interviews with different employees in the head office and at TNP.

22. Interview with outreach manager, TNP, October 8, 2002.

23. LAMP was initiated in 1988 in Babati District by SIDA (Swedish International Development Agency) as a community-based program to assist districts and communities to manage natural resources (United Republic of Tanzania [URT] 2005).

24. There was a lot of confusion over these beacons. Oltukai Village government feared they were part of a plan by AWF to grab their land, inhibiting them from gaining legal village title.

25. Interview, December 16, 2003.

26. Interview, November 23, 2003.

27. Interview on his return from Pasiansi Wildlife Training Institute, Mwanza (2003). Also reflects statements he made at several meetings during my presence (2005).

28. Also referred to as the village executive officer (VEO) or *mtendaji* in Swahili, he is employed by the government, in charge of village bookkeeping and meant to act as a counterpart to the elected village chairman.

29. From regular conversations during transect work, during harvest time, and while walking past the new elephant "corridors" in Endepesi.

30. Because of the drought of 2005/6, people in both villages didn't farm. In speaking to a friend from Oltukai who farmed a plot in Kisongo, he said the elephants seem to have gone out to the Kisongo and Lolkisale area. "They have gone looking for maize. We haven't seen them at all this year [in Oltukai] because there are no farms for them to raid."

31. Presentation, Charles Foley, Wildlife Conservation Society meeting, Arusha 2003. Foley runs the Tarangire Elephant Project.

32. From Foley 2002.

33. From conversations with the Foleys and MR manager regarding elephant movements through the ranch.

34. Group interview with seven Landis (varying in age from late twenties to late thirties), Oltukai, September 2002. Words in brackets indicate questions asked by me or clarifications/translations.

35. He is referring here to the specific location shown on maps. See discussion in chapter 2.

36. In Maa, *a-do* means both "I say" and "I think."

37. "A Maasai citizen," this statement draws from several hundred hours of conversation with men and women in Oltukai Village.

38. Interview, 2003.

39. This was nearly always how it was said in Swahili: *wakiamua kuhama,* if they decide to move.

40. This second segment comes from separate interviews and from observations during nights spent at the boma.

41. Interview, July 12, 2003.

42. Interview, April 24, 2002.

43. From a group interview with ten women of varying ages, led by the chairwoman of the cultural boma, Esilalei. The cultural boma was created by AWF to bring tourists to the area and includes a building to sell jewelry, along with a collection of Maasai houses (*enkaji* sg., *inkajijik* pl.), built in the old-fashioned style (i.e., without grass roofs).

44. Interview, November 8, 2003.

45. Drawing from several hundred hours of conversations with men and women in Esilalei Village, but mostly men of the Seuri, Makaa, and Landis age-set.

46. Interview, October 2002.

47. Interview, September 2003.

48. From conversations with the ranch manager, AWF newsletters, and participation in meetings.

49. Tanzania Land Conservation Trust (TLCT) 2002. See also "Manyara Ranch: A Corridor—and More," accessed May 29, 2020, https://www.awf.org/news/manyara-ranch -corridor-and-more.

50. Interview with three *ilmurran,* members of the Korianga age-set, in Esilalei, October 2003.

51. This and the following statement come from an interview with father and son, November 28, 2003.

52. Interview, December 10, 2003.

53. Interview, November 29, 2003, repeated in another interview with a Makaa elder.

54. African Wildlife Foundation (AWF) and Jeshi Kitiafi Tanzania (JKT), Tanzanian National Army.

55. Interview, November 13, 2003.

56. Interview, November 26, 2003.

57. When I asked elders in interviews about the placement of a corridor (a specific protected area for the passage of wildlife), more than half of the responses reflected this sentiment (in exact or similar words).

58. Interview, November 9, 2003.

59. Interview with the elder, Esilalei.

60. Combined words of two interviews with a young Landis (December 2, 2003) and a middle-rank Makaa (November 8, 2003).

61. Interview, December 13, 2003.

62. Interview, November 26, 2003.

63. Combined from interview on December 9, 2003, and comments made by speaker at meeting in AWF Arusha office, May 2005.

64. From words voiced by this speaker and others at meetings regarding KEEP, 2005.

65. Interview, December 16, 2003.

66. Interview, July 7, 2003.

67. Interview, November 2003.

68. From meeting in AWF office, April 2005.

69. From Gamassa 1989 and interview, March 2002. See also Newmark 1993 on corridor design.

70. Interview, November 12, 2003. He worked for many years in the Ngorongoro Conservation Area and participated in research with U.S. and Kenyan collaborators on pastoralist-wildlife relations.

71. This last part is not from an interview with the speaker but with other people at TANAPA headquarters and TNP.

72. Meeting, AWF office Arusha, April 2005.

73. Meeting, AWF office Arusha, April 2005.

74. Meeting, AWF office Arusha, April 2005.

75. From a telephone conversation/interview, February 7, 2004.

76. These words come from a combination of a direct reply (email first and then in person) to the statement by Landis M (2005), which I relayed to him, and other responses to Maasai reactions to KEEP from 2003–5.

77. See note 75.

78. They were called such, but in some cases were just rich elders hand-picked by government leaders.

79. From an explanation he gave on two separate meetings between KEEP representatives and Oltukai Village government, 2005.

80. From conversations with many people in both villages and observations.

81. This statement draws from comments made at different times, but mostly during the KEEP village meeting, April 2005.

82. From a combination of conversations and statements made at meetings.

83. Meeting about KEEP, April 2005, that the villagers called and asked me to attend.

84. From a village meeting, April 2005.

85. Despite talk of KEEP for a year, my explanation of an easement was the first that people of Oltukai had heard. AWF staff explained to me that the concept was too complicated for Maasai to understand.

86. From the views of many young men active in farming as discussed at this meeting and elsewhere.

87. Meeting, Oltukai, April 2005.

88. Meeting, Oltukai, April 2005.

89. Meeting, Oltukai, April 2005.

90. This statement summarizes statements made by the speaker and other Maasai throughout the village whenever discussing the possibility of conservation corridors.

Interlude III

1. See Goldman and Milliary 2014.

Chapter 6

1. The *Emanyara* Maasai will say, "*Mapeti olcani*," Let's go to the tree, though I also heard *enkiguena*, which is used across Maasailand, along with regional variations. In Kenya, the *Ilka-putiei* used *entumo* (to meet); the Purko in Maasai Mara used *Orkiu* (termite mound), which was only used in *Emanyara* when a conflict or claim was involved.

2. The word for news and visitor is the same (news: *ilomon*, visitor: *ilomon/engamoni* for male/female).

3. A priest working with Maasai in Kenya shared with me the following story. He was ill, and a group of elders paid him a visit. They asked him how he was. He responded that he was not well but quite sick. The elders were not happy with this response and explained how he should respond to this question. If he wakes up in the morning and is still alive, then he is well, because he is alive, and so he must always respond that he is well when asked. The priest was ashamed of himself, thinking, "And I came here to teach *them* about God?"

4. This responsive listening is so central to Maasai communication that young children who are learning to talk practice telling one another *tedo ooó* or *tedo eeé*.

5. I observed a village assembly meeting (2005) where a government representative from the ward was present who had not been invited. Her requests that they follow "Tanzanian Law" and conduct the meeting in Swahili were ignored, as were her complaints about the meeting following "Maasai" style.

6. Saning'o Milliary, personal communication.

7. I was often placed in this position and did not realize it was the norm until I observed it happening with other "guests," Maasai and non-Maasai alike.

8. See Goldman and Little 2015. Differences are related to NGO and church presence. See below in this chapter for more on changing gender dynamics.

9. Saning'o Milliary, personal communication.

10. Elder, Oltukai Village, 2009.

11. In the past it was extremely rare for *ilmurran* to marry prior to *eunoto*, though the huge range of ages within an age-group meant that while some were ready to settle down and act like elders after *eunoto*, others were still quite young and wanted to stay being "warriors." By the time that most men reach *Olng'esher*, they have already been acting like elders for quite a while, with their own cattle, wives, and children. Nonetheless, some *ilmurran* remain under the patronage of their fathers. The group is considered mature and capable of providing blessings only once they have officially become elders.

12. Regarding the creation of yet more *ilaigwenak*, a village government leader commented that "this business of the *ilaigwenak* is foolish. We (the village government) are working hard—building dams, dips, bringing development. What are they doing? Just calling meetings. What does that help?"

13. After learning this phrase, I would bring it up in other parts of Maasailand (Tanzania and Kenya), which always brought laughter and agreement that yes, this is often what happens.

14. The words in quotes come from Saning'o Milliary, who described the process to me in this way.

Conclusion

1. I presented the ideas in this book, including the use of the *enkiguena* framework, to Maasai civil society forums in Kenya and Tanzania and have copublished on the ideas with two Maasai civil society actors (Goldman, Sinandei, and DeLuca 2014; Goldman and Milliary 2014).

2. On the varied ways in which decolonization is being discussed, see Sium et al. 2012.

3. Minutes, meeting, January 10, 2017, Manyara Ranch.

4. Personal conversation with UCRT director. Also see http://www.ujamaa-crt.org/uploads /1/2/5/7/12575135/ucrt_ccro_brief_2014.pdf, accessed September 20, 2019.

References

Adams, Jonathan, and Thomas O. McShane. 1992. *The Myth of Wild Africa: Conservation Without Illusion*. New York: W. W. Norton.

Anderson, David, and Richard Grove, eds. 1987. *Conservation in Africa: People, Polices and Practice*. Cambridge: Cambridge University Press.

Arhem, K. 1985. *The Symbolic World of the Maasai Homestead*. Working Paper Series in African Studies Programme, edited by Uppsala University. Uppsala, Sweden: Uppsala University.

Barad, Karen. 2007. *Meeting the Universe Halfway: Quantum Physics and the Entanglement of Matter and Meaning*. Durham, N.C.: Duke University Press.

Barad, Karen. 2014. "Diffracting Diffraction: Cutting Together-Apart." *Parallax* 20 (3): 168–87. https://doi.org/10.1080/13534645.2014.927623.

Basso, Keith H. 1996. *Wisdom Sits in Places: Landscape and Language Among the Western Apache*. Albuquerque: University of New Mexico Press.

Behnke, R. H., I. Scoones, and C. Kerven, eds. 1993. *Range Ecology at Disequilibrium: New Models of Natural Variability and Pastoral Adaptation in African Savannas*. London: Overseas Development Institute.

Beinhart, W. 1987. "Introduction to Part One." In *Conservation in Africa: People, Polices and Practice*, edited by D. Anderson and R. Grove, 15–19. Cambridge: Cambridge University Press.

Bell, Richard H. V. 1971. "A Grazing Ecosystem in the Serengeti." *Scientific American* 225 (1): 86–93.

Benjaminsen, Tor A., Mara J. Goldman, Maya Y. Minwary, and Faustin P. Maganga. 2013. "Wildlife Management in Tanzania: State Control, Rent Seeking and Community Resistance." *Development and Change* 44 (5): 1087–109. https://doi.org/10.1111/dech.12055.

Bevenger, Gregory S. 2004. *Tarangire National Park Precipitation Analysis*. USDA Forest Service.

Blaser, Mario. 2010. *Storytelling Globalization from the Chaco and Beyond*. Durham, N.C.: Duke University Press.

Bonner, Raymond. 1993. *At the Hand of Man: Peril and Hope for Africa's Wildlife*. New York: Alfred A. Knopf.

Borner, Markus. 1985. "The Increasing Isolation of Tarangire National Park." *Oryx* 19 (2): 91–96.

Botkin, Daniel. 1990. *Discordant Harmonies: A New Ecology for the Twenty-First Century*. New York: Oxford University Press.

Brockington, Dan. 2002. *Fortress Conservation: The Preservation of the Mkomazi Game Reserve, Tanzania*. Bloomington: Indiana University Press.

Brockington, Dan, and Jim Igoe. 2006. "Eviction for Conservation: A Global Overview." *Conservation and Society* 4 (3): 424.

Bryan, Joe. 2009. "Where Would We Be Without Them? Knowledge, Space and Power in Indigenous Politics." *Futures* 41 (1): 24–32.

Bryan, Joe. 2011. "Walking the Line: Participatory Mapping, Indigenous Rights, and Neoliberalism." *Geoforum* 42 (1): 40–50.

Bluwstein, Jevgeniy, Francia Moyo, and Rose P. Kicheleri. 2016. "Austere Conservation: Understanding Conflicts over Resource Governance in Tanzanian Wildlife Management Areas." *Conservation and Society* 14 (3): 218–31.

Büscher, Bram, Robert Fletcher, Dan Brockington, Chris Sandbrook, William M Adams, Lisa Campbell, Catherine Corson, Wolfram Dressler, Rosaleen Duffy, and Noella Gray. 2017. "Half-Earth or Whole Earth? Radical Ideas for Conservation, and Their Implications." *Oryx* 51 (3): 407–10.

Cameron, Emilie. 2012. "New Geographies of Story and Storytelling." *Progress in Human Geography* 36 (5): 573–92.

Caughley, Graeme, and A. R. E. Sinclair. 1994. *Wildlife Ecology and Management*. Cambridge, Mass.: Blackwell Science.

Collard, Rosemary-Claire, Jessica Dempsey, and Juanita Sundberg. 2015. "A Manifesto for Abundant Futures." *Annals of the Association of American Geographers* 105 (2): 322–30. https://doi.org/10.1080/00045608.2014.973007.

Collet, D. 1987. "Pastoralists and Wildlife: Image and Reality in Kenya Maasialand." In *Conservation in Africa: People, Policies, and Practice*, edited by D. Anderson and R. Grove, 129–48. Cambridge: Cambridge University Press.

Cooke, Amy. E. 2007. "Subdividing the Savanna: The Ecology of Change in Northern Tanzania." PhD diss., University of North Carolina.

Coughenour, Michael B. 1991. "Spatial Components of Plant-Herbivore Interactions in Pastoral, Ranching, and Native Ungulate Ecosystems." *Journal of Range Management* 44 (6): 530–42.

Crampton, Jeremy W. 2009. "Cartography: Performative, Participatory, Political." *Progress in Human Geography*, no. 336, 840–48. https://doi.org/10.1177/0309132508105000.

Davis, Alicia. 2011. "'Ha! What Is the Benefit of Living next to the Park?' Factors Limiting In-Migration next to Tarangire National Park, Tanzania." *Conservation and Society* 9 (1): 25.

Davis, Alicia, and Mara J. Goldman. 2019. "Beyond Payments for Ecosystem Services: Considerations of Trust, Livelihoods and Tenure Security in Community-Based Conservation Projects." *Oryx* 53 (3): 491–96. https://doi.org/10.1017/S0030605317000898.

de Boer, W. F., and Herbert H. T. Prins. 1990. "Large Herbivores That Strive Mightily but Eat and Drink as Friends." *Oecologia*, no. 82, 264–74.

de la Cadena, Marisol. 2015. *Earth Beings: Ecologies of Practice Across Andean Worlds.* Durham, N.C.: Duke University Press.

Deihl, C. 1985. "Wildlife and the Maasai: the Story of East African Parks." *Cultural Survival Quarterly* 9 (1): 37–40.

Diamond, J. M. 1975. "The Island Dilemma: Lessons of Modern Biogeographic Studies for the Design of Natural Reserves." *Biological Conservation*, no. 7, 129–46.

Duffy, Rosaleen. 2014. "Waging a War to Save Biodiversity: The Rise of Militarized Conservation." *International Affairs* 90 (4): 819–34.

Ellis, J., M. Coughman, and D. Swift. 1993. "Climate Variability, Ecosystem Stability, and the Implications for Range and Livestock Development." In *Rangeland Ecology at Disequilibrium: New Models of Natural Variability and Pastoral Adaption in African Savannas*, edited by R. H. Behnke, I. Scoones, and C. Kerven. London: Overseas Development Institute.

Escobar, Arturo. 2007. "Worlds and Knowledges Otherwise: The Latin American Modernity/ Coloniality Research Program." *Cultural Studies* 21 (2–3): 179–210.

Estes, Richard D. 1991. *The Behavior Guide to African Mammals.* Berkeley: University of California Press.

Finnegan, Ruth. 2007. *The Oral and Beyond: Doing Things with Words in Africa.* Chicago: University of Chiago Press.

Foley, Charles. 2004. "What Is the Future of Tarangire National Park?" *Miombo*, no. 27, 12–14.

Foley, Laura. S. 2002. "The Influence of Environmental Factors and Human Activity on Elephant Distribution in Tarangire National Park, Tanzania." In *Natural Resource Management, Rural Land Ecology.* Enschede, The Netherlands: International Institue for Geo-information Science and Earth Observation.

Fosbrooke, Henry A. 1948. "An Administrative Survey of the Maasai Social System." *Tanganyikan Notes and Records*, no. 26, 1–50.

Fryxell, J. M., and A. R. E. Sinclair. 1988. "Causes and Consequences of Migration by Large Herbivores." *Trends in Ecology & Evolution*, no. 3, 237–41.

Furniss, G., and L. Gunner, eds. 1995. *Power, Marginality and African Oral Literature.* Cambridge: Cambridge University Press.

Galaty, John. 1981. "Land and Livestock Among Kenyan Maasai." *African and Asian Studies* 16 (1–2): 68–88.

Gamassa, D. M. 1989. "Land Use Conflicts in Arid Areas: A Demographical and Ecological Case Study: The Kwakuchinja Wildlife Corridor in Northern Tanzania." Master's thesis, Agricultural University of Norway.

Gardner, Benjamin. 2012. "Tourism and the Politics of the Global Land Grab in Tanzania: Markets, Appropriation and Recognition." *Journal of Peasant Studies* 39 (2): 377–402.

Gardner, Benjamin. 2016. *Selling the Serengeti: The Cultural Politics of Safari Tourism.* Athens: University of Georgia Press.

Garland, Elizabeth. 2006. "State of Nature: Colonial Power, Neoliberal Capital, and Wildlife Managment in Tanzania." PhD diss., University of Chicago.

Gereta, Emmanuel, Godwell Elias Ole Meing'ataki, Simon Mduma, and Eric Wolanski. 2004. "The Role of Wetlands in Wildlife Migration in the Tarangire Ecosystem, Tanzania." *Wetlands Ecology and Management* 12 (4): 285.

Goldman, Mara. 1998. "Wildlife Conservation and Pastoral Development in the Semi-Arid Savanna Lands of Tanzania: Changing Views of the Role of Maasai Pastoralists." Master's thesis, University of California.

Goldman, Mara. 2003. "Partitioned Nature, Privileged Knowledge: Community-Based Conservation in Tanzania." *Development and Change* 34 (5): 833–62.

Goldman, Mara. 2007. "Tracking Wildebeest, Locating Knowledge: Maasai and Conservation Biology Understandings of Wildebeest Behavior in Northern Tanzania." *Environment and Planning D: Society and Space*, no. 25, 307–31.

Goldman, Mara. 2009. "Constructing Connectivity? Conservation Corridors and Conservation Politics in East African Rangelands." *Annals of the Association of American Geographers* 99 (2): 335–59.

Goldman, Mara. 2018. "Circulating Wildlife: Capturing the Complexity of Wildlife Movements in the Tarangire Ecosystem in Northern Tanzania from a Mixed Method, Multiply Situated Perspective." In *The Palgrave Handbook of Critical Physical Geography*, edited by Rebecca Lave, Christine Biermann, and Stuart N. Lane, 319–38. New York: Springer.

Goldman, Mara. Forthcoming. "The Problem with Tradition Is That It Keeps on Changing: Making Sense of Maasai 'Traditional' Leadership in the Twenty-First Century."

Goldman, Mara, Alicia Davis, and Jani Little. 2016. "Controlling Land They Call Their Own: Access and Women's Empowerment in Northern Tanzania." *Journal of Peasant Studies* 43 (4): 777–97.

Goldman, Mara, and Jani S. Little. 2015. "Innovative Grassroots NGOS and the Complex Processes of Women's Empowerment: An Empirical Investigation from Northern Tanzania." *World Development*, no. 66, 762–77.

Goldman, Mara, and Saning'o Milliary. 2014. "From Critique to Engagement: Re-Evaluating the Participatory Model with Maasai in Northern Tanzania." *Journal of Political Ecology* 21 (1): 408–23.

Goldman, Mara, Joana Roque de Pinho, and Jennifer Perry. 2010. "Maintaining Complex Relations with Large Cats: Maasai and Lions in Kenya and Tanzania." *Human Dimensions of Wildlife* 15 (5): 332–46.

Goldman, Mara, Joana Roque de Pinho, and Jennifer Perry. 2013. "Beyond Ritual and Economics: Maasai Lion Hunting and Conservation Politics." *Oryx* 47 (4): 490–500.

Goldman, Mara, and Fernando Riosmena. 2013. "Adaptive Capacity and Vulnerability to Drought in Tanzanian Maasailand: Changing Strategies to Navigate Across Fragmented Landscapes." *Global Environmental Change* 23:588–97.

Goldman, Mara, Makko Sinandei, and Laura DeLuca. 2014. "Conflict Resolution, Land Disputes and Peace Building in Northern Tanzania: The Role of Customary Institutions." In *Building Peace from Within: Community-Based Peace Building in Africa*, edited by S. Maphosa, L. DeLuca, and A. Keasle, 153–71. Pretoria, South Africa: Africa Institute of South Africa.

Green, Lesley, ed. 2013. *Contested Ecologies: Dialogues in the South on Nature and Knowledge.* Cape Town, South Africa: Human Sciences Research Council.

Gustavo, Esteva. 1996. "Hosting the Otherness of the Other: The Case of the Green Revolution." In *Decolonizing Knowledge: From Development to Dialogue*, edited by Frederique Apffel-Marglin and Stephen A. Marglin, 249–78. Oxford: Clarendon Press.

Haraway, Donna. 1989. *Primate Visions: Gender, Race, and Nature in the World of Modern Science*. New York: Routledge.

Haraway, Donna. 1991. *Simians, Cyborgs and Women: The Reinvention of Nature*. New York: Routledge.

Haraway, Donna. 1994. "A Game of Cat's Cradle: Science Studies, Feminist Theory, Cultural Studies." *Configurations*, no. 1, 59–71.

Haraway, Donna. 1997. *Modest_Witness@Second_Millennium*. New York: Routledge.

Harding, Sandra. 1988. *Is Science Multicultural? Postcolonialisms, Feminisms, and Epistemologies*. Bloomington: Indiana University Press.

Harris, Leila M., and Helen D. Hazen. 2006. "Power of Maps: (Counter) Mapping for Conservation." *ACME* 4 (1): 99–130.

Hobart, Mark. 1993. "Introduction: The Growth of Ignorance?" In *An Anthropological Critique of Development: The Growth of Ignorance*, edited by Mark Hobart, 1–30. New York: Routledge.

Hobbs, N. T. 1996. "Modification of Ecosystems by Ungulates." *Journal of Wildlife Management* 60 (4): 695–713.

Hodgson, Dorothy. 2001. *Once Intrepid Warrior: Gender, Ethnicity and the Cultural Politics of Maasai Development*. Bloomington: Indiana University Press.

Hodgson, Dorothy. 2005. *The Church of Women: Gendered Encounters Between Maasai and Missionaries*. Bloomington: Indiana University Press.

Hodgson, Dorothy. 2011. *Being Maasai, Becoming Indigenous: Postcolonial Politics in a Neoliberal World*. Bloomington: Indiana University Press.

Hodgson, Dorothy, and Richard A. Schroeder. 2002. "Dilemmas of Counter-Mapping Community Resources in Tanzania." *Development and Change*, no. 33, 79–100.

Homewood, Katherine, and Alan Rodgers. 1991. *Maasailand Ecology: Pastoralist Development and Wildlife Conservation in Ngorongoro, Tanzania*. New York: Cambridge University Press.

Hughes, L. 2006. *Moving the Maasai: A Colonial Misadventure*. New York: Palgrave Macmillan.

Hulme, D., and M. Murphee, eds. 2001. *African Wildlife and Livelihoods: The Promise and Performance of Community Conservation*. Portsmouth, N.H.: Heinemann.

Hutton, J., W. M. Adams, and J. C. Murombedzi. 2005. "Back to the Barriers? Changing Narratives in Biodiversity Conservation." *Forum for Development Studies* 32 (2): 341–37.

Igoe, Jim. 2000. "Ethnicity, Civil Society, and the Tanzanian Pastoralist NGO Movement: The Continuities and Discontinuities of Liberalized Development." PhD diss., Boston University.

Igoe, Jim. 2004. *Conservation and Globalization: A Study of National Parks and Indigenous Communities from East Africa to South Dakota*. Case Studies on Contemporary Social Issues, edited by John A. Young. Belmont, Calif.: Wadsworth/Thompson Learning.

Igoe, Jim. 2006. "Becoming Indigenous Peoples: Difference, Inequality, and the Globalization of East African Identity Politics." *African Affairs* 105 (420): 399–420.

Igoe, Jim. 2017. *The Nature of Spectacle: On Images, Money, and Conserving Capitalism*. Tucson: University of Arizona Press.

Igoe, Jim, and Dan Brockington. 1999. *Pastoral Land Tenure and Community Conservation: A Case Study from North-East Tanzania*. Pastoral Land Tenure Series. London: International Institute for Environment and Development.

Igoe, Jim, and B. Croucher. 2007. "Conservation, Commerce, and Communities: The Story of Community-Based Wildlife Management Areas in Tanzania's Northern Tourist Circuit." *Conservation and Society* 5 (4): 432–49.

Iliffe, John. 1979. *A Modern History of Tanganyika*. Cambridge: Cambridge University Press.

Ingold, Tim. 2000. *The Perception of the Environment: Essays in Livelihood, Dwelling and Skill*. New York: Routledge.

Jachmann, Hugo. 1999. *Estimating Abundance of African Wildlife: An Aid to Adaptive Management*. Norwell, Mass.: Kluwer Academic Publishers.

Jacobs, Alan H. 1965. "The Traditional Political Organization of the Pastoral Masai." PhD diss., Oxford University.

Jacobs, Alan H. 1975. "Maasai Pastoralism in Historical Perspective." In *Pastoralism in East Africa*, edited by T. Monad, 406–22. Oxford: Oxford University Press.

Jacobs, Alan H. 1978. *Development in Tanzania Maasailand: The Perspective over 20 Years, 1957–1977*. USAID Mission in Tanzania.

Jacobs, Alan H. 1980. "Pastoral Development in Tanzania Maasailand." *Rural Africana*, no. 7, 1–14.

Kahurananga, J., and F. Silkiluwasha. 1997. "The Migration of Zebra and Wildebeest Between Tarangire National Park and Simanjiro Plains, Northern Tanzania, in 1972 and Recent Trends." *African Journal of Ecology*, no. 35, 179–285.

Kicheleri, Rose, George C. Kajembe, Thorsten Treue, Felister Mombo, and Martin Nielsen. 2018. "Power Struggles in the Management of Wildlife Resources: The Case of Burunge Wildlife Management Area, Tanzania." In *Wildlife Management: Failures, Successes and Prospects*. IntechOpen.

Kipury, Niomi. 1983. *Oral Literature of the Maasai*. Nairobi, Kenya: Heinemann Educational Books.

Kristjanson, P., M. Radeny, D. Nkedianye, Russell L. Kruska, Robin S. Reid, H. Gichohi, Fred Atieno, and R. Sanford. 2002. *Valuing Alternative Land-Use Options in the Kitengela Wildlife Dispersal Area of Kenya*. ILRI Impact Assessment Series 10. Nairobi, Kenya: International Livestock Research Institute.

Laltaika, Elifuraha. 2013. "Pastoralists' Right to Land and Natural Resources in Tanzania." *Oregon Review of International Law* 15 (1): 43.

Lamprey, H. F. 1963. "Ecological Separation of the Large Mammal Species in the Tarangire Game Reserve, Tanganyika." *East African Wildlife*, no. 1, 63–92.

Lamprey, H. F. 1964. "Estimation of the Large Mammal Densities, Biomass and Energy Exchange in the Tarangire Game Reserve and the Maasai Steppe in Tanganyika." *East African Wildlife*, no. 2, 1–46.

Law, John. 2004. *After Method: Mess in Social Science Research*. International Library of Sociology, edited by John Urry. New York: Routledge.

Law, John, and Annemarie Mol, eds. 2002. *Complexities: Social Studies of Knowledge Practices*. Durham, N.C.: Duke University Press.

LEAT (Lawyers Environmental Action Team). 1998. *Socio-Legal Analysis of Community-Based Conservation in Tanzania: Policy, Legal, Institutional and Programmatic Issues, Considerations and Options.* EPIQ/Tanzanian Natural Resource Management Programme.

Little, Peter D. 1994. "The Social Context of Land Degradation ('Desertification') in Dry Regions." In *Population and Environment: Rethinking the Debate,* edited by L. Arizpe, M. P. Stone, and D. C. Major, 209–51. San Francisco, Calif.: Westview Press.

Little, Peter D. 1996. "Pastoralism, Biodiversity, and the Shaping of Savanna Landscapes in East Africa." *Africa* 66 (1): 37–51.

Loth, Paul E., and Herbert H. T. Prins. 1986. "Spatial Patterns of the Landscape and Vegetation of Lake Manyara National Park." *ITC Journal* 1986 (2): 115–30.

Lovell, E. 2018. "Range of Lines: Exploring the Mobilities, Maps, and Technologies That Shape Tanzania's Northern Rangelands." PhD diss., University of Colorado Boulder.

Lunstrum, Elizabeth. 2014. "Green Militarization: Anti-Poaching Efforts and the Spatial Contours of Kruger National Park." *Annals of the Association of American Geographers* 104 (4): 816–32.

Margules, C., A. J. Higg, and R. W. Rafe. 1982. "Modern Biogeographic Theory: Are There Any Lessons for Nature Reserve Design?" *Biological Conservation,* no. 24, 115–28.

Massek, A., Ol'oisolo, and J. O. Sidai. 1974. *Wisdom of Maasai (Eneno o lMaasai).* Nairobi, Kenya: Transafrica.

Mbembe, Achille. 2001. *On the Postcolony.* Berkeley: University of California Press.

Mbembe, Achille. 2015. "Decolonizing Knowledge and the Question of the Archive." Lecture presented at the University of the Witwatersrand, Wits Institute for Social and Economic Research, Johannesburg, South Africa, April 22. https://wiser.wits.ac.za/system/files/Achille%20Mbembe%20-%20Decolonizing%20Knowledge%20and%20the%20Question%20of%20the%20Archive.pdf.

McCabe, J. Terrence. 2003. "Disequilibrial Ecosystems and Livelihood Diversification Among the Maasai of Northern Tanzania: Implications for Conservation Policy in Eastern Africa." *Nomadic Peoples* 7 (1): 74–92.

McCabe, J. Terrence, Paul W. Leslie, and Laura DeLuca. 2010. "Adopting Cultivation to Remain Pastoralists: The Diversification of Maasai Livelihoods in Northern Tanzania." *Human Ecology* 38 (3): 321–34.

McCabe, J. Terrence, S. Perkin, and C. Schofield. 1992. "Can Conservation and Development Be Coupled Among Pastoral People? An Examination of the Maasai of the Ngorongoro Conservation Area, Tanzania." *Human Organization* 51 (4): 353–66.

McNaughton, S. J. 1979. "Grassland-Herbivore Dynamics." In *Serengeti: Dynamics of an Ecosystem,* edited by A. R. E. Sinclair and M. Norton-Griffiths, 46–81. Chicago: University of Chicago Press.

McNaughton, S. J. 1984. "Grazing Lawns: Animals in Herds, Plant Form, and Coevolution." *American Naturalist* 124 (6): 863–87.

McNaughton, S. J. 1985. "Ecology of a Grazing Ecosytem: The Serengeti." *Ecological Monographs* 55:259–94.

McNaughton, S. J., and Nicholas J. Georgiadis. 1986. "Ecology of African Grazing and Browsing Mammals." *Annual Review of Ecology and Systematics,* no. 17, 39–65.

Ministry of Natural Resources and Tourism. 1998. *The Wildlife Policy of Tanzania*. Dar es Salaam: Government Printer.

Mol, Annemarie. 2002. *The Body Multiple: Ontology in Medical Practice*. Durham, N.C.: Duke University Press.

Mol, Frans. 1972. *Maa: A Dictionary of the Maasai Language and Folklore, English-Maasai*. Nairobi: Marketing and Publishing.

Mol, Frans. 1981. "The Maasai and Wildlife." *Swara* 4 (2): 24–27.

Mol, Frans. 1996. *Maasai: Language and Culture*. Narok, Kenya: Mill Hill Missionary.

Msoffe, Fortunata, Fatina A. Mturi, Valeria Galanti, Wilma Tosi, Lucas A. Wauters, and Guido Tosi. 2007. "Comparing Data of Different Survey Methods for Sustainable Wildlife Management in Hunting Areas: The Case of Tarangire–Manyara Ecosystem, Northern Tanzania." *European Journal of Wildlife Research* 53 (2): 112–24.

Mwalyosi, R. B. B. 1981. "Notes and Records: Utilization of Pastures in Lake Manyara National Park." *African Journal of Ecology*, no. 21, 135–37.

Mwalyosi, R. B. B. 1990. "Integrated Resource Management for Lake Manyara Catchment Basin." In *Project 3755*. Dar es Salaam, Tanzania: Institute of Resource Assessment, University of Dar es Salaam.

Mwalyosi, R. B. B. 1991. "Ecological Evaluation for Wildlife Corridors and Buffer Zones for Lake Manyara National Park, Tanzania, and Its Immediate Environment." *Biological Conservation* 57 (2): 171–86.

Mwalyosi, R. B. B. 1992. "Influence of Livestock Grazing on Range Condition in South-West Masailand, Northern Tanzania." *Journal of Applied Ecology* 29 (3): 581–88.

Nadasdy, P. 2005. "The Anti-Politics of TEK: The Institutionalization of Co-Management Discourse and Practice." *Anthropologica* 47 (2): 215–32.

Nadasdy, Paul. 1999. "The Politics of TEK: Power and the 'Integration' of Knowledge." *Artic Anthropology* 36 (1–2): 1–18.

Nagar, Richa. 2014. *Muddying the Waters: Coauthoring Feminisms across Scholarship and Activism*. Urbana: University of Illinois Press.

Nagar, Richa. 2019. *Hungry Translations: Relearning the World Through Radical Vulnerability*. Urbana: University of Illinois Press.

Naughton-Treves, Lisa, Rebecca Grossberg, and Adrian Treves. 2003. "Paying for Tolerance? The Impact of Depredation and Compensation Payments on Rural Citizens' Attitudes Toward Wolves." *Conservation Biology* 17 (6): 1500–11.

Ndagala, Daniel K. 1992. *Territory, Pastoralists, and Livestock: Resource Control Among the Kisongo Maasai*. Uppsalla, Sweden: Almqvist and Wiksell.

Neumann, Roderick. 1995a. "Local Challenges to Global Agendas: Conservation, Economic Liberalization and the Pastoralists' Rights Movement in Tanzania." *Antipode* 27 (4): 363–82.

Neumann, Roderick. 1995b. "Ways of Seeing Africa: Colonial Recasting of African Society and Landscape in Serengeti National Park." *Ecumene* 2 (2): 149–69.

Neumann, Roderick. 1998. *Imposing Wilderness: Struggles over Livelihood and Nature Preservation in Africa*. Berkeley: University of California Press.

Neumann, Roderick. 1997. "Primitive Ideas: Protected Areas Buffer Zones and the Politics of Land in Africa." *Development and Change*, no. 28, 559–82.

Newmark, William D. 1993. "The Role and Design of Wildlife Corridors with Examples from Tanzania." *Ambio* 22 (8): 500–4.

Ngoitiko, Maanda, Makko Sinandei, Partalala Meitaya, and Fred Nelson. 2010. "Pastoral Activists: Negotiating Power Imbalances in the Tanzanian Serengeti." In *Community Rights, Conservation and Contested Land: The Politics of Natural Resource Governance in Africa*, edited by Fred Nelson, 269–90. Washington, D.C.: Earthscan.

Norton-Griffiths, M. 1978. *Counting Animals*. Serengeti Ecological Monitoring Programme, edited by J. J. R. Grimsdell. Nairobi, Kenya: African Ecological Monitoring Programme.

Nyerere, Julius K. 1968. *Ujamaa: Essays on Socialism*. New York: Oxford University Press.

Oba, Gufu, Niles C. Stenseth, and Walter J. Lusigi. 2000. "New Perspectives on Sustainable Grazing Management in Arid Zones of Sub-Saharan Africa." *BioScience* 50 (1): 35–51.

ole Ndaskoi, Navaya. 2002. "Maasai Wildlife Conservation and Human Need: The Myth of 'Community-Based Wildlife Management.'" *Fourth World Journal* 5 (1): 150–91.

Parkipuny, M. L. 1989. "Pastoralism, Conservation and Development in the Greater Serengeti Region." Occasional Paper 1. Ngorongoro Conservation and Development Project, IUCN.

Parkipuny, M. L. Ole. 1979. "Some Crucial Aspects of the Maasai Predicament." In *African Socialism in Practice: The Tanzanian Experience*, edited by Andrew Coulson. Nottingham: Spokesman.

Parkipuny, M. L. Ole, and Dhyani J. Berger. 1993. "Maasai Rangelands: Links Between Social Justice and Wildlife Conservation." In *Voices from Africa: Local Perspectives on Conservation*, edited by Dale Lewis and Nick Carter. Washington, D.C.: World Wildlife Fund.

Potkanski, Tomasz. 1994. *Property Concepts, Herding Patterns and Management of Natural Resources Among the Ngorongoro and Salei Maasai of Tanzania*. London: International Institute for Environment and Development.

Potkanski, Tomasz. 1999. "Mutual Assistance Among the Ngorongoro Maasai." In *The Poor Are Not Us: Poverty and Pastoralism*, edited by D. Anderson and Broch-Due Vigdis, 199–218. Athens: Ohio University Press.

Pratt, D. J., and M. D. Gwynne, eds. 1977. *Rangeland Management and Ecology in East Africa*. Huntington, N.Y.: Robert E. Krieger.

Prins, Herbert H. T. 1987. "Nature Conservation as an Integral Part of Optimal Land Use in East Africa: The Case of the Masai Ecosystem of Northern Tanzania." *Biological Conservation*, no. 40, 141–61.

Prins, Herbert H. T. 1992. "The Pastoral Road to Extinction: Competition Between Wildlife and Traditional Pastoralism in East Africa." *Environmental Conservation* 19 (2): 117–23.

Prins, Herbert H. T. 2000. "Competition Between Wildlife and Livestock in Africa." In *Wildlife Conservation by Sustainable Use*, edited by Herbert H. T. Prins, J. G. Grootenhuis, and T. Dolan, 51–80. Boston: Kluwer Academic.

Prins, Herbert H. T., and I. Douglas-Hamilton. 1990. "Stability in a Multi-Species Assemblage of Large Herbivores in East Africa." *Oecologia*, no. 83, 392–400.

Prins, Herbert H. T., and Paul E. Loth. 1988. "Rainfall Patterns as Background to Plant Phenology in Northern Tanzania." *Journal of Biogeography*, no. 15, 451–63.

Reid, R. 2012. *Savannas of Our Birth: People, Wildlife, and Change in East Africa*. Berkeley: University of California Press.

Reid, R. S., D. Nkedianye, M. Y. Said, D. Kaelo, M. Neselle, O. Makui, L. Onetu, S. Kiruswa, N. Ole Kamuaro, and P. Kristjanson. 2009. "Evolution of Models to Support Community and Policy Action with Science: Balancing Pastoral Livelihoods and Wildlife Conservation in Savannas of East Africa." *Proceedings of the National Academy of Sciences* 113 (17): 4579–84.

Reid, Robin S., David Cambell, Louis N. Gachimbi, Jeff Worden, Edna E. Wangui, Stephen Mathai, Simon M. Mgatha, Bilal Butt, Joshep M. Maitima, H. Gichohi, and Eric Ogol. 2004. "Likages Among Changes in Land Use, Biodiversity and Land Degradation in the Loitokitok Area of Kenya." In *Land Use Change Impacts and Dynamics (LUCID) Project Working Paper*. Nairobi: International Livestock Research Institute.

Reid, Robin S., M. Rainy, J. Oguto, Russell L. Kruska, M. McCartney, M. Nyabenge, K. Kimani, M. Kshatriya, Jeff Worden, L. Ng'ang'a, J. Owuor, J. Kinoti, E. Njuguna, Cathleen J. Wilson, and R. Lamprey. 2003. "People, Wildlife and Livestock in the Mara Ecosystem: The Mara Count 2002." In *Report, Mara Count 2002*. Nairobi: International Livestock Research Institute.

Rohde, Richard, and Thea Hilhorst. 2001. *After the Fall: Political Ecology and Environmental Change in the Lake Manyara Basin, TZ.* Edinburgh: International Institute for Environment and Development Drylands Programme.

Roque de Pinho, J. 2009. "Staying Together: People-Wildlife Relationships in a Pastoral Society in Transition, Amboseli Ecosystem, Southern Kenya." PhD diss., Colorado State University.

Roque de Pinho, Joana, Clara Grilo, Randall B. Boone, Kathleen A. Galvin, and Jeffrey G. Snodgrass. 2014. "Influence of Aesthetic Appreciation of Wildlife Species on Attitudes Towards Their Conservation in Kenyan Agropastoralist Communities." *PloS one* 9 (2): e88842.

Rugumayo, Caroline R. 1997. "The Politics of Conservation Area Management: On Actors, Interface and Participation: The Case of Ngorongoro Conservation Area, Tanzania." PhD diss., Norwegian University of Science and Technology.

Saitoti, Tepilit Ole. 1980. *Maasai.* New York: Harry N. Abrams.

Sayre, Nathan F. 2008. "The Genesis, History, and Limits of Carrying Capacity." *Annals of the Association of American Geographers* 98 (1): 120–134. https://doi.org/10.1080/00045 600701734356.

Schroeder, R. A., and R. P. Neumann. 1995. "Manifest Ecological Destinies: Local Rights and Global Environmental Agendas." *Antipode*, no. 27, 321–24.

Schroeder, Richard A. 1999. "Geographies of Environmental Intervention in Africa." *Progress in Human Geography* 23 (3): 359–378. https://doi.org/10.1177/030913259902300302.

Scoones, I., ed. 1995. *Living with Uncertainty.* London: Intermediate Technology Publications.

Semali, Ladislaus M., and Joe L. Kincheloe, eds. 1991. *What Is Indigenous Knowledge? Voices from the Academy.* Indigenous Knowledge and Schooling, edited by Joe L. Kincheloe and Ladislaus M. Semali. New York: Falmer Press.

Shetler, J. B. 2007. *Imagining Serengeti: A History of Landscape Memory in Tanzania From Earliest Time to Present.* Athens: Ohio University Press.

Shivji, I. 1998a. "Contradictory Perspectives on Rights and Justice in the Context of Land Tenure Reform in Tanzania." *Tanzania Zamani* 4 (1/2): 1–56.

Shivji, I. G. 1998b. *Not Yet Democracy: Reforming Land Tenure in Tanzania.* London/Dar es Salaam: IIED/HAKI ARDHI/Faculty of Law, University of Dar es Salaam.

Simpson, D. 2008. *Milking the Rhino*. Oley, Pa.: Bullfrog Films.

Simpson, Leanne Betasamosake. 2001. "Aboriginal Peoples and Knowledge: Decolonizing Our Processes." *Canadian Journal of Native Studies* 21 (1): 137–48.

Simpson, Leanne Betasamosake. 2004. "Anticolonial Strategies for the Recovery and Maintenance of Indigenous Knowledge." *American Indian Quarterly* 28 (3/4): 373–84.

Simpson, Leanne Betasamosake. 2017. *As We Have Always Done: Indigenous Freedom Through Radical Resistance*. Minneapolis: University of Minnesota Press.

Sinclair, A. R. E. 1983. "The Function of Distance Movements in Vertabrates." In *The Ecology of Animal Movement*, edited by I. Swingland and P. J. Greenwood, 240–58. Oxford: Clarendon Press.

Sinclair, A. R. E., and Peter Arcese, eds. 1995. *Serengeti II: Dynamics, Management, and Conservation of an Ecosystem*. Chicago: University of Chicago Press.

Sium, Aman, Chandni Desai, and Eric Ritskes. 2012. "Towards the 'Tangible Unknown': Decolonization and the Indigenous Future." *Decolonization: Indigeneity, Education & Society* 1 (1): I–XIII.

Sletto, Bjørn Ingmunn. 2005. "A Swamp and Its Subjects: Conservation Politics, Surveillance and Resistance in Trinidad, the West Indies." *Geoforum*, no. 36, 77–93.

Smith, Linda Tuhiwai. 2013. *Decolonizing Methodologies: Research and Indigenous Peoples*. London: Zed Books.

Smith, Nicole M. 2016. "'No Cow Makes This Sort of Profit': Capital, Success, and Maasai Gemstone Traders in Tanzania." *Extractive Industries and Society* 3 (2): 442–49.

Spear, Thomas. 1993. "Being 'Maasai,' but not 'People of Cattle': Arusha Agricultural Maasai in the Nineteenth Century." In *Being Maasai: Ethnicity and Identity in East Africa*, edited by Thomas Spear and Richard Waller, 120–36. Athens: Ohio University Press.

Spear, Thomas. 1997. *Mountain Farmers: Moral Economies of Land and Agricultural Development in Arusha and Meru*. Berkeley: University of California Press.

Spencer, Paul. 2003. *Time, Space, and the Unknown: Maasai Configurations of Power and Providence*. New York: Routledge.

Spencer, Paul, and Richard Waller. 2017. "The Maasai Age System and the Loonkidongi Prophets." *Journal of Eastern African Studies* 11 (3): 460–81.

Strathern, Marilyn. 1991. *Partial Connections*. Savage, Md.: Rowman and Littlefield.

Sumba, Daudi, Patrick Bergin, and Clive Jones. 2005. "Land Conservation Trusts: A Case Study of Manyara Ranch, Tanzania." *AWF Working Papers*. Washington, D.C.: African Wildlife Foundation.

Talbot, Lee M., and Martha Talbot. 1963. *The Wildebeest in Western Masailand, East Africa*. Washington, D.C.: Wildlife Society.

Talle, Aud. 1988. "Women at a Loss: Changes in Maasai Pastoralism and Their Effects on Gender Relations." PhD diss., University of Stockholm.

Tanzania Land Conservation Trust (TLCT). 2002. *The Manyara Ranch: A Reality Check*. Arusha: AWF.

Tarangire Conservation Project (TCP). 1998. *Final Report on the Analysis of Wildlife Movements in Tarangire National Park*. Insubria, Italy: OIKOS and University of Insubria, Italy.

Tarangire-Manyara Conservation Project (TMCP). 2000. *Procedure Manual: Data Collection, Storage and Organization*. Instituto Oikos, Tanzania Branch, and University of Insubria, Varese Branch, in cooperation with TANAPA (Tanzanian National Parks Authority).

Tarangire-Manyara Conservation Project (TMCP). 2002a. "Participatory Land Use Maps and Associated Data," in Tarangire-Manyara Conservation Project, final report, prepared by Instituto Oikos Tanzania Branch and University of Insubria, Varese Branch, in Cooperation with Tanzania National Parks Association.

Tarangire-Manyara Conservation Project (TMCP). 2002b. "Mapping of the Distribution and Numbers of Large Mammals in the Tarangire-Manyara Area," in Tarangire-Manyara Conservation Project, final report, prepared by Instituto Oikos Tanzania Branch and University of Insubria, Varese Branch, in Cooperation with Tanzania National Parks Association.

Thompson, M., and K. Homewood. 2002. "Entrepreneurs, Elites and Exclusion in Maasailand: Trends in Wildlife Conservation and Pastoralist Development." *Human Ecology* 30 (1): 107–38.

Todd, Zoe. 2016. "An Indigenous Feminist's Take on the Ontological Turn: 'Ontology' Is Just Another Word for Colonialism." *Journal of Historical Sociology* 29 (1): 4–22.

Turnbull, David. 2000. *Masons, Tricksters and Cartographers: Comparative Studies in the Sociology of Scientific and Indigenous Knowledge.* Amsterdam: Harwood Academic.

Turner, Matthew D. 1993. "Overstocking the Range: A Critical Analysis of the Environmental Science of Sahelian Pastoralism." *Economic Geography*, no. 69, 402–21.

Turner, Matthew D. 1998. "Long-Term Effects of Daily Grazing Orbits on Nutrient Availability in Sahelian West Africa: 1. Gradients in the Chemical Composition of Rangelands Soils and Vegetation." *Journal of Biogeography*, no. 25, 669–82.

United Republic of Tanzania (URT). 1999a. *The Village Land Act, 1999.* Dar es Salaam: Government Printer.

United Republic of Tanzania (URT). 1999b. *The Land Act, 1999.* Dar es Salaam: Government Printer.

United Republic of Tanzania (URT). 2005. *Poverty and Human Development Report.* Dar es Salaam: Mkuku na Nyota Publishers.

United Republic of Tanzania (URT). 2009. *The Wildlife Conservation Act.* Dar es Salaam: Government Printer.

Van de Vijver, C. A. D. M., P. Poot, and Herbert H. T. Prins. 1999. "Causes of Increased Nutrient Concentrations in Post-Fire Regrowth in an East African Savanna." *Plant and Soil*, no. 214, 173–85.

Verran, Helen. 1998. "Re-Imagining Land Ownership in Australia." *Postcolonial Studies: Culture, Politics, Economy* 1 (2): 237–54.

Verran, Helen. 2001. *Science and an African Logic.* Chicago: University of Chicago Press.

Verran, Helen. 2002. "A Postcolonial Moment in Science Studies: Alternative Firing Regimes of Environmental Scientists and Aboriginal Landowners." *Social Studies of Science* 32 (5–6): 729–62.

Voeten, Margje M. 1999. "Living With Wildlife: Coexistence of Wildlife and Livestock in an East African Savanna System." PhD diss., Wageningen University.

Voeten, Margje M., and Herbert H. T. Prins. 1999. "Resource Partitioning Between Sympatric Wild and Domestic Herbivores in the Tarangire Region of Tanzania." *Oecologia* 120 (2): 287.

Wa Thiong'o, Ngugi. 1992. *Decolonising the Mind: The Politics of Language in African Literature.* Oxford: James Curry.

Walker, B., and R. J. Scholes. 1993. *An African Savanna: Synthesis of the Nylsvley Study*. Cambridge: Cambridge University Press.

Waller, Richard. 1979. "The Lords of East Africa: The Maasai in the Mid-Nineteenth Century, c. 1840–1885." PhD diss., Cambridge University.

Waller, Richard. 1988. "Emutai: Crisis and Response in Maasailand, 1883–1902." In *The Ecology of Survival: Case Studies from North East African History*, edited by D. Johnson and D. Anderson, 73–113. London: Lester Crook Academic Publishing.

Watson, A., and O. H. Huntington. 2008. "They're Here—I Can Feel Them: The Epistemic Spaces of Indigenous and Western Knowledges." *Social and Cultural Geography* 9 (3): 257–81.

Watson-Verran, Helen, and David Turnbull. 1995. "Science and Other Indigenous Knowledge Systems." In *Handbook of Science and Technology Studies*, edited by Sheila Jasanoff, Gerard E. Markle, James C. Peterson, and Trevor Pinch, 115–39. Thousand Oaks, Calif.: SAGE.

Western, David. 1982. "The Environment and Ecology of Pastoralists in Arid Savannas." *Development and Change* 13 (2): 183–211. https://doi.org/10.1111/j.1467-7660.1982.tb00117.x.

Western, David. 1989. "Conservation Without Parks: Wildlife in the Rural Landscape." In *Conservation for the Twenty-first Century*, edited by D. Western and M. Pearl, 158–65. New York: Oxford University Press.

Western, David. 1997. *In the Dust of Kilimanjaro*. Washington, D.C.: Island Press.

Western, David, and Helen Gichohi. 1993. "Segregation Effects and the Impoverishment of Savanna Parks: The Case of Ecosystem Viability Analysis." *African Journal of Ecology* 31 (4): 269–81.

Westoby, M., B. Walker, and I. Noy-Meir. 1989. "Opportunistic Management for Rangelands Not at Equilibrium." *Journal of Range Management* 42 (4): 266–74.

Whatmore, S., and L. Thorne. 1998. "Wild(er)ness: Reconfiguring the Geographies of Wildlife." *Transactions of the Institute of British Geographers*, no. 23, 435–54.

White, F. 1983. *Vegetation of Africa: A Descriptive Memoir to Accompany the UNESCO/AETFAT/UNSO Vegetation Map of Africa*. Paris: UNESCO.

Wiley, Liz A. 2003. *Community-Based Land Tenure Management: Questions and Answers About Tanzania's New Village Land Act, 1999*. Dry Lands Issue Paper 120. London: International Institute for Environment and Development.

Woodroffe, Rosie, Simon Thirgood, and Alan Rabinowitz, eds. 2005. *People and Wildlife: Conflict or Coexistence?* Cambridge: Cambridge University Press.

Wright, V. Corey. 2017. "Turbulent Terrains: The Contradictions and Politics of Decentralised Conservation." *Conservation and Society* 15 (2): 157.

Zimmerer, K. 2000. "The Reworking of Conservation Geographies: Nonequilibrium Landscapes and Nature-Society Hybrids." *Annals of Association of American Geographers* 90 (2): 356–69.

Index

wenak), 206; helpers to, 83. *See also* *enkiguena*; *enkutoto*

ilaigwenak le nkaji (clan leader), 25, 203, 205. *See also ilaigwenak*

iloibonok (ritual leader; sg., *oloiboni*), 28, 226, 232n35; defined, 28

iloshon (sections; sg. *olosho*), 16, 23, 68, 81, 83, 148, 205, 226; as Maasai sociospatial category of management, 81–83; historically managed as separate common-property transhumant grazing systems, 81; as territorial sections, 16; previously viewed as distinct social group or "tribes," 23; porous boundaries of, 81; seven territorial sections in Tanzania, 23; utilized and changed with villagization within Tanzania, 83. *See also* *enkutoto* (sub-section)

ilmurran (sg., *olmurrani*), 8, 9, 25, 26, 27, 59, 62, 65, 66, 79, 81, 84, 85, 86, 93, 96–97, 124, 125, 128, 130, 132, 139, 142, 153, 154, 156, 161, 179, 197, 198, 201, 203, 204, 211, 226, 227, 231–32nn34–35, 236n34, 244n50, 246n11; at times hesitant to speak at an *enkiguena*, 179; knowledge of wildlife and pastures, 179; commanded the admiration and/or scorn from tourists, scholars, and administrators, 25; conflict between junior and senior members within age-set, 204; contemporary changes in the social and economic position of, 204; deterrence from killing lions (*olng'atuny*), 9, 130, 142; elders limit access to wives, cattle (*inkishu*), and political decision-making for, 204; male warrior age-set, 8, 25; lion (*olng'atuny*) hunting by, as evidence of ability to protect the community, 202; participate in *enkiguena*, 198; past existence of *enmayata* (separate villages for), 198; table summarizing time and history of different age-sets, 26. *See also* Maasai society

impoorri/empoor (hard ground where no grass grows), 50, 69, 120, 225; Maasai prevent cattle (*inkishu*) from creating, 120; wilde-beest (*oingat*) creating, 120; zebras' (*oloi-tikoshi*) role in, 120. *See also* cattle (*inkishu*); wildebeest (*oingat*); zebra (*oloitikoshi*)

inkishu. *See under* cattle

inkutot (sub-section/spatial unit of organization; sg., *enkutoto*), 16, 23, 68, 81, 82, 83, 88, 148, 151, 157, 226, 231n30, 235n16; and Maasai mobility, 148; a subdivision within an *iloshon/olosho* territorial section, 16; also applied to space within a Maasai house, 231n30; clan relations within, 23, 205; customary property management and grazing rules at the level of, 81, 82; those of *Ilkisongo olosho*, 23; each has its own *ilaigwenak* (customary leader), 23; geographic and social overlap across, 23; rarely recognized by NGOs working on land-use planning, 81; relevant for Maasai cultural events and resource management, 81. *See also ilaigwenak; iloshon; Maasai society*

International Council on Monuments and Sites (ICOMOS), xiii

International Union for the Conservation of Nature (IUCN), xiii

Jeshi kujenga Taifa (JKT, Tanzania National Army), xxiii, 180, 234n40, 244n54

kilometric index of abundance (KIA), 40–41, 45, 46; animals' relative abundance table, 47; chart of common wildlife, 46; described, 45, 46

Kwa Kuchinja Environmental Easements Project (KEEP), xxiii, 161, 189; "*Kwa Kuchinja* wildlife corridor", 31, 88–89, 161, 164, 166, 172, 175, 179, 183, 184, 185; *Kwa Kuchinja/* to slaughter, 88. *See also* wildlife corridor

Lake Manyara National Park (LMNP), xvii, xxiii, 60, 89, 114, 155, 165, 166, 167, 168, 169, 170, 175, 177, 178, 184, 190, 234n47, 239n55, 242n11, 242n14

Lalamilama, 74

About the Author

Mara J. Goldman is an associate professor in the Department of Geography at the University of Colorado Boulder, where she is a faculty affiliate with the Institute for Behavioral Science, the Women and Gender Studies Program, and the Center for Native American and Indigenous Studies. She received her BA in geography from Clark University (1994), her MA in geography from the University of California, Los Angeles, (1998), her MS in conservation biology and sustainable development from the University of Wisconsin, Madison (2001), and her PhD in geography from the University of Wisconsin, Madison (2006). She co-edited the book *Knowing Nature: Conversations at the Intersection of Political Ecology and Science Studies* (University of Chicago Press, 2011). Goldman's work has appeared in various academic journals, such as *Journal of Peasant Studies, Area, Oryx, World Development, Journal of Political Ecology,* and *Global Environmental Change.* She has received grants from the Fulbright U.S. Scholar Program (for Tanzania and India), the National Science Foundation, and the French National Research Agency. She lives in Boulder, Colorado, with her husband, Shankar Ayyalasomayajula, and their two children, Anisha and Aanya.